The Real Story of the USS JOHNSTON DD-821

Part 2

As told by the officers and sailors who served aboard her

Editor & Contributing Author: George A. Sites

Special Thanks

This book would not be complete without a special thanks to all the readers of the first USS Johnston book, the Johnston officers and sailors who provided their stories for inclusion in this book and to all of you who have encouraged me to put together "Part 2". Like the first book, this has been a labor of love and I hope you enjoy the stories provided by your fellow shipmates.

I have also included some biographies of our fellow shipmates. If you are like me, you like knowing what a former shipmate's life continued to be after serving with him. Some of these have appeared in the Johnston Newsletter.

Thanks to all! George A Sites, Editor

Dedication and In Memory Of

This book is dedicated to all the officers and sailors who served aboard the USS Johnston DD-821 during her 35 years of service to the greatest Navy in the world and to the United States of America.

Your service and sacrifices are appreciated by all of America.

Not to be forgotten, our beloved fallen shipmates. May you rest in peace.

Copyright 2013

George A. Sites
5653 Haydens Reserve Way
Hilliard, Ohio 43026 USA

All rights reserved. No part of this publication may be reproduced, stored in a retrieval system or transmitted in any form or by any means — electronic, mechanical, photocopying, recording, and scanning or any other means now known or hereafter invented without the prior written permission of George A. Sites.

While the editor and the publisher believes that the information given in this book is correct, all parties must rely upon their own judgment when making use of it. Neither the editor nor the publisher assumes any liability to anyone for any loss or damage caused by any error, misrepresentation or omission in this book, whether such is the result of negligence or any other cause. Any and all such liability is disclaimed.

ISBN-13: 978-0-9790746-4-6

ISBN-10: 0-9790746-4-9

NOTES

Editor and contributing author:

George A. Sites, RD2
USS Johnston DD821, 1969-1971

Assistant Editor: Alida L. Breen

Cover designed by: Roy A. Sites

CONTRIBUTING AUTHORS

(Names are in alphabetical order and the rates shown are during the sailor's Johnston service)

Argonti, John
(FTG-2) 1966-1968

Batsche, David
(FTG-2) 1960-1963

Beebe, Glen
(QMSN) 1955-1957

Benjestorf, Gary "Benje"
(RD-2) 1966-1969

Buckle, Edward
(HM) 1950-1954

Carden, Milner
(QM-2) 1954

Cook, Billy
(FTG-3) 1965-1968

Crichton, Alva "Al"
(RDSN) 1949-1953

Damm, Art
(F1/c) 1946-1947 (Plank-Owner)

Demmel, Phil
(TE-3) 1948-1953

Engelien, John
(FTG-3) 1960-1961

Fanzone, Mike
(DK-3) 1953 - 1954

Foley, Francis D.
(Rear Admiral) U.S. Naval Institute

Frost, Bob "Frosty"
(RM-3) 1952-1955

Garrison, Morrow "Gary"
(BT-1) 1949-1952

Guere, Leonard "Lenny"
(SA) 1952-1955

Harris, Daun "Harry"
(RD-3) 1968-1970

Hocking, Ralph
(DC-2) 1951-1955

Hughes, Jack
(LTJG) 1962-1965

Jensen, A. D.
(Tin Can Sailor Magazine)

Johnston, Paul
(MM-3) 1965-1967

Mack, Jonathan "Toby"
(LTJG) 1966-1968

McCaffree Jr, Burnham C. "Mike"
(Commander) 1970-1972

McIntosh, Stu
(Colonel) USAF Retired

Mynatt, Ginger
(Texas Co-Op Power Magazine)

Nava, Robert "Bob"
(SM-3) 1957-1959

Nugent, George
(Ensign) 1950-1951

Obst, James
(FP-1) 1954-1957

Phillps, Jeffery
(MM-3) 1980

Potter, John "Mick"
(FTG-1) 1967-1971

Pringle, Robert
(Commander) 1964-1965

Raygor, John
　(SN1/c) 1953-1954

Rawlins, Vinny
　(USMC)

Rosenthal, Harold
(YN-2) 1957

Sauerwine, Bruce
　(QM-2) 1971-1975

Savage, David G.
　(Wisconsin Journal Sentinal)

Sites, George A.
　(RD-2) 1968-1971

Sudholz, Herman O.
　(LT) 1959-1963

Takesian, Eli
　(Chaplain) 1964-1967

Turner, Bruce
　(LCDR) Triad Navaires San Diego Magazine

Watson III, William P. "Bill"
　(Midshipman 3rd Class) 1970

Williams, Carl
　(MM-1) 1976-1980

Williams, Donna
   (Wife of Carl Williams)

Zenes, Stephen
   (RM-1) 1975-1977

LIST OF NEWSPAPER/MAGAZINE ARTICLES
(In order of publishing date)

"JICPAC 0819 Sailor Non-Stop Adventurer"
By: LCDR Bruce Turner, KICPAC 0819 PAO, The Triad Navaires San Diego magazine, June 1962

"Blistered Gun Barrels Mark DesDiv 42's Long Vietnam Voyage"
The Cruiser-Destroyerman magazine August, 1968

"Footnotes in Texas History: Orange's World War II Shipbuilding Boom" By: Ginger Mynatt, Texas Co-Op magazine, October 2011

"Going into battle over cross"
By: David G. Savage, Tribune Washington Bureau, Milwaukee, Wisconsin Journal Sentinel, March 20, 2012

"Destroyer History Notebook, Evolution of the 5-Inch/38-Caliber Gun"
The Tin Can Sailor newspaper Vol. 36, No. 4

"USS JOHNSTON (DD-557) and the Battle off Samar"
By: A.D. Jensen, The Tin Can Sailor newspaper, October, November, December 2012

TABLE OF CONTENTS

Chapter 1 - History of the USS Johnston

Chapter 2 - Technical details

Chapter 3 - Years 1945 through 1949

Chapter 4 - Years 1950 through 1959

Chapter 5 - Years 1960 through 1969

Chapter 6 - Years 1970 through 1983

Chapter 7 - Jolly "J" Ports of Call

Chapter 8 - A Sailor's Life

Chapter 9 - On the Lighter Side

FOREWORD

The purpose of this book is to continue memorializing the stories and experiences of the officers and sailors who served aboard USS Johnston DD-821.

As with the first book, it is not intended to be a "History Book" in the true sense of the words. It is simply a collection of Johnston stories as told by those who served aboard her in their **own words**! Keep in mind each story is how the author remembers it. Some new as well as previous contributors have made this second "Johnston" book possible.

Like it, love it or hate it and without question the two books contain the most complete story of the USS Johnston DD-821 available anywhere.

We hope you enjoy it!

Chapter 1

HISTORY OF THE USS JOHNSTON DD-557 & DD-821

(Much of this chapter is available in the public domain.

Editor's Note: As most of us know our beloved DD-821 would not have been built without the terrible sinking of the original USS Johnston DD-557. The following story and reports are based upon the words of the senior surviving Officer after his ship is destroyed and sunk during the battle off Samar. As I typed these reports into this book, I just couldn't imagine what the feelings of the crew must have been like. So many terrible things were happening at the same time, explosions, shipmates killed and wounded, it goes on and on. It reads like a movie script.

USS JOHNSTON (DD-557) and the Battle off Samar

By: A. D. Jensen

Editor's note: This story appeared in "The Tin Can Sailor" newspaper Dated October, November, and December 2012.

Named for Civil War naval hero John Vincent Johnston, DD-557 was launched by the Tacoma Shipbuilding Company of Seattle, Washington, on 25 March and commissioned on 27 October 1943. Three months later, on 1 February 1944, the new destroyer was in the Marshall Islands bombarding the beaches at Kwajalein. She was at Eniwetok in late February with the HALL (DD-583), AYLWIN (DD-355), MACDONOUGH (DD-351), MONAGHAN (DD-354, and MCCORD (DD-534), supporting the invasion. She subsequently took part in bombardments at Kapingamarangi Atoll in the Carolines and off Bougainville in the Solomon Islands.

The JOHNSTON then joined the HAGGARD (DD-555), Hailey (DD-556), and FRANKS (DD-554) on antisubmarine patrol. On 15 May 1944 they successfully ended a twenty-hour search when the HAGGARD made sonar contact and launched her depth-charges. The JOHNSTON and FRANKS joined her and at 0015, the FRANKS' depth charges produced a thunderous explosion. They confirmed the destruction and identity of the I-76 when daylight revealed her scattered remains.

The USS JOHNSTON (DD-557) was a FLETCHER-class destroyer built by Seattle-Tacoma Shipbuilding and commissioned on 27 October 1943. Two days before her first birthday, she was sunk by Japanese warships at the Battle Off Samar in what has been called the bravest and most daring charge ever made by a destroyer against other ships. Her commanding officer, CDR Ernest Evans, was an American Indian of Cherokee and Creek ancestry from Oklahoma. His bravery had already been recognized in 1944 with a Bronze Star. When Evans realized the size of the force that he intended to attack, he got on the 1MC and told his crew, "A large Japanese fleet has been contacted. They are fifteen miles away and headed in our direction. They are believed to have four battleships, eight cruisers, and a number of

destroyers. This will be a fight against overwhelming odds from which survival cannot be expected. We will do what damage we can." Despite knowing that they would not survive, the JOHNSTON's crew did their jobs well and helped to convince Admiral Kurita, commander of the Japanese force, that his fleet was not superior after all and that he needed to flee.

On 21 July 1944, following patrols in the Solomons, Marshalls, and Marianas, the JOHNSTON joined the battleship PENNSYLVANIA (DD-38) for the bombardment of Guam where she fired more than 4,000 rounds. By October 20, the JOHNSTON was operating with Escort Carrier Task Unit 77.4.3, identified as "Taffy 3". The unit included Rear Admiral Clifton A.F. Sprague's flagship FANSHAW BAY (DVE-70), five other escort carriers; the destroyers, JOHNSTON, HOEL (DD-533), and HEERMANN (DD-532); and the destroyer-escorts DENNIS (DE-405), JOHN C. BUTLER (DE-339) RAYMOND (DE-341), and SAMUEL B. ROBERTS (DE-413).

On 25 October 1944, the JOHNSTON was firing on enemy airfields on the island of Samar when American planes reported a Japanese force of four battleships, seven cruisers, and eleven destroyers descending on Sprague's group. The rest of the U.S. Fleet was steaming in their direction but wouldn't reach Samar before the Japanese did. The ships of Taffy 3 were all that stood between the enemy and Leyte Gulf. ADM Sprague launched his planes to meet the oncoming enemy and sent his ships at top speed toward the Leyte Gulf. When the destroyers and destroyer escorts arrived off San Bernardino Strait east of Samar they prepared to protect their escort carriers from the enemy force bearing down on them. The Japanese were planning a three-pronged attack. Their cruisers would attack the American ships from the east, their destroyers from the west, and their battleships down the center.

A slightly smaller hero, the destroyer escort USS SAMUEL B. ROBERTS (DE-413) also stood up to the much larger Imperial Japanese force that could have crushed the underdog Americans had their commanders realized that it was not Admiral William Halsey's main force as they had thought. The American ships fought so fiercely that the Japanese were confounded. Admiral Kurita decided to save his

force and fled back the way they had come. DE-413 was a JOHN C. BUTLER-class ship built at Houston's Brown Shipbuilding and commissioned on 28 April 1944. When the ship sank at the Battle Off Samar, she took with her 89 of her crew. The other 120 floated for more than two days in three lifeboats before being rescued.

The JOHNSTON's gunnery officer, LT Robert C. Hagen, said later, "We felt like little David without a slingshot." But they had smoke. Proceeding under fire from the Japanese, the JOHNSTON followed a zigzag course as she laid a 2,500-yard-wide smoke screen between their escort carriers and the enemy's guns. Then, with 5-inch guns blazing, the JOHNSTON's captain, CDR Ernest E. Evans, took on the nearest cruiser. After firing 200 rounds, the destroyer fired ten torpedoes, turned sharply, and disappeared into the smoke screen. She emerged a minute later, to see the cruiser KUMANO burning furiously. The enemy ship was doomed, but the JOHNSTON's situation was little better. She'd been struck three times by a battleship's 14-inch shells and three times more by a light cruiser's 6-inch shells.

The JOHNSTON had lost all power to her steering engine and her three 5-inch guns. Her gyro compass was useless. She was able to disappear briefly into a rain squall to assess damage and make some rapid repairs, but essentially, she was out of the action. She'd fired all her torpedoes and, with just one engine, wouldn't be able to keep up with the others.

The USS MACDONOUGH (DD-351) was a FARRAGUT-class destroyer built at the Boston Navy Yard and commissioned 15 March 1935. The MACDONOUGH was also at Leyte Gulf for the Battle Off Samar but remained with the highly vulnerable troop ships that Kurita's Center Force had come to destroy. Smaller than most of her Japanese counterparts, the spunky MACDONOUGH acquitted herself admirably on many occasions during the war at Guadalcanal, the Gilberts, the Marshalls, and New Guinea, among others and was active in the assaults leading to the recapture of the Philippines. In all, the MACDONOUGH received 13 battle stars for World War II.

But CDR Evans had other ideas. He took his ship in with the other destroyers, dodging and returning salvos, but when she emerged from the blinding smoke he discovered she was headed for a collision with the destroyer HEERMANN. The captain ordered all engines back full, but with one engine, that did little more than slow the ship down. With full power, the HEERMANN was able to back out of danger. The two ships passed with less than 10 feet between them and turned their attention again to the battle.

Because the smoke made it impossible to see, Evans ordered gunnery officer Hagen to hold his fire unless he could see the target. He didn't have to wait long. At 0820, a massive battleship loomed out of the smoke just off the JOHNSTON's port beam. Hagan immediately recognized the ship's distinctive pagoda mast as belonging to a KONGO-class battleship and gave the order to fire. He was certain that at least 15 of the 30-round barrage hit the pagoda. The battleship fired her 14-inch guns in return but failed to hit the destroyer.

Moments later, the JOHNSTON came upon the GAMBIER BAY (CVE-73) under attack by a heavy cruiser and badly damaged. CDR Evans ordered his gunners to open fire on the Japanese ship, hoping to draw her fire away from GAMBIER BAY. The JOHNSTON's diversionary action wasn't enough to save the carrier, but she was able to score four hits on the Japanese ship. The sudden appearance of a Japanese destroyer squadron, cause the JOHNSTON to end that fight and turn her guns on the new arrivals, attacking the first and second destroyers in rapid succession. The Japanese destroyers that remained hadn't expected a fight and moved out of range of the JOHNSTON's guns. Once they reached a safe distance, the squadron regrouped and fired their torpedoes. All missed, but their gunners were able to knock out one of the JOHNSTON's forward guns and damage another. They also hit her bridge where the fires and explosions caused CDR Evans to shift his command to the fantail. From there, he yelled orders down through an open hatch to the men who were turning her rudder by hand.

Besides fighting to save their ship, the JOHNSTON's crew hoped to keep the Japanese force from reaching the remaining five American carriers before help arrived. The best they could do was delay the Japanese. But by 0930, the JOHNSTON was in serious trouble. She had lost all power and at 0945, CDR Evans had no choice but to give the order to abandon ship.

At 1010, as the JOHNSTON rolled over and began to sink, a Japanese destroyer approached to fire one last shot making sure she sank. According to one of the survivors, as she went down, the Japanese captain saluted her. In the final reckoning only 141 of the 327 officers and crew were saved. Of the 186 lost, about 50 were killed by enemy action, 45 died on the rafts from their injuries, and 92, including CDR Evans, were alive in the *water after the destroyer sank, but were never seen again.*

The HOEL and SAMUEL B. ROBERTS were also lost trying to save the escort carriers and protect the landings at Leyte. Despite the losses of men and ships, the Americans turned back the Japanese from Leyte Gulf and bought time for the larger U.S. force to arrive. It was later learned that the Japanese admiral had ordered his ships to retire because he believed that Leyte Gulf was defended by a force of ESSEX-class carriers and cruiser escorts, not a half-dozen "baby flat-tops" and what Adm. Sprague called "small boys."

"Copyright 2012, Tin Can Sailors, Inc. Used with Permission."

DD-557 at the Battle off Samar

Action & Damage Reports Provided By: Jonathan "Toby" Mack, LTjg, Years on USS Johnston: 1966 - 1968

ACTION REPORT - USS JOHNSTON DD-557

DD557/A16-3

Serial 04 14 November 1944

C-O-N-F-I-D-E-N-T-I-A-L

From: The Senior Surviving Officer
To: The Commander-in-Chief, United States Fleet

Via:

(1) Commander Task Unit 77.4.33

(2) The Commander Carrier Division TWENTY-FIVE

(3) The Commander Carrier Division TWENTY-TWO

(4) The Commander SEVENTH Fleet

(5) The Commander-in-Chief, U.S. Pacific Fleet

Subject: Action Report - Surface engagement off Samar, P.I., 25 October 1944

Reference:

(a) Pacific Fleet Confidential Letter No. 2CL-44

(b) ComCarDiv 25 Special Action Report of 29 October, 1944, Serial 00100

Enclosure:

(A) Diagram of torpedo attack

(B) Report of Ship's Damage

(C) Report of Destruction of Publications

(D) Medical Report

Part I

1. (a) This ship went to general quarters at about 0650, 25 October, 1944, (zone minus 9 time), on the TBS information that we were being pursued by a major portion of the Japanese fleet. For the next three hours we engaged the enemy, attempting to keep constantly

interposed between the enemy force and our carriers. Maximum use was made of all weapons at our disposal, mainly torpedoes, five inch thirty-eight caliber guns, and smoke. At about 0945 (zone minus 9 time) the order to "ABANDON SHIP" was given as a result of heavy enemy gun fire damage, and the JOHNSTON was observed to sink at about 1010 (zone minus 9 time).

(b) The results of the action were as follows:
(1) The enemy was unable to destroy more than a small part of this Task Unit.
(2) The enemy was turned away before he could reach Leyte Gulf.
(3) Torpedo and five inch hits were obtained on several enemy units by this ship.

2. (a) This ship was a unit of the screen of Task Unit 77.4.3, Commander Task Unit 77.4.3 and OTC was in USS FANSHAW BAY. The screen Commander, Task Unit 77.4.33 was in the USS HOEL. The screen was designated Task Unit 77.4.33. This Unit sortied from Seadler Harbor, Manus Island, Admiralty Group, on 12 October 1944. This Unit proceeded to Leyte Island, P.I., in company with Task Group 77.2 (Fire Support group), and the other units of Task Group 77.4 (Escort Carrier Group), on 18 October, 1944, this task unit began operating independently as the Northern Air Support Group. Carrier aircraft furnished air support for the preliminary bombardment, landings,

and subsequent occupation of Leyte Island in accordance with air operation plan of Commander Task Group 77.4 Operation Order 2-44. From 18 October until 25 October the USS JOHNSTON acted as part of the anti-submarine screen for this unit.

(b)   This ship's mission was to act as part of the antisubmarine screen for the carriers of Task Unit 77.4.3. In absence of specific orders, doctrine used in the engagement was in accordance with General Tactical Instructions and Destroyer Torpedo Doctrine contained in DTB 4-44. Tactical respects and assumptions of the situation on the CVO of the action were clearly outlined in reference (b).

(c)   Own forces at the outset of the action were the surface and accompanying air units of Task Unit 77.4.3, namely the CVE's FANSHAW BAY, ST. LO, WHITE PLAINS, KALININ BAY, GAMBIER BAY and KITKUN BAY; the destroyers, HOEL, HEERMANN and JOHNSTON; the destroyer escorts ROBERTS, RAYMOND, DENNIS and BUTLER. This Task Unit was in formation 5R. The position of the unit at the outset of the action and the ensuing track during the action were as outlined in reference (b).

(d)   Enemy force encountered consisted of four battleships (two KONGO and two ISE), four to six cruisers, and seven or more destroyers (TERUTSURI class).

The battleships were to the eastward and appeared to be in echelon formation to the right. The cruisers were forward of the beam of the leading battleships in echelon to the right. There appeared to be an interval of several thousand yards between the cruisers and battleships. The destroyers were to be westward of the cruisers with an interval of several thousand yards. This enemy force was bearing about 345 (true) from this ship at the outset of the engagement.

(e) Sea was calm with a wind velocity of 6-8 knots from the northeast. The sky was about 3/10 covered with cumulus clouds, with widely scattered showers. In the following detailed account of the action all times will be local time zone. Item (minus 9) time zone is used. This report is made by the Gunnery Officer, the senior surviving officer of the USS JOHNSTON. Valuable assistance was obtained from the communication officer, who was the officer of the deck, from the damage control officer, from the Captain's recorder and from all surviving personnel. As no log of records was saved when the ship sunk, all times stated are approximate.

Part II

This ship had secured from morning alert, the first carrier's plane strike, ASP and C.P. patrols had been launched. At about 0650 word was received by TBS "We are being pursued by a large portion of the Jap fleet." General Quarters was sounded and this task unit headed in an easterly direction to launch planes. At this time the enemy fleet was about thirty four thousand yards distant bearing approximately 345 from us. The Japanese force was closing the range rapidly, their speed being 22 - 25 knots. The Captain immediately gave orders to the engine room to light off all boilers and make maximum speed. The Captain also ordered the engine room to commence making funnel smoke and ordered the smoke screen generator detail to make FS smoke. This ship then commenced zig-zagging back and forth between the enemy and our own formation, laying heavy smoke screen. By 0700 the carriers had launched all available planes and the formation turned to a southwesterly course. Ships were informed by TBS at this time for destroyers to make smoke. This unit had been under fire by the Japanese fleet since 0650.

At 0710 the range to the nearest cruiser had closed to eighteen thousand yards and fire was opened with the five inch battery on this cruiser. The planes were, at this time, striking the Japanese force, completing their strike at about 0715. As soon as this ship commenced firing on the enemy, we in turn were taken under heavy fire from more than one Jap unit. This ship was straddled during this period. As a result of the heavy enemy gun fire, the Captain gave the order to stand-by for torpedo attack to starboard and turned and headed toward the enemy. Torpedoes were set on low speed because of heavy fire to insure being within torpedo range and to insure being able to fire our torpedoes even though this heavy fire should put the ship out of action before the range had closed. The ship closed to within ten thousand yards of the enemy before torpedoes were fired. The point of aim was the leading cruiser, the target angle was 040, the target speed 25 knots. The torpedoes were fired on low speed, a depth of six feet set, and a spread of one degree was used. Torpedo mount one was trained to 110 relative, and torpedo mount two was trained to 125 relative. Then torpedoes were fired, the torpedoes in mount one were fired with 35 degrees right gyro angle and torpedoes in mount two were fired with 25 degrees right gyro angle. A torpedo tube off-set of 2 ½ degrees was used. All ten torpedoes were fired at three second intervals and were observed to run hot, straight and normal. During the run in, the five inch guns fired in rapid salvo fire with the leading cruiser as the point of aim. Over two hundred rounds were fired at this cruiser. An excellent solution was contained throughout and numerous hits were visually observed. No direct spotting was necessary. A continuous ladder of two hundred yards, subsequently cut to one hundred yards, was used. It is believed that this heavy cruiser was severely damaged by at least forty five-inch shells. Common projectiles were used throughout this run.

Results of the torpedo attack were not observed visually, as this ship was retiring behind a heavy smoke screen when the torpedoes were scheduled to hit. It can be positively stated, however, that two and possibly three heavy underwater explosions were heard by two officers and many enlisted men in the repair parties at the time our torpedoes were scheduled to hit. Upon emerging a minute later from the smoke screen the leading cruiser was observed to be burning furiously astern.

At this time, about 0730, this ship was hit for the first time. It is believed we were hit by three fourteen inch projectiles, followed thirty seconds later by three 6 inch projectiles. Those hits knocked out the after fire room and engine room, all power to the steering engine, all power to the after three five inch guns and rendered the gyro compass useless. Maximum speed was now slowed to seventeen knots. Steering was done manually at steering aft, orders being received from the bridge via JV phones. The stable element and FD radar were out of commission during this time for about five minutes. The SC radar antenna was snapped off by the force of shells hitting, rendering that radar inoperative. For the next two hours our ship's course had to be applied manually on the computer. Five inch guns numbers three and five were still receiving indicating signals. The gun crews would match pointers, shift to telescope control and set sight angle and sight deflection received from plot in by hand.

Five inch gun number four fired in local control the remainder of the action, firing at the same target as the remainder of the battery. A providential rain storm was entered immediately after receiving this heavy damage and a valuable ten minutes respite was gained to estimate extent of damage. As soon as FD radar and stable element were back in operation the leading Jap destroyer was taken under fire at a range of ten thousand yards in modified radar control. This ship then observed by radar two cruisers to be closing the formation rapidly and proceeded to take the nearest cruiser under fire in modified radar control at a range of eleven thousand yards. Approximately one hundred rounds were fired at these two targets which were not actually seen at any time. At 0750 received orders by TBS for small boys to make torpedo attack. CTU 77.4.33 then ordered small boys to form one eight. This ship then proceeded to fall in astern of the USS HOEL, HEERMANN and ROBERTS and furnish fire support for these ships as they made their torpedo attack. Firing was continued intermittently on the closest enemy cruiser. Difficulty was experienced by gunnery control in staying on the target due to radical movements of the ship and loss of own ship's course. As we turned to retire after the other destroyers had fired their torpedoes, range closed to six thousand yards on the leading Japanese cruiser and many hits were obtained on it at this time. Retirement was commenced with the aid of a heavy smoke screen. At approximately 0810 the

JOHNSTON emerged from a heavy smoke screen only to find the USS HEERMANN on our starboard bow on a collision course with us at a distance of about two hundred yards. The Captain backed full on the one remaining engine and the HEERMANN was observed to back full on all engines. A collision was thus averted by the narrowest possible margin. The HEERMANN was observed to backing at a speed of at least fifteen knots, thus naturally aiding in avoiding us. As soon as the HEERMANN cleared us, all possible speed was again made. At about 0820 there suddenly appeared out of the smoke a battleship of the KONGO class, seven thousand yards distant, on our port beam. This target had been reported to control combat and was immediately taken under fire. By this time the Captain had given the order not to fire on any target unless we could see it, the reason for this order being that enemy and friendly ships were now in the melee. Approximately forty rounds were fired at the Jap battleship, at our necessarily reduced rate of fire, before retiring behind our own smoke screen and before being taken under fire by this battleship. Several hits were observed on the pagoda superstructure.

During this period the ship was heading, in general, to southwestward, several miles astern of our main body. As we headed in southwesterly direction, in general, we had the Jap cruiser and battleship force on our port quarter and the Jap destroyers on our starboard quarter. This picture was held clearly in mind by the Captain at all times. Ranges varied from seven to twelve thousand yards to all those Jap units. Liberal use was being made of a smoke screen protection throughout this period. At about 0830 the GAMBIER BAY was observed to be under heavy fire by a Japanese heavy cruiser and listing heavily to port. This ship attempted to draw fire away from the GAMBIER BAY by taking the cruiser under fire at this time. The range was closed to six thousand yards and maximum fire was brought to bear on this heavy cruiser. This attempt, as was to be expected, was unsuccessful, despite numerous hits being observed. At about 0840 fire was checked when it became apparent that the Japanese destroyers on our port hand were closing rapidly on the carriers. Upon receiving this information from combat, the Captain directed our course toward the enemy destroyers who were deployed in a column with the apparent destroyer leader in the van, followed by two divisions consisting of three destroyers apiece. The Japanese destroyers were sighted at a range of about ten thousand yards and fire was immediately opened on the destroyer leader. Our fire appeared to be extremely effective and the range continued to close to about seven thousand yards. This ship was hit several times during this encounter by five inch projectiles. Approximately twelve hits were obtained on the leading Japanese destroyer before a most amazing thing happened. The destroyer leader proceeded to turn ninety degrees to the right and break off the action. Fire was immediately shifted to the second destroyer and hits were observed at initial range of around eight thousand yards. During firing on this second destroyer the Captain attempted to cross the "T" on the Jap column. However, before this was accomplished, amazingly enough, all remaining six Jap destroyers turned ninety degrees to the right and the range began to open rapidly.

The TBS transmission had been received just prior to our opening fire on those Jap destroyers, directing the small boys to interpose between the carriers and Japanese cruisers on their port quarter. We checked fire as the Jap destroyers retired, turned to the left and proceeded to close the range on the Jap cruisers. For the next half hour this ship proceeded to engage first the cruisers on our port hand and then the destroyers on our starboard hand, alternating between the two groups in a somewhat desperate attempt to keep all of them from closing the carrier formation. The ship was getting hit with disconcerting frequency throughout this period. Finally at about 0930 we found ourselves with two cruisers dead ahead of us, several Jap destroyers on our starboard quarter and two cruisers on our port quarter. The battleships were still well astern of us. At this fateful time numerous Japanese units had us under very effective fire, all of these ships being within six to ten thousand yards of us. Shortly after this an avalanche of shells knocked out our lone remaining engine room and fire room. Director and plot lost power. All communications were lost throughout the ship. All guns were out of operation with the exception of five inch gun number four that was still shooting in local control. As the ship went dead in the water and its fate long since inevitable, the Captain gave the order to abandon ship at about 0945. The ship was abandoned by approximately 0955 and the ship was observed to roll over and sink at 1010. The ship was under constant fire up to the time it actually rolled over and sank. A Japanese destroyer was observed to close the range to one thousand yards to insure the ship's final destruction.

Part III

Performance of own ordnance material and equipment.
(a) Ordnance material in general was very good. Considerable difficulty was experienced with oversized powder cases. A large part of this trouble undoubtedly can be attributed to the necessity of ramming by hand the after three guns during the major part of the engagement.

However, four powder cases had to be extracted after attempting to ram with power still available on the rammer.

The full-empty indicator linkage on the 5" gun projectile hoist jammed the entire hoist on #3 guns making it impossible to hoist shells manually. It is recommended that this linkage be removed from the projectile hoists as unnecessary.

This ship had been in commission one year. It had not fired a practice surface problem or any torpedo practice since shakedown. Fortunately, realistic drills, including all casualties that actually occurred during the engagement were invaluable.

The pointers and trainers all required reliefs during the two hours the after guns were in manual. Excellent results were observed from the after guns however, with them in telescope control, after having matched indication pointers to locate the target. Sight angles and sight deflection were given constantly over the JQ phone circuit and were set in accurate.

This ship had made no advanced provision for replacing men killed on the 5: guns. This oversight became apparent when all men in #3 - 5" upper handling room were killed or badly burned by hot steam from after engine room. Eventually, men were brought in from 20 MM guns to supply this gun.

This ship had non-tracer, non-self-destructive 40 MM ammunition. It is believed this would have been effective on the cruisers and destroyers that came within 6000 yards of us. However, this opportunity to inflict damage on the enemy was overlooked. The Gunnery Officer was cognizant of this potential weapon, but felt that his full attention was required with the 5" guns. This ship was rigged to fire two 40 MM from main battery director.

The performance of the lookouts was disappointing. Very little was seen of them after the Machine Gun Officer and Lookout Officer were killed on the first hit received. The Gunnery Officer acted as Chief Lookout on the disengaged side. CIC supplied invaluable dope constantly as to the whereabouts of the enemy units. A large part of the time, however, it was a problem of firing at the closest ship visible through the smoke. Fire discipline was remarkably excellent. On one occasion we trained on one of our DE's as it came out of the smoke screen close abroad. Then the ship was identified as friendly, the director was trained off target. One hot gun had a powder case "cook-off" at that instant and a near miss resulted just ahead of the DE.

Hot load guns normally were ordered fired out with no delay upon being reported after checking fire.

Communications were maintained with four of the five guns and with Plot up to the very last.

The first hits received knocked out the ship's gyro and grounded out the firing circuit. All firing after the first hit was rapid continuous fire with the gun pointer firing either by Local Battery or by percussion. The first hits tumbled the stable element and the entire IC board tripped out for about two minutes. After power was regained, the stable element was set back in the vertical position by hand and placed in operation.

The first shell hits sheared off the FD radar antenna shearing off pin, slewing the antenna into the elevation stops, and elevation control of the FD radar was lost. The antenna was then grabbed and pointed in general at the horizon and ranges were again obtained. Radar ranges were used throughout.

Standard gunnery doctrine was used throughout except that only limited firing was done in modified radar control after the own ship's course went out.

(b) Ten torpedoes and over 800 rounds of 5" ammunition were fired during the action. Seven smoke screen generators were expended.

(c) Effectiveness of gunnery was great, and it should have been, as the targets were large, were not moving too radically, and the range was in most cases disconcertingly short.

2. The effectiveness of the Japanese gunnery was not impressive. While they were good enough to sink us, with gunfire they had available, our staying afloat as long as we did is nothing short of remarkable. Their reactions seemed very slow, and we continually succeeded in throwing many salvos into both Jap cruisers and destroyers before they would retaliate. At the medium ranges at which they were engaged their percentage of hits was unbelievingly low. No fire control radar was apparent and no effective search radar seemed able to help them anticipate us, as we continually surprised them as we came out of the smoke screen.

Green and red projectile bursts were observed closely. The battleships were firing AP projectiles.

The Japanese destroyer torpedo attack was ineffective as a result of their unexplainable failure to take a favorable position on the bow of the carriers before launching their attack.

In general the Japanese appeared hesitant and uncertain as to what to do, both in their maneuvering and in their gunnery, and as a result ended up doing very little.

Part IV

(1) See enclosure (B) for report of ships damage.
(2) Enemy Battle Damage.

(a) 0715-0730 Fired at enemy heavy cruiser with common projectiles. Believe seriously damaged with at least 40 hits.

0720 - Ten torpedoes fired with same heavy cruiser as point of aim. Believe scored two torpedo hits on this cruiser, leaving it dead in the water and blazing furiously astern. A fainter underwater explosion heard about a minute after the two explosions were heard on the heavy cruiser lends to the possibility that a battleship was hit by one torpedo. See diagram of torpedo problem in Enclosure (A).

0750 - 0800 A second heavy cruiser was hit by at least 10 5" AA common projectiles.

0820 - Fired at battleship of KONGO class. Scored at least 15 hits with 5" AA Common shells.

0830 - Fired at heavy cruiser sinking GAMBIER BAY. Scored 5 hits with AA Common projectiles.

0840 - 0850 Fired at second destroyer. Scored 5 hits - moderate damage.

0900 - 0940 Firing intermittently at cruisers and destroyers, scoring numerous individual hits during this period with no approximation of damage possible.

(b) (1) Most significant effect of damage was probably noticed on the enemy destroyers. The fact that they eventually, about (0920) launched their torpedo attack from the starboard quarter of the carriers - well abaft their beam - is testimony of their respect for our gunfire. Undoubtedly our constant disappearing and reappearing thru the smoke screen gave the impression that more than one destroyer was engaging them. If they had moved up on the bow of our carriers, the carrier's complete destruction would have been inevitable. The Jap destroyers did not launch a typical torpedo attack - it was more a last desperate shot before they retired.

(2) The heavy cruiser hit by torpedoes and numerous 5" projectiles is believed to have been seen to sink by flyers.

(3) Structural damage to the Jap cruisers and one battleship that hits were scored on undoubtedly had the effect of knocking out a great many anti-aircraft guns on their topsides rendering them more vulnerable to subsequent air strikes.

(c) No accurate estimate can be made of enemy material and personnel casualties, but it is certain that they were extensive.

Part V

1. (a) Internal communications were in general very good throughout, considering the number of hits taken. However, there was a distinct weakness in communicating with steering aft. When all communications from the bridge were finally lost, and remaining on the bridge became unbearable from the fire from #2 5" gun, the commanding officer went to the fantail and continued to conn the ship from there. Communications within the task unit were excellent throughout the battle. All maneuvering was by TBS. Circuit discipline was good, and use of the circuit was restricted to necessary communications. It is interesting to note that in spite of the terrific punishment taken and a direct hit in radio control, the TBS was operational to the very end.

Communications between the forces is what appears to have been fouled up. We had received numerous contact reports of the enemy force coming toward San Bernardino Straits but it was assumed that Task Force 38 was guarding the Straits. The greatest failure of communications was the failure of CTF 30 to notify CTF 77.4 that he was leaving the Straits for the Escort Carrier Group to protect. Report of destruction of publications is attached hereto, as Enclosure (C). The radar equipment held up unusually well. The first hit snapped off the SC radar antenna, but it was the only radar that was permanently out. The SG and FD were out temporarily, when power was lost, but both went back on very shortly, and both operated to the very end.

(c) - - - - -

(d) - - - - -

(e) The use of smoke appeared to be effective, and when the ship was behind a screen the enemy firing was very ineffective. One very providential rain squall made an effective screen when it was most needed, right after the first hit.

(f) CIC kept control and the bridge well informed as to the location of enemy targets, and the sole failure was their failure to give any warning of the approach and near collision with the USS HEERMANN.

(g) - - - - -

(h)   Performance of engine room personnel and equipment was excellent throughout. Handling of casualties left nothing to be asked for. At the beginning of the action JOHNSTON had on 12,000 gals of fuel oil and 10,000 gals of diesel oil. No DD should ever be allowed to run that low.

(I) - - - - -

(j) - - - - -

As this report was written by the coordinated efforts of all the surviving officers no other comment is necessary. There should be more adequate communications with steering aft, it is recommended that a 21MC be installed there. It is also recommended that a magnetic compass be installed in steering aft. It was extremely difficult to maintain a steady course when cruising on one engine, and steering by hand from aft, giving directions by phone from the bridge. Each 5" gun should have two short powder cases available for emergency use. A scientific study of ships' silhouettes and constant drill estimating target angles and target speeds paid big dividends.

After this ship lost own ships course, and the action turned into a melee, very little time was had for the plotting room to improve on the "solution" estimated by the Gunnery Officer.

The 5" guns should be rigged to receive casualty power more efficiently. Recommend that a riser cable be installed from the main deck to steering aft on all 2100 ton destroyers.

The 141 survivors of this ship clung to three rafts and two floater nets for fifty hours before being rescued. It is recommended provisions resembling the very efficient manner in which downed fliers are picked up be made for rescuing ship survivors. This group of survivors was "zoomed" by three different friendly planes within two hours after the ship sunk. No life rafts or food were dropped by them and no help arrived for two days and two nights. During this period forty five officers and men died as a result of wounds, shock, and exposure. In another day without help there would have been no survivors of this ship. The Captain and Executive Officer are missing in action. Five additional officers and 87 men are missing in action. All these Officers and men were seen alive in the water after abandoning ship, but have not been heard from since. With only a few exceptions the only group of survivors picked up were those gathered together by the Gunnery Officer immediately after the ship sunk.

Part VI

1. (a) Personnel performance, in general left nothing to be desired. A well-trained crew fought its ship in an inspired manner in accordance with the highest traditions of the Navy. See Medical Report attached as Enclosure (A).

Signed: R.C. HAGEN

DAMAGE – DD 557

DAMAGE

A16-3 USS Johnston (DD557)
Serial 03 c/o Fleet Post Office
San Francisco, Calif.
13 November 1944
C-O-N-F-I-D-E-N-T-I-A-L

From: The senior Surviving Officer
To: The Chief of Bureau of Ships

Subject: Damage to the USS Johnston in Battle Off Samar on 25 October 1944, Report of:

1. The following account is a chronological report of gun fire damage that resulted in the sinking of the USS JOHNSTON in the Battle Off Samar on 25 October 1944. All times are local time (-9 time zone) and are approximate only, as no record or logs were saved when the ship sank.

0650 General Quarters

0655 Commenced making FS and funnel smoke. All damage control equipment broke out and ready for use. Two boilers lighted off.

0720 All four boilers on the main steam line with superheat temperature at 900

0730 Ship sustained first hits which were composed of a salvo of three 14" or 16" projectiles, followed very closely by three 6" projectiles. No. 1 14" hit at Frame 156 under #6 Depth Charge Projector, hitting between bulkhead C-202 and C-203 breaking open on depth charge and tearing a hole in the main deck 3' wide and 6' long. Shell hit bench along forward bulkhead of the machine shop tearing a hole about 4' in diameter in bulkhead and hitting main reduction gear port engine and detonating. On passing through main deck, shell cut plumbing and main drain from ship's head. Compartment C-202 commenced flooding through ruptured sea ghost at end of main drain from head. Flooding was controlled by stuffing rags and wooden plugs into ruptured sea ghost. Compartment C-203 was flooding due to ship's zig-zag motions. Water was passing through hole in main deck passing into C-202 and into C-203 through large hole in bulkhead between C-203 and C-202. Water would wash up into hole in main deck when ship would turn to starboard. This motion put 3 to 4 inches of water in C-203. Several salt water lines and the main leading to deck plug frame 137 were shattered by shrapnel, also electrical wiring leading from #2 engine room through C-202 aft. This hit slowed speed to 17 knots and turns on starboard engine was increased to 350 RPMs which was sustained until emergency astern signal later. No. 2 14" hit frame 144 port side between #2 and #4 Depth Charge Projector passing through main deck about 1' inboard down into #2 engine room detonating on hitting main steam turbine. On passing through the deck this shell cut main steam strainer, main steam line to cruising turbine, one of the two main steam lines leading to the HP turbine and cut all electrical cable running aft that came through the bulkhead near main cruising turbine. All lights were extinguished and the after engine room filled with escaping steam. Seams were ruptured in hull of ship near frame 146 below reduction gear and compartment and started slow flooding. No. 3 14" hit penetrated main deck and uptake space at junction of uptake space vertical bulkhead and main deck from 127 - 128 port side. On passing through deck shell sheared auxiliary steam line in uptake space, passing down into #4 boiler and detonating. Boiler was demolished and the compartment filled with steam. On detonating shell ruptured bulkhead leading to #2 engine room port side about 5' up from bottom of shell plating. Fires under both boilers, except one burner in #3 boiler was extinguished by concussion. Master fuel oil valve was closed from topside by hand and all topside steam valves were closed. Ship had been on split plant operation and all valves leading aft from #1 engine room were closed. No. 4 6" shell hit #2 stack under director platform. Binnacle was demolished and platform bent upward on both sides of stack. Shell detonated after hitting stack but location cannot be ascertained. No. 5 and No. 6 6" shells hit port side of bridge, one detonating on bridge and one passing bridge deck aft of port director.

ADDITIONAL DAMAGE AND DAMGE CONTROL MEASURES

S.C. Radar antenna was snapped by whipping motion of mast and fell on yard arm. Master Gyro frame was broken in half and power was out to gyro. Repair parties evacuated wounded from bridge and commenced evacuation of wounded men from #2 fire room and #2 engine room. Several men from #2 fire room had escaped immediately after hits but rescue measures could not be attempted for about 10 minutes due to steam. The first hits caused #3 Upper Handling room to be abandoned temporarily due to steam escaping through hatch leading from #2 engine room, port side Compartment B-111/114, and filling the handling room with steam. All power aft of #2 engine room was out and steering was commenced in manual in steering engine room. Guns 54 and 55 began loading by hand and passing shells to gun mounts by hand. All projectile hoists had been jammed or damaged from shock and could not be operated manually. Casualty power was lost from #1 engine room distribution board. The cause of power failure cannot be ascertained though repeated attempts were made to complete the circuit. Evacuation of #2 engine room and #2 fire room was accomplished by men descending into the spaces equipped with asbestos suits and breathing apparatus. About 10 minutes after all wounded were evacuated from engineering spaces, electrical fires broke out in #2 fire room and #2 engine room. Those fires were quickly extinguished with 15 pound CO_2 bottles by men in asbestos suits, but for a period of 30 minutes repeated electrical fires broke out before they were finally completely extinguished. Those first were due to an attempt to supply the after guns and steering engine room with normal or stand-by power supply. When it was ascertained that all cables leading aft were out, all breakers leading aft were opened. The slow flooding resulted in water about 3' deep in #2 E.R. when a submersible pump was rigged, but no power supply was available within reach of the pump cable. A longer lead was spliced on the pump and lead to passage B-101 which had a casualty power switch connected to #1 engine room board. Again it was not possible to get power. Apparently there was a rupture or faulty hookup from #1 engine room board to the casualty power switches. Both 3 5" magazines began to flood slowly and water was 6' deep in the compartment one hour later.

0810 Hits were received in the Supply Office, Emergency Radio room to and forward of gun #4. Those hits demolished the places hit but did not affect the fighting efficiency of the ship. Many men in the vicinity were killed and injured.

0910 Sustained three 5" or 6" hits. One exploded in the coding Room. It demolished the Coding Room, chart Storage, wrecked all gear in Radio Control (except the TBS), killed or wounded all persons in Radio Control, set fire to #1 40 MM ready service magazine. A few 40 MM shells exploded and dense smoke resulted. The second projectile hit #2 5" gun by the pointers seat, wrecking the mount, killing or wounding all the gun crew, started fires in #2 5" upper handling room. Heavy smoke resulted increasing the difficulties of the bridge and control personnel. The third projectile hit just forward of #1 5" gun penetrating the deck and caused flooding to begin in #1 5" magazine. Two fire hoses and sprinkling system extinguished the fire in #1 40 MM ready service magazine. A fire hose succeeded in extinguishing fires in #2 5" mount and upper handling room. All of these fires were put out 5 - 10 minutes after the fires started. As a result of these hits all communications was lost with steering aft. Orders to the wheel were then sent back by A16-3 messenger until about 0920. At this time the Captain went to the fantail and conned the ship from there with only his seaman's eye and knowledge of the relative position of enemy ships to guide him. From 0910 on we sustained innumerable hits up and down the length of the ship.

0920 - 0930 All depth charges in the stern racks were scuttled.

0940 Sustained hits in #1 fire room which stopped starboard engine. The ship slowed down and finally went dead in the water.

0945 The Captain gave order to "Abandon Ship".

0955 All personnel capable to do so had left the ship. The gig and four life rafts were successfully launched. However, the gig was apparently filled with shrapnel, as it sank shortly after it was in the water. Considerable difficulty was experienced in getting two floater nets over the side. The floater nets are not easily removed from the ship. Those we did not get off went down with the ship as the ship rolled over before she sank.

1010 The ship was observed to roll over and sink bow first.

Signed: R.C. HAGEN

L – R, Eli Taksian, ADM Bill Crowe and Bill Mercer at the Navy Memorial in 2003

The previous photo is of Bill Mercer (right), survivor of DD-557, with ADM Bill Crowe (center), former Chairman of the Joint Chiefs, and CAPT Eli Takesian, who was DESRON 4 Chaplain and rode the USS Johnston (DD-821) in 1966-1967. Bill Mercer attended our US Navy Memorial plaque dedication in 2003 – see the second picture of the plaque – it is proudly on display at the Navy Memorial today. Bill Mercer also shared in considerable detail his experiences that day and while in the water the next two.

It was a riveting story. Bill plays a prominent role in Jim Hornfischer's book. Both Mercer and Crowe passed away several years ago.

> **USS JOHNSTON DD557 - DD821**
> The Officers and Men of USS Johnston (DD821)
> Salute the Crew of USS Johnston (DD557)
>
> Sunk during their heroic defense of TU 77.4.3 (Taffy 3)
> Battle of Leyte Gulf - Battle off Samar - 25 October 1944
>
> Honors Ceremony At the Site: 11° 50'N - 126° 10'E
> While enroute to Vietnam - 26 December 1967

Footnotes in Texas History: Orange's World War II Shipbuilding Boom

Editor's note: This article was written by Ginger Mynatt and appeared in "Texas Co-Op Power" magazine, October 2011. Consolidated Steel in Orange Texas is where DD-821 was built.

The city of Orange, on Texas' eastern border, was nearly wiped out by the Depression despite a proud history of lumbering and shipbuilding on the banks of the Sabine River near the Gulf of Mexico. In the 1930s, Orange was broke. The population had dwindled. A mere 8 percent of residents had jobs. Businesses were shuttered, and farms were repossessed.

But then the Japanese attacked Pearl Harbor, and the United States entered World War II. Overnight, Orange became a bustling metropolis; helping supply the largest navy in the world as one of the nation's leading shipbuilding towns.

Because Orange already had shipbuilding infrastructure, U.S. Navy officials arrived with lucrative contracts in hand. Steel fabricator Consolidated Western Steel Corp. built a shipyard, and the existing Levingston and Weaver shipbuilding companies expanded. Within a few months, these three companies created thousands of jobs. People came from everywhere:

nearby communities and farms, East and North Texas, the swamps of Louisiana and hills of Oklahoma. From 1941 to 1945, Orange's population ballooned from a few thousand to about 70,000.

Production churned around the clock. The bright lights of the shipyards illuminated the revamped downtown 24 hours a day. The bustle of people coming and going at all hours, the hammering and drilling of sheet metal and the pneumatic pounding of rivets made night like day. Young boys stood at the gates of shipyards at midnight hawking newspapers, shoeshines and anything else they could find to sell.

New service businesses opened up. Cleaners, shoe repairs, auto shops, barbershops and grocery stores could not keep up with demand. Employers opened early, closed late and tried to keep wages competitive with those of the shipyards to retain help. Every commodity was in short supply: dry goods, canned goods, clothing, auto parts, construction materials and fresh food. Local gardeners and farmers sold produce before it ripened and eggs before they were laid.

A housing shortage drove people to live in tents, fields, barns and sheds. To solve the problem, the federal government bulldozed sand into a marsh and built more than 4,500 temporary homes in a development called Riverside. Because Riverside bordered the Sabine River, the ground was always wet. Concrete streets, designed as drains, channeled the water when it rained, but there was nowhere for it to go. Even if a Riverside resident could afford a car, it couldn't make it through the streets; therefore, people walked barefoot to their homes.

Educated locals filled office and supervisory positions, mingling with naval officers and administrators from other parts of the country. Uneducated workers attended school and trained for specific jobs. They became machinists, welders or fabricators in a matter of weeks. Even with all of the workers descending on the town, Orange needed more. Women entered the workforce.

Young single women from farms and widowed women whose husbands were killed overseas - many with children to support - joined the ranks. Even townswomen lined up to work, donning pants and hardhats to the shock of some of their neighbors.

To the surprise of many men, women proved to be great workers in the shipyards, eagerly learning, paying attention to detail and taking their jobs seriously. In small areas, women's smaller hands and statures were big assets. But women weren't restricted to dainty work. They tackled grueling projects and didn't complain, even when shooting hot rivets deep in the hull of a ship, enduring 100-degree heat.

Collectively, the community of Orange produced hundreds of ships, including the USS Aulick - the first warship from Texas to enter active service. Consolidated Steel produced 39 destroyers and 110 destroyer escorts, well-armed, fast-moving warships that protected troop carriers and other large ships. In four years, Levingston Shipbuilding built 160 vessels: barges, small river and large ocean tugboats, tenders to ferry supplies and messages. Weaver Shipbuilding completed 135 minesweepers made from wood to deter German magnetic explosives.

Nine other major U.S. shipbuilders bolstered the American fleet during World War II, most of them near large cities such as Pittsburgh, Jacksonville, Florida, Los Angeles and Houston, areas that touted huge workforces. Per capita, however, the once tiny town of Orange out produced them all.

Chapter 2

TECHNICAL DETAILS
Destroyer History Notebook
Evolution of the 5-Inch/38-Caliber Gun

Editor's note: This story appeared in "The Tin Can Sailor" newspaper Vol. 36, No 4.

Since at least 1933 the main guns installed on U.S. Navy destroyers have been some version of the 5-inch. By far the largest number was the famed 5-inch/38-caliber guns, either in single or dual mounts. The first were the FARRAGUT's (DD-348 to DD-355) each of which carried five of the guns. They were followed by the GEARING Class ships which were built with six guns in three dual mounts. The 5-inch/38, as it is normally called, was installed as the main battery in some 512 destroyers. In addition, the gun was installed on many other ship types, from cruisers and battleships as the secondary battery to aircraft carriers as antiaircraft batteries. The USS ATLANTA-class cruisers had 16 of the guns in 8 twin mounts as the main battery.

The 5-inch gun has been the mainstay of American destroyers for more than 75 years and is still in use today though the guided missile has replaced the naval gun as their main battery. Shown in this picture is a ship equipped with two 5-inch twin mounts forward. She is moored next to a ship with two 5-inch single mounts forward. Because the two guns of twin mounts operate as a unit, their advantage lies in the number of projectiles that can be put on target at any given amount of time.

No destroyers were built after the 156 CLEMSON-class ships of 1919 until the FARRAGUTs. The CLEMSONs carried the 4-inch/50 caliper main guns but they were not effective against aircraft and lacked director control. The intervening 14 years gave naval engineers and designers time to come up with a workable replacement for the old 4-inch stand-by. The 5-inch provided everything the navy wanted in projectile lethality, range, and accuracy and in the switch to a separate projectile and power for improved storage and handling.

After their FRAM 1 conversion, most GEARING-class ships lost their second mount, leaving only one twin mount forward. Here the USS NEWMAN K. PERRY (DD-883) fires her forward guns at a target in Vietnam in 1966. With a range of 9 miles, most coastal targets were within range of a destroyer's guns. The speeds of jet aircraft ended the usefulness of these guns as antiaircraft batteries which forced the navy to pair the ships with guided missile destroyers

or cruisers when operating in a potentially hostile area.

Following the 8 FARRAGUTs in 1934 were 8 PORTERs and 16 MAHANs in 1936. Four small classes appeared in 1937, the DUNLAP (2), GRIDLEY (4), BAGLEY (8), and SOMERS (5). As construction ramped up after Japan's 1936 termination of the London Naval Treaty that set limits on construction of warships for the United States, Great Britain, and Japan, American shipbuilding designs incorporated ever more of the new 5-inch guns. In 1939 came the 10 BENHAMs and 12 SIMS but with war threats in 1940, building increased drastically with 30 BENSON-class and 66 GLEAVES-class destroyers (the latter was also known as the BRISTOL or LIVERMORE-class.) Finally, a design that nearly everyone could agree upon was approved and beginning in 1942, the FLETCHER Class began to enter the fleet ultimately totaling 175 ships. They were the last of the single-mount 5-inch/38-cal guns and were followed by 58 ALLEN M. SUMNER-class and 98 GEARING-class destroyers as well as 12 destroyer minelayers which were SUMNER hulls converted before commissioning.

Until that time, the maximum range of the 5-inch projectile was 9 miles fired from the unstable platform of a destroyer at sea. As shore installations shifted from manually-aimed shore batteries and mobile artillery to radar-directed guns, different weapons were needed. A greater stand-off distance was needed as defense against the improved shore batteries. The solution was the appropriately timed MK57 RAP or Rocket Assisted Projectile with its MK62 rocket motor that provided a 2-second burn which increased the rocket's range by 50% without diminishing its accuracy. They were used in the Vietnam War beginning as early as 1969.

In this action painting on a U.S. Navy recruiting poster, a sailor is ready to load a 4-inch shell into a gun. The 4-inch was the largest diameter fixed cartridge used. In the 5-inch and larger shells, the powder and projectile were separate. In the smaller guns, the powder is in a shell casing whereas the powder in larger weapons is loaded in silk bags. A single powder casing holding 19-20 pounds of powder could propel a 50-55 pound projectile out to a full nine miles but the powder necessary to hurl a battleship's 16-inch projectile, weighing as much as 2,700 pounds, took more than 600 pounds of powder to reach the maximum range of 23 miles. The navy had stopped equipping ships with the 4-inch guns by 1935.

But all things manmade eventually come to the end of their usefulness. The manpower-intensive 5-inch/38 cal gun eventually became a candidate for replacement, not so much with a superior weapon as a more automated one. As many as 38 men, by some accounts, were needed to fully man the gun, its handling room, and magazine. It was replaced by the 5-inch/54-caliber gun, which was, at least, partially automated with no one in the gun mount and only a 3-man crew below deck to oversee, operate, and feed the automatic loader. The old 5-inch/38 continued in use for more than a decade but all future construction incorporated automated naval guns.

"Copyright 2012, Tin Can Sailors, Inc. Used with Permission."

Chapter 3

YEARS 1945 THROUGH 1949

Kilroy Was Here!

KILROY WAS HERE

For those of you who served during WWII you likely remember this. It made no difference what city; town, burg, state, island or what country you went to, Kilroy had already been there. During World War II, the saying "Kilroy Was Here!" began to appear as graffiti at home and wherever the American military traveled overseas. Eventually the saying and the cartoon character that often accompanied it came to represent America's worldwide presence. Today, it remains a whimsical symbol of the achievements made by Americans during the 20th century's darkest hour.

PHIL'S ADVENTURES - Part Deux
By: Phil Demmel, Teleman (TE-3)

Years on board the Johnston: 1948 to 1953

Hello George - I just finished that latest newsletter and I thought that I would take you up on writing about some of the interesting things that I vividly remember. I was on board the Johnston from November 1948 until January of 1953. My rate was TE3 and I was also the ship's mailman from May 1949 until I left the ship in January 1953. I came onboard while the ship was in the Boston Navy Yard being repaired from the collision with the carrier KEARSAGE. I was with several other guys and we were all directed to the mess hall for some coffee and then told to find some place to hit the rack. In the mess hall I saw a mess cook rubbing his feet and toes with his hands so I passed on the coffee. Another time while we were in Newport, I made a mail run in the motor launch to pick up our mail. We were told that we would be stuck on the beach for the day because the ship would be late getting back into port. I put the mail into the launch and headed for the Blue Moon bar on Thames Street. I met a woman there and talked her into staying with me for the day. We got a room and did the big nasty and then went out for chow. I asked her if she was game again and she said yes so we did it again. I asked her if she would like to go to a show and she said OK. After the show I asked if she was still game and she said GAME ON. Finally it was time to go back to the fleet landing and return to the ship. On the way I heard someone say "HEY SAILOR!" but I kept on walking. Then I heard that voice again and I turned to see who was being called. It was two Newport Police officers and they wanted me. They asked me how long I had known this woman and I said that we had just met that morning. I naturally left out some of the details. I was then told this woman was a 16 year old runaway from Boston and that I should shove off RIGHT NOW!

   I have never forgotten those great days. I was on Johnston's softball team for the 1951-1952 seasons. We won the SOPA trophy and went undefeated. Our record for the year was 48 wins and 3 losses. Our main pitcher was Al "red" Miller and he was un-hittable. I played third base and was a part of a great bunch of guys who only played to win.

Having been the mailman, I heard a lot of stories and was involved in a lot of things that I just don't have time for now. Oh yes, while we were in Trieste, Italy I had to go in to the airport to meet the airplane with our mail. I rode in a large army truck and had to sit on the mail bags because the seats were really hard. When we arrived at the airport, I only had one sack of mail instead of two. Ralph Hocking was with us and he suggested that we stop back in one of the towns that we had driven through and sure enough at the police station we found our lost sack of mail. I "NEVER" said a word, but I made certain that on the next mail run this sack of mail was delivered. That was the original snail mail.

The best years of my life were from 1948 until my discharge in 1953. No regrets. The chief torpedo man that swore me in during 1948 later came aboard in 1952 and we hit it off just great. Holy hell, I could keep on going and going but this time I will quit.

(Editor's note: I asked Phil what the "TE" rate was and what his job on the ship was because I was unfamiliar with it. Here is what he said)

The TE rating was abolished not long after I left the Navy and was changed to Postal Clerk (PC). My time was spent in the radio shack or ship's office, mostly just hanging out in the cubby-hole near the ships store. After all of the modifications to the Johnston after I left you may not know where the ship's store was. It was originally near the aft officer's quarters. I don't have a picture of the insignia that I wore on my shoulder, but it was a combination of the radioman and yeoman. My GQ station was a loader for one of the 40 mil guns. It was a tough job but someone had to do it!

Bio - F1/C Art Damm

Served on USS Johnston: 1946 to 1947 (Plank-Owner)

When my enlistment was up, I was sent to the Brooklyn Naval Yard for discharge. They gave me $100.00 mustering out pay and $4.17 for trainfare to the North Philly station.

Home looked different on Oct 10. 1947. My time in the service was up and I was in another world.

I can remember I was lying on the sofa when my Dad came home from work. First thing he asked me was, "Are you retired?" What he meant was go out and get a job. I did get work at Edward Budd Company making door post dies for the 1948 Kaiser Frazer autos. I left there in a year and got a job with

Derbyshire Machine and Tool Company as a machinist. They make specialized parts for the Navy such as custom valves, pumps and strainers. These products are made from bronze, stainless, aluminum and any other none-corrosive material. I remained at Derbyshire for 31 years and retired in 1990.

In that time I got married, had 3 kids, got divorced and am now happily married to Shirley for the past 13 years. We have a great life together with plenty of trips, vacations and long distant visits with friends and relatives.

Bio - Morrow Brown Garrison

Years on the Johnston: 1949 to 1952

Editor's Note: It is a real pleasure to present this bio of former Johnston shipmate, Morrow Garrison. Although I never met Morrow, I have the pleasure of knowing his wife Trudy, daughter Brenda Gail (BG for short) and his son-in-law Ward Hinds as a result of the USS Johnston DD-821 Association reunions. They never miss a year! They are all very fine people and I consider it an honor to know each of them

MORROW BROWN GARRISON (Gary) Born in Danville, Alabama on March 21, 1930 to Leldon D. and Grace Lorraine Garrison. Gary as most of his friends knew him attended the Winton Alabama Grammar School and Cotaco High School.

In 1948, he volunteered and served his country in the Navy with active duty until 1952 including a tour of duty in Korea and two in the European Theater as engineer aboard the Destroyer USS Johnston. He earned the rank of first class petty officer and received an honorable discharge with a good conduct medal and captain's commendation. While his ship was refitting for six months at her home port of Newport, Rhode Island, Gary met a charming young woman from the Boston area and began to commute there with increasing frequency. Returning to civilian life, he married his sweetheart, Gertrude Bouzan (Trudy) on June 13, 1953.

Trudy's family and his desire to complete his education brought him back to New England to Northeastern University where he received the degree of Bachelor of Science with a major in accounting in 1957. He took jobs as a painter and as an apprentice building superintendent to make ends meet while he went to college during the day.

The late 50's saw him begin his career both as a father with the arrival of Brenda Gail Garrison and as an accountant with a staff audit position at Arthur Anderson and then an internal auditor position at client company, Avildsen Tool and Machines.

In 1964, he took a position as controller of Snow Manufacturing Company, a manufacturer of automated high speed drilling, tapping and threading machines in Bellwood, Illinois and shortly after the company's sale by founder, Herman Goldberg to Wallace Carroll. With this transition began an association that was to form the major portion of his working career.

His dedication and loyalty to the enterprise was soon recognized and in 1972, he was promoted to Vice President / Controller of American Machine and Science Company, a new home office being set up to manage independent Carroll companies including Snow. During his tenure as group controller, he inspired such confidence in his employer that additional accounting and administrative duties were transferred to his office. These included a large number of Carroll family trusts and the maintenance and management of family-owned real estate including investment properties such as land and building in Kansas City, Reno, Arkansas, Texas, Massachusetts, Palm Beach and Minneapolis and Elgin, Barrington, Chicago and Lake Forest, Illinois.

He served during the 1970's and '80s as vice president and director of AMSI, and as president and director of Metetellic Corp., LeWa Co., Chelco Co., Building Management Corp., Illinois Property Management Corp., Manufacturers Acceptance Corp., secretary/treasurer and director of Chicago Capital Corp., and president of Park Safe Deposit Co., all headquartered in Elgin, Illinois. He was president and director of Master Machine Tools, Inc. in Hutchinson, Kansas, and Quasar Contemporaries in Mt. Prospect, Illinois and Director of Gaertner Scientific Co. in Chicago, Illinois.

In 1982, he negotiated a deal which was essentially the swap of a suburban Chicago bank in the AMSI Group for a residential development in Third Lake, Illinois that had been foreclosed by a Chicago bank. He completed and sold out this 380+ home site project in the next three (3) years and established AMSI as a significant real estate enterprise. Based on his research and strong advocacy, one of the Carroll enterprises bought the Quinlan & Tyson Company in October 1982, the largest-with over 20 offices and 450 sales associates-suburban residential real estate brokerage firm in the Chicago area. Gary, who had earlier obtained his brokerage license and joined the National Association of Realtors became president of Quinlan and Tyson and orchestrated the rapid turnaround in this recession-battered business and restored it to its previous position as a profitable industry leader. In 1985, he helped negotiate it sale to Merrill Lynch Real Estate on very favorable terms. He was elected to the position of Director of RELO in early 1984, serving a three-year term on the Board of this, the world's largest residential relocation network with 1039 affiliated firms in 1300 communities and 18 foreign countries.

When Gary was appointed President of AMSI Group of companies, he took direct responsibility for AMSI subsidiaries including Hinz Lithographing Company plus machine tool companies, Snow Manufacturing Company, Standard Automatic, Master Machine Tool, Johnson Drill Head Company, Mills Jennings Company in Chicago, later Reno, Hawthorne Bank of Wheaton, Illinois and Taft-Pierce in Cumberland, Rhode Island. In 1985 in the merger of the two Wallace E. Carroll groups of companies, American Machine & Science Inc. and International Metals & Machines, Inc., Gary became Vice Chairman of CRL, the combined company.

Even before the passing of his longstanding friend and employer, Wallace Carroll in 1990, Gary had begun to lay the groundwork for the development of large tracts of property owned by the LeWa Company (another Carroll company with primarily passive real estate assets). Appointed head of this group in the 1980s, he played a significant role in the joint venture development of International Plaza with Opus Corporation, a 275,000 square foot 10-story class A office building just south of the Minneapolis Airport. He had a major part in the platting of Lake Forest farmland to help solidify the inherent residential real estate values.

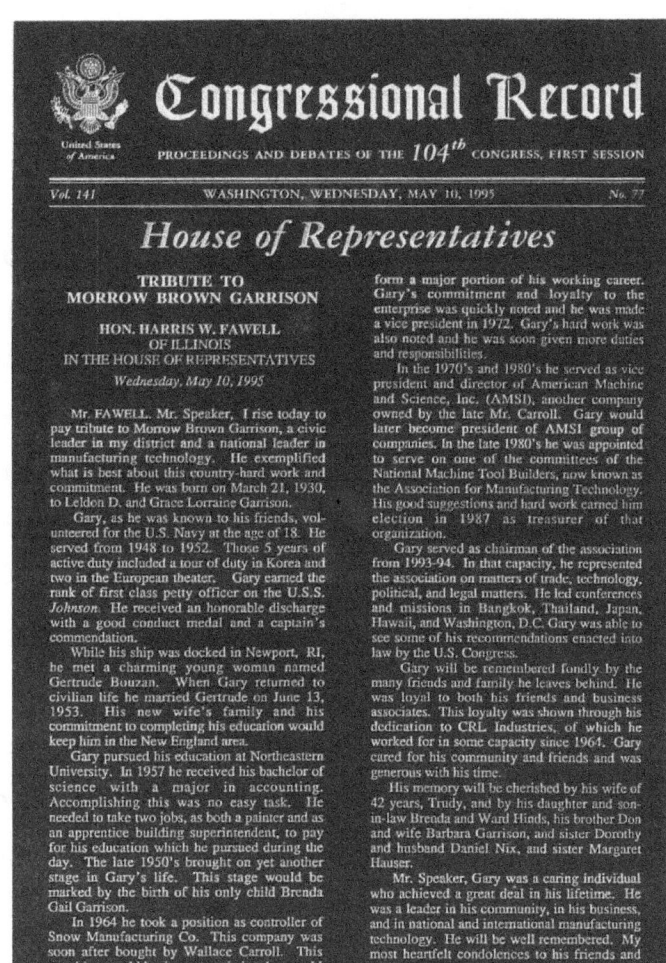

In the late 1980s, he was appointed to serve on one of the committees of the National Machine Tool Builders, now known as the Association for Manufacturing Technology. His good suggestions and active service earned him election in 1987 as treasurer of that organization representing most of the machine tool manufacturers and distributors in this $3 billion industry. Soon he was in the succession for Chairman and served in 1993 and '94 as head of this organization publicly representing the association in matters of trade, technology, political and legal matters. He led conferences and missions in Bangkok, Thailand, Japan, Hawaii and Washington D.C. during his tenure and had the satisfaction of seeing some of his recommendations enacted into law by the U.S. Congress. In 1994 and '95, he continued an active advisory role as immediate past president of this organization.

He also continued as consultant, advisor and director to the Carroll International Corporation and related entities despite his declining health.

Gary will be remembered fondly by the many friends he made in his business and personal life. He was a gentleman with a warm sense of humor, gracious under pressure, tough and insightful but always fair in business, scrupulously honest, trustworthy and loyal to his business associates and friends. He was a kind and generous person - never quick to take offense or rush to judgment on the character or motives of others. His keen and broad intelligence led him into numerous careers in which he excelled, fortunately without ever having to leave his one employer of some 30 years. He cared for his community and friends and gave generously of his time and advice when called upon in organizations such as the St. Andrews Society. His memory is cherished by his wife of 42 years, Trudy Bouzan Garrison, and daughter and son-in-law, Brenda and Ward Hinds and brother, Don and Barbara Garrison, and sister Dorothy and Daniel Nix, brother Arlin Bruce, brother Jack and wife Nancy Garrison, and sister Margaret Hauser.

His life profoundly affected the lives of many other people for the better and he will be deeply and widely missed. Gary passed away on May 2, 1995.

The Best Cruise I Ever Had
By: Alva H. "Al" Crichton, Radarman (RDSN)

Years on board the Johnston: 1949 to 1953

While aboard the Johnston on the deck force and then the radar gang, I made two cruises to the Mediterranean, two Midshipman cruises (one to Canada and one to Scotland and Holland). We made many cruises to Cuba and the Caribbean.

When I left the ship in 1953 she was off to a Northern Europe cruise. But the best duty I had was in January thru March of 1951. We were to go to Korea with the Fisk and Rush. However at the last moment we were replaced with a DDR and reassigned to another Division.

It was cold in Newport and we went to Pensacola, Florida to do plane guard duty for the pilots learning to land on the USS Monterey. We were in warm weather all winter. I used to pull liberty at Mobile, Alabama and on one three day liberty, two shipmates and I hitch-hiked to New Orleans. During 1951 on the return cruise to Newport we pulled into Savanna, Georgia and some of our men marched in the Saint Patrick's Day Parade. Some of the guys tore up the town. One of our officers told us the mayor told our skipper the USS Johnston is not welcome in Savannah anymore. This was the best cruise I ever had on the "Jolly J".

Chapter 4

YEARS 1950 THROUGH 1959

THE CURE ALL

By: Edward I. Buckle, Hospital Corpsman (HM)

Years on board the Johnston: 1950 to 1954

Editor's Note: This is a story frequently told by Ed to his family and 8 grandkids as recalled by his son Edward J. Buckle. Unfortunately, Corpsman Buckle passed away on March 19, 2013.

While in port, there was apparently a daily work detail to perform maintenance and whatever else you do on a destroyer while it's in port. At the time, Pop remembered one section of sailors on the boat that would show up in droves at sick bay when it was their turn for this duty. So before it was their turn one day, the Chief had my dad go to the PX and get three bottles of empty capsules. In three different colors (dad was colorblind, so no telling what color they were). He then filled them with sugar.

The story goes that as the ill sailors reported with their various ailments, they were quickly diagnosed with any one of several nefarious 'diseases' and prescribed some 'medication'. Some got yellow, some got blue, some got red. The general program was 'take two of these and if you're not feeling better in 30 minutes we will begin a series of injections", or something like that. Pop reported that all managed to make a quick recovery and help on the work detail.

SUMMER OF '51

By: George Nugent, Ensign

Years on board the Johnston: 1950 to 1951

The only episode I can recall occurred during a visit to Rotterdam I believe in the summer of '51. It goes like this.

One of our crew members was gone overnight and appeared in the morning under escort of a giant Dutch  policeman. It appears that the lady he visited in the night claimed that he failed to pay her. A quick trip below produced a carton of cigarettes, which the police officer accepted as compensation for the alleged transgression. The offender, being a member of the wardroom, was sufficiently chastised and embarrassed. Isn't it strange what we remember? There must have been far more important things that happened during my brief year on the Jolly J, but that particular one sticks in my mind.

EXPANDED ITINERARY

By: Ralph Hocking, Damage Controlman (DC-2)

Years on board the Johnston: 1951 to 1955

Let's see now---it was early 1953 (March? April?) and we had tied up in Portsmouth, England. I had applied for a few days' leave during our stay to visit my mother's relatives in Merrie Olde England.

Wait. Wait. Back up a bit for some biographical background. My mother was born in Sheppey, England and arrived in America in the early 1920s with the rest of her family. Her extended family, aunts, uncles, cousins remained in the city of Walsall.

Okay, back to Portsmouth. As luck would have it there were several English naval vessels at nearby docks. My mother had written her relatives that the Johnston was to visit Portsmouth in the course of our cruise. Shortly after our arrival a British sailor boarded the Johnston and asked for me; it was my mother's cousin Harold, who was serving aboard one of those English ships. A few minutes after our meeting, I was given permission to leave the Jolly J and visit his floating home. It was some time in the afternoon; time for an English naval tradition--a serving of rum. Rather a spot of luck, what?

I didn't see any more of Harold; his ship got underway the following day.

A day or so later I was given my leave to visit family in Walsall. Prior to my packing for the journey I prevailed on one of the cooks (who shall remain nameless) to give me a canned ham as a gift for my hosts. This turned out to be a stroke of genius as, unknown to me; England was still in the days of meat-rationing. Damn! Am I brilliant?

A ride in one of those typical English black taxis got me to the station where I boarded a train to London, then a ride to Birmingham, a large city not too far from my destination. It was interesting to ride in those trains which were divided into small compartments rather than the usual rows of seats for two so common in this country - and a vendor aboard kept making the rounds selling tea. He had a tank on his back and from a short hose attached to same he dispensed tea into a paper cup for a penny. It was a surprise to me that the tea was served with milk in it. A short trip from Birmingham to Walsall and I was greeted by my hosts. After arrival at the house the greeting became a celebration when I presented the ham. I was treated royally, though I'm sure that had more to do with my "engaging personality" than the H-A-M.

After a few days of sightseeing, including an evening at the cinema, it was time to end a delightful, informative visit and head back to Portsmouth. It was truly a marvelous opportunity to meet and learn from my extended family; Portsmouth was/is obviously high on my list of wondrous ports-of-call.

Although I never saw cousin Harold again, his sister and her daughter visited me in the early 70s when I lived in New Jersey.

And daughter, Stephanie, with husband Peter spent part of their honeymoon trip to the USA with me here in South Carolina in 1996.

Just thought I'd share what I believe is an unusual side-trip in the course of a Med/Europe cruise. How many others have had the chance to visit relatives in foreign countries while on one of Uncle Sam's cruises? Let's hear those stories.

---

3 1/2 YEARS ON THE JOLLY "J"

By: Bob Frost, Radioman (RM-3)

Years on board the Johnston: 1952 to 1955

I went aboard the Johnston in January 1952 and then went to Gitmo, Cuba followed by Radioman school. Following that in 1953 I met the Johnston in Londonderry, Ireland. Listed below are the rest of the ports we went to through September, 1955.

In 1953 we visited:

Athens, Greece
Piraeus, Greece
Argostoli, Greece - an island that sunk after we left due to an earthquake

Rhodes, Greece

Rock of Gibraltar

Oran, Africa

Izmir, Turkey - that is where we went wild boar hunting

Halifax, Nova Scotia

San Juan, Puerto Rico

St. Thomas, Virgin Islands

In 1954 we visited:

St. George, Bermuda

Trieste, Italy

Venice, Italy

Augusta Bay, Sicily

Athens, Greece

Rock of Gibraltar

Londonderry, Ireland

Wilhelmshaven, Germany - we were the first American ship to go there since 1939. We were treated like kings. People took us into their homes for meals, free taxi rides and the night club allowed us to have a jam session using their instruments. It was raining the day we left but the dock was just loaded with their residents waving us goodbye. It was a great port.

Bremerhaven, Germany - we came into port the same time as the USS United States. We looked like a small canoe next to it. I went aboard the USS United States to visit my wife's uncle, who was a Lt. Commander on board her and in charge of the Engineering Department.

Lorient, France - they didn't want any Americans there. Men were picked to go on liberty. Many fights broke out, so the Captain got everyone back on board and we got underway around midnight to avoid any more trouble.

Cardiff, Wales

Newcastle, England

Dundee, Scotland

Amsterdam, Holland - during a flood we helped people pile sand bags to hold back the water. We were honored by the Mayor for the help we gave them.

Portsmouth, England

Argentia, Newfoundland

In 1955 we visited:

Gitmo, Cuba

Kingston, Jamaica

Santiago, Cuba

San Juan, Puerto Rico

I don't know if anyone else ever listed the ports they went to with the Johnston. I spent 3 1/2 years on the ship and we were all family. It was a great time in my life. I married my wife when she was 17 and still had two weeks of high school left. I remember going to the Executive Officer and requesting overnight liberty to see my wife graduate from high school. He stated, "I never heard that excuse before!" and granted me overnight liberty.

OH SHIT, COURTMARSHAL
By: Mike Fanzone, Dispersing Clerk (DK-3)

Years on board the Johnston: 1953 to 1954

I became Ship's Store Operator early in December 1953. Stan Drier was the disbursing clerk and I was his assistant. We were at sea and the line at the store was quite long. As usual, I was selling Oreo cookies and Hershey candy bars. LT. Rankowski stepped to the front of the line and asked, "How much are the candy bars?"

I replied, "Twenty-four cents each or four for a dollar." He said, "I'll take four with almonds." He gave me a dollar and left.

Less than five minutes later he was back and very upset. He said, "You over-charged me. Twenty-four cents each should be ninety-six cents for four. Give me my four cents!"

I replied, "Sorry sir." and returned his four pennies. The guys in line witnessed this exchange of words and within a few minutes word spread throughout the ship.

A few days later it was payday. I was given the pay chit and the money, told to go to the bridge and pay the Captain. I requested permission from the Master at Arms to go to the bridge. I had never been on the bridge before. I approached the Captain, saluted and said, "Payday, Sir!" I presented him with the clipboard to sign the chit. He signed it; I gave him his money and was ready to leave.

He said, "Fanzone, I understand you had a misunderstanding with LT. Rankowski?" My first thought was "OH-SHIT, COURTMARSHAL". The Captain hesitated, looked me in the eye and said with a Cheshire cat grin, "DISMISSED."

Any Merchandise Left in the Ship's Store?

By: Mike Fanzone, Dispersing Clerk (DK-3

We were in Paris which was part of the ship's tour arranged by American Express. Norm Heise and I wanted to go on a tour of the night spots and at the last minute Norm cancelled out so I decided to go alone.

I arrived at the Lido Club around 1900 and proceeded to the bar. The bartender was very nice, suggested I move further down so I could see the show better. I told him I was limited in money. He said, "No problem, enjoy the show." A short time later, two women in full makeup and obviously B-girls or shills, sat next to me.

I repeated what I had said to the bartender, "No money."

They said, "OK, slow night!"

Just before the show started, the tour group from the ship arrived. There I was, sitting on the best seat in the house with a "hottie" on each side of me. I acknowledged their presence by saying, "Hello."

The officer in charge (I don't remember his name) came up to me and asked, "Is there any merchandise left in the ship's store?"

I smiled and said, "I think I left a little bit, sir!" and gave him a big smile.

A Short Duty Assignment
By: John Leo Raygor, Seaman (SN1/c)

Years on board the Johnston: 1953 to 1954

John served on the USS Johnston from January 1953 till his discharge September 1954. On 7 January 1953 he departed from Newport, RI for NATO operations in the North Atlantic. The Johnston aided the Dutch after storms in the North Sea had caused extensive flooding in the Netherlands. He then sailed for duty in the Mediterranean for 2 months and then along the Atlantic coast from New England to Cuba until his discharge. While on the Johnston he visited ports in Great Britain, France and Scandinavia.

Some Time During 1954
By: Leonard "Lenny" Guere, Seaman Apprentice (SA)

Years on board the Johnston: 1952 to 1955

Sometime during 1954 I was on restriction (for what I don't remember) and I heard over the P.A. System "Muster all P.A.L.'s and restricted men to the Quarter Deck. I was on the "OI" level and in my hurry to get there quickly, I fell down the ladder. The result was a broken right arm. We were in Newport, R.I. so I was sent to the hospital. When I returned I had a cast on my arm and went on light duty. Six weeks later I had to go back to the hospital to have the cast taken off. While having the cast removed, the nurse (LTjg) accidently knocked a scalpel off her work table and it landed point first on my foot. The blade went in the top of my shoe into the middle toe. It really hurt. As a result, I came back to the ship minus a cast but had 2 stitches in my toe, large bandage and one shoe in my hand. Light duty again!

A SHORT STAY
By: Milner Carden, Quartermaster (QM-2)

Year on board the Johnston: 1954

I am a retired teacher and coach, 82 years old and not in good health (cancer - 8 years). I only served a bit less than one year on the 821 but had a wonderful time.

We left Norfolk in early January 1954 and 28 days later we sailed into Trieste, Italy. We then sailed between Sicily and the toe of Italy. We were lucky and were selected to do a "Good Will" tour of Italy; Austria; Athens, Greece; Naples, Italy; Gibraltar; Spain; Lisbon; Germany; France and most of the British Islands. We returned to the United States in late 1954.

While in Europe, we met with politicians and talked to clubs and promoted the United States as much as we could. We also played Basketball in several countries. It was **"The Best Duty Ever!"**

The Adventures of James Obst
By: James "Jim" Obst, Pipefitter (FP-1)

Years on board the Johnston: 1954 to 1957

I came aboard the Johnston on August 25, 1954 after graduating from Pipefitter's school at Norfolk, Virginia. Being the last person to come aboard, I ended up on mess duty. So much for 3 months of schooling! Since almost everything on the Johnston was shut down for repairs, we were birthed and ate on the APL-32. I was hoping that

the ship was based at Philadelphia as I had an older brother working there. However being based at Newport, Rhode Island I could still make it down to visit on a long weekend, so that wasn't that bad.

After the overhaul period, we set sail for GITMO. One nice thing about it, we were heading south in the middle of the winter. The bad thing for me was that I ended up with a mid-watch while going around Cape Hatteras. That was the roughest ride I've ever been on.

On my first Mediterranean cruise, we were refueling at sea prior to entering the Fjord leading to Londonderry, Ireland. Fueling was going well until the hose came out of the fueling trunk. Practically all of the port side of the ship had a coat of oil on it. Talk about a mess. It was scrubbed down before we entered the Fjord.

Later, on a Midshipman cruise, we decided to take it easy for the 6 week cruise. We only worked on emergency things; routine maintenance would have to wait. That was different for us because we normally found something to do all the time. The best part of that cruise was having the Midshipman put on the coffee while keeping the shop clean.

I believe it was on this cruise that we pulled into GITMO for a few days. The base had a festival of some kind going on. Anyhow, the Captain had picked up a palm tree and had it by his sea cabin. It was sitting in a water bucket. After several days at sea, it began to wither. The XO put a note in the "Plan of the Day" asking if anyone had knowledge of keeping a palm tree alive and if so, see the Captain. Our first class came up with the idea to fabricate a watering can. I got a couple of one-gallon cans from the cooks, made a partial cover on one of the cans and formed a handle for it. Then I fabricated a spout with a sprinkling head and got some paint from the deck crew. Actually it turned out pretty good. We talked to the Engineering Officer about what we had done and was wondering if the Captain would come down to the shop since we had something that might help his palm tree. Arrangements were made, the shop was cleaned up, fresh coffee was made and the Captain came down. We had a nice chat with him. I have a couple of pictures with him watering the tree. I don't remember whether it helped the tree or not.

The 3 years I was on the Jolly J had us home-ported at Newport, Rhode Island. Most of that time, we would tie up to a buoy which was anchored in the bay. Normally there were four Destroyer's tied together at each buoy. One morning the Captain had the XO take the ship out. After just getting underway, the XO executed a turn to port only it was too quick and the spray shield on the port side was hit by the bow of the ship we were pulling away from. Needless to say, there was some damage done to the spray shield. The Captain took over the rest of the way out of the bay. The XO came down to survey the damage and asked us if we would be able to repair it. We told him we probably could but that if he ever did that again, we would take his driver's license!

On my last cruise we operated in the North Sea with a group of NATO country naval ships. This was during the fall of the year. The North Sea is not the place to be in the fall. It is so rough up there you can't do any work. Most of the time we were traveling at 6 or 8 knots, just enough speed to control the direction of the ship. Several times I saw ships we were operating with where the forward one-third was completely out of the water. That is an eerie feeling when you realize your ship is probably doing the same thing.

During one of the cruises an Admiral on a Cruiser invited all of the Commanding Officers in the Task Group to have lunch with him on board the Cruiser. We had to transfer the CO's from ship to ship to the Cruiser and back again later in the day without getting them wet. What a job that was!

During the 1957 Med Cruise we visited: Gibraltar; Valencia; Cartagena; Marseilles; Cannes; Palma; Lisbon and Barcelona. In addition to that, we conducted Drone Shoots, Refueled, ASW Ops, Carrier OPS, Barrier Patrol, helped with a Carrier Fire and found a downed plane on May 13th.

On or about November 26, 1957 I was relieved of my duties on the Jolly J and was sent to the Newport News Naval base for discharge with the rank of FP1. Thanks to the Government cutting the Navy's budget I was released 60 days early. Thinking back now, the time spent on the Jolly J wasn't all that bad.

Behind the Spray Shield on the starboard side, main deck we had a small bench that we could use for welding or cutting with an oxyacetylene outfit without worrying about anything catching on fire.

One day I was cutting some steel pipe with the outfit and the Engineering Officer came by and asked if he could watch. I gave him a pair of goggles to wear and told him not to stand too close because of sparks and molten metal flying around. He watched for a while and then asked if he could try cutting a piece of pipe. The trick to start cutting a hole in pipe is that you want to have the spot you are heating hot enough so that when you open the oxygen valve it blows through the pipe. If it is not hot enough it will blow back at you.

I got a welding apron and jacket for the officer, lit the torch for him and watched as he was heating the spot. He hit the oxygen valve a little early and it blew back at him. We had a good laugh about it but he said "No more cutting for him!"

As most of you know, in the early and mid 50's, most of the Navy destroyers tied up to permanently anchored buoys in the bay. WE usually tied 4 ships to each buoy. One morning the Captain decided to let the X.O. get the ship underway for the day's exercises.

We were the first ship to get underway and either the X.O. started turning to port or the wind blew us and the last 6 or 8 feet of the port side spray shield hit the bow of the ship we were pulling away from. We heard the crunch and came topside to wee what had happened. The X.O. had come down off of the bridge to look at the damage. He then asked if we thought we could repair it. If a repair order would have to be sent to the Tender the accident would probably go on his record and that wouldn't look good. We nonchalantly told him we thought we could but the next time it happens we would take away his Driver's License.

One final note on my time on the "Jolly J" - my Discharge Date should have been February 4, 1958. So instead of coming home for Christmas 1957 I had taken all my leave time during the summer of '57 since I would be discharged about 6 weeks after Christmas. Sometime in October or November of '57, Congress cut the Navy's budget and I was to be discharged 60 days early on December 4, 1957. The only bad thing about that, I had taken all my leave days up to February 4, 1958 so I owed them 5 days' pay. I told them they could take those 5 days' pay out of my mustering out money and I would still go home early.

On December 1, 1957 I received my FP 1 rating and was discharged on December 2nd. I consider myself lucky to have only missed one Christmas at home. That Christmas Eve was my first shore patrol duty at Cannes France.

Going Into Battle Over Cross
By: David G. Savage, Tribune Washington Bureau
Originally Published in the Milwaukee, Wisconsin Journal Sentinel - March 20, 2012
Provided by: Glen Beebe, Quartermaster (QMSN)

Years on board the Johnston: 1955 to 1957

WASHINGTON - The Obama administration is asking the Supreme Court to allow a 43-foot-tall cross that serves as a war memorial to remain atop Mount Soledad near San Diego, arguing the cross that has been there since 1954 is not an endorsement of religion.

The government should not be required "to tear down a cross that has stood without incident for 58 years as a highly venerated memorial to the nation's fallen service members." Solicitor General Donald Verrilli Jr. said in a new appeal to the high court.

He urged the justices to reverse a decision of the 9th U.S. Circuit Court of Appeals that held last year that the cross was primarily a Christian symbol and unconstitutional. Its prominent display on public land in La Jolla amounted to an official "endorsement of religion" in violation of the First Amendment, the judges said in a 3-0 ruling.

If the justices take up the case this year it could force them to resolve whether religious symbols can be displayed on public land.

Critics say the cross is a religious symbol, not a universal symbol that honors all fallen soldiers. The 9th Circuit judges said the cross "has never been used to honor all American soldiers in any military cemetery."

The 9th Circuit judges also noted that until the 1980's, Mount Soledad's cross was a gathering place for Christians and a scene for Easter Sunday services. Its role as a war memorial came only after the litigation began, the judges said.

Defenders of the cross say it serves as a symbol of sacrifice and a memorial to honor the nation's fallen soldiers dating back to World War I. In 2006, Congress moved to take possession of Mount Soledad and its cross to preserve the war memorial.

A Selectee for the Navy
By: Harold Rosenthal, Yeoman (YN-2)

Years on board the Johnston: 1957

For the Army, you are a draftee. -For the Navy, a selectee. Law school finished, my student deferment was gone. "Every tenth man" blared an order at the draft Center "step forward. Your bus is outside on its way to Boot Camp, Bainbridge, Maryland." Then one year at NAS Brunswick, Maine learning about -30 degree weather, snow that never stops or melts and soft shell lobsters at 69 cents a pound.

Enough of being a landlubber; I'm a sailor. There is a tin can, USS Johnston (DD821), the "Jolly J," home port Newport, Rhode Island, that is short a Yeoman. Tag, you're it.

"*Permission to come aboard*" "Why?" asked the OOD. "You're missing a Yeoman." "Hell, we got seven and the ship's office only has room to seat four. "So hang around" I was ordered, "until the 'Old Man' decides what to do with you."

Hang around I did - mostly on the fan tail. Where, as a 25 year old and married, I was asked to lecture to erotically curious virgin 17 year olds. They asked "What does it look like? How do you get her to say yes and how do you do it?" I also read a lot, took turns in the ship's office, handled the little legal work aboard and for sea duty, was Captain's talker.

Cruise preparations: We were scheduled to go on a four month cruise. My First Class put me in charge of dealing with the changes and sub changes that came in daily to modify our planned deployment. At first it was to be a Med cruise. Scrub that! We were headed for the

North Sea. The crew was measured for foul weather gear for the expected bitter cold. Scrub that! We are going to the Straits of Hormuz. There it is as hot as the North Sea is cold. Because our desalinators that make fresh water are inefficient at warm sea temperatures, two more were ordered to be brought on board and welded to the fan tail deck. Scrub that! Gone is the foul weather gear. No desalinators. We are going on a Med cruise. I checked. It was in detail the very cruise which we had first received.

Time for rumors: Everyone, and the Navigator, was confused by the many changes in our proposed deployment. -Time for my skill as a rumor monger. After 'anchors away,' I spread the word we would be the first man o' war to steam into the harbor of Madrid. The best rumors are based on a bit of truth. We would have been the first of any kind of ship to steam into the harbor of Madrid. The Spanish Capitol is 40 miles from any navigable stream. The Navigator believed the rumor. He ordered me to get a book of world maps from our little library. When he finally spotted land locked Madrid, he banged the book on the deck and stormed out. If he reads this, I confess. I started the rumor.

A Typical Spanish Naval Vessel

But we were the first American man o' war to steam into a harbor. It was the harbor of Cartagena, the Spanish naval base. There we saw Spain's well-kept fleet of WW1 German destroyers. They leave port for a day or so about once a year. Their sides look like they had been simonized. A snipe aboard us opened a sea valve causing bunker C to coat the Spanish ship that lay beside us. He was sent over the side on a stage with buckets, brushes and degreasers. He spent the entire day scrubbing the Spanish antique clean.

The sea can be beautiful and can be ugly: You take what it gives and steam on. Every sunrise and sunset is unique and magnetic. They demand to be watched. The sea can be mirror flat reflecting every cloud in the sky or

Sunrise at Sea

it can be dangerous. While acting as captain's talker, for more than a day we plowed through a storm that would hide our bow and number one turret and splash against the wheel house windows. With amazing skill our Captain, who kept the helm the entire time, steered us into 40 foot waves. They fought him. They tried to turn us so they could hit us abaft and lay us flat in the sea. Knowing a 49 degree list would send cold water down the stacks and crack the boilers, we watched the inclemiter as it indicated we were slowly tilting 37 degrees port to 37 degrees starboard. A good part of the crew had the dry heaves. It was duty canned pork sandwiches for the rest of us.

Sunset at Sea

On a moonless night with ASW set, we knifed through blobs of phosphorescent life. -Some faintly glowing blue, some pink, some red. They varied in size from the ship's length to about a half mile. Without a horizon, because the sea between them was as inky black as the sky, it seemed they were sometimes below and sometimes they were above us. Has any other ship seen this North Atlantic phenomenon? With running lights lit and a moon glowing, the answer would be no.

Steam through the Straits of Gibraltar, that tight opening to the Med, again no moon and ASW. At the same time you see the lights of Spain and the lights of Morocco.

A Captain on Board is always …." Arleigh Burke, then Commander of the United States Navy, was on board the USS Salem, the cruiser in charge of the 5th Fleet, the Mediterranean command. He invited every captain in the Med for lunch. Our Captain, only a Lieutenant Commander, the junior ranking captain of every 6th fleet ship, was ordered to pick them up. For a day and a half we steamed all over that bathtub to pick up the captains. Since they outranked everyone on the Jolly J, they took over our officers' staterooms who then shoved the Chiefs out of their quarters.

When we finally hove to, starboard to the Salem, we high lined the captains onto the cruiser. Our Captain was on the quarter deck saying goodbye. An Ensign was OOD and I was captain's talker. Since the Captain was too big to fit into the breaches boy, he was still on our quarter deck when the Salem ordered us to make turns for 15 knots from our 11, and "away." The OOD then gave a "left standard rudder" command. The helmsman properly echoed the command which was repeated by the OOD. "Left standard rudder, aye," called the helmsman as I watched water increasing between us and the Salem in a V pattern. The Captain was suddenly up in the wheelhouse. He shoved the helmsman knocking him to the deck and spun the wheel to the right to its chocks. Vehicles on water, such as ships, do not answer direction changes as well as vehicles on land. We slid in front of the Salem. She outweighed our 2,200 by her 20,000 ton. Her bow was as high as our wheelhouse. We could not see water between us. "If she touches our fan tail," someone said, "we will go down in a minute." I'm telling the story; it did not happen.

The Salem ordered us back under her command. A letter was to come to be part of the Captain's jacket. A helicopter delivered that letter. Without reading it, we all knew what it said.

As legal Yeoman, I prepared papers indicating the UCMJ charges for which the ensign might be made to answer. The Captain ordered me to tear up all copies and bring the ensign to his stateroom. He told the quivering ensign this was the last cruise for some of our officers. They were retiring. Since we were port and starboard watches, they would not be able to go ashore in each port unless someone would volunteer to stand watch each time. "I will!" cried the ensign. "Fine," said the Captain, "then you're dismissed." After obtaining permission to stay, I asked the Captain why he had treated the ensign the way he did. His answer – "My Naval career is destroyed. How does it help to destroy another man's career? He has learned a lesson and will be the better for it." Many years later by chance I met the Captain. From the Johnston he was put in charge of security at the Panama Canal. From there he captained a supply ship and then back to security at the Canal where he ended his career. I hope the Captain was right. I hope the ensign went on to be the better for having destroyed the Captain's career.

Teasing the Russians: Italy's toe sticks far into the Mediterranean. But for the Med's mouth drinking from the Atlantic Ocean and its butt at the Black Sea, the toe creates the narrowest point between Europe and Africa.

"I wonder how much Russian submarine traffic exists in the Mediterranean?" an Admiral pondered from his cushy Pentagon chair. "We got these tin cans in that bathtub. Let's find out."

Each of us was given a sector between the toe and Africa that overlapped the ships above and below us by two nautical miles. For two days the Sonarmen cleaned the wax from their ears and listened. Sometimes it was a school of fish, sometimes an undersea stream of cold water and sometimes it was a submarine.

"Fish bearing 5 degrees to port, 500 yards" my captain's talker headphones squawked. "She's turned and is coming straight at us, 5 knots to our 15. -400, 300, 200. She is making a hard left turn," announced the reports. "Hard to port," yelled our OOD as we skidded more than a mile past that contact. Sonar, "We've lost her." "Keep looking" was the order.

When Sonar found her again, she played the same game. She came straight at us and then made a hard turn right or left as we skidded past her. At the sub's slower speed and covered with the friction of the encompassing water, she could turn on a dime. We, at a higher speed and on the surface couldn't turn on a ten dollar bill. In the two days we had at least seven frustrating contacts. Only one broke periscope, did not identify, then went down and disappeared.

Several times we dropped hand grenades at 30 second intervals – an international signal to surface and identify. These subs were diesel with limited oxygen and fuel. What were their captains thinking? "Were those hand grenades or are the Americans firing at us? Should we fire at them?"

On our fan tail the depth charge rack had been unchained. Any sailor back there could have shoved the lever and rolled one into the sea.

Why were we playing chicken with the Russians? These were international waters. I hoped a spring in that cushy Pentagon chair would break free and spear that Admiral in his fan tail.

Captain and White Hat Playing Chess

Hopson's choice: It can now be told. I had open gang way. On port calls I could stay ashore as long as the officers. I almost lost it. We had a chess tournament on board. I was to play against the Captain. On the QT, he told me if I beat him I would lose my privilege. I worked for the Exec. He was four months junior to the Captain. Both were Lieutenant Commanders. There was a bit of rivalry. I got the same QT from the Exec. "If I valued my privilege …." The Captain and I played to a draw. Every sailor on the ship believed I engineered the draw. Everyone I have since told it to believes I engineered it. How do you engineer a draw?

The Little Car in Marseille

At liberty: With what do sailors start liberty in a foreign port? Freeiz cervatis! Cold beer! In Marseille they have these cute little cars. Loaded with and by cervatis, warm or cold, four sailors can pick one up and wedge it, - a perfect fit - between a light and a telephone pole. I wonder if it is still wedged there.

Beach at Cannes & Caves of Drach

I wonder if the women on the beaches of Cannes still strip bear and then rummage in their bags for their bathing suits, oops' I mean bare. I would not have been as enthralled if they only stripped a bear. Did you see what the blond in the photo was holding by the hand? I admit when projecting the slides to friends, one of them pointed out what she was holding which I had not noticed before.

I wonder if in the Caves of Drach on Majorca, they still row you across an underground lake while playing Schubert waltzes.

I wonder if when buying chocolate in Valberg, France, which is just across from the Swiss border, anyone else is told it is "imported." Then after paying triple Swiss chocolate prices you learn it is from Brooklyn, New York.

I close with a photo of DesDiv 8, with our Johnston and four of her sisters tied against our destroyer tender. It was 1957. It was between Vietnam and Korea. It was peace time. My duty was easy and of no danger. I salute those who served upon our tin can in time of conflict. I thank you. Thank you everyone!

Johnston with Sister Ships of DesDiv 8

BECOMING A BLUENOSE BY CROSSING THE ARCTIC CIRCLE
By: Bob Nava, Signalman (SM-3)

Years on board the Johnston: 1957 to 1959

We returned from our Med Cruise on August 1st, 1957 after a month in our Homeport, we headed back out to Sea. This time we cruised to the North Atlantic. We had ports-of-call in Plymouth and Portsmouth, England and then on to Glasgow, Scotland. We then met up with our NATO partners and proceeded north towards the Arctic Circle. We spent a lot of time patrolling the waters looking for Russian Submarines and sometimes we actually found them. While playing the Cold War games we used to play we crossed the Arctic Circle on September 20, 1957 and became members of the Bluenose Society. The entire crew received a scroll and we had a small celebration. Also at this time there was a historic occurrence happening.

The USS Nautilus SSN 571 was the first nuclear submarine to go under the ice pack at the North Pole and it surfaced while our squadron was operating in the area. Also at this time, I was on the deck force, 1st Division and was standing the 12 to 4 a.m. lookout watch on the starboard side. It was 40 degrees below zero and while being relieved I took off my foul weather hat to do a pass down to my relief. My ears were sweating from the foul weather gear and the extreme cold made my ears freeze immediately. I suffered frost bite on both ears immediately from this incident. This was quite an experience for a young sailor who was just 18 years old at the time. We finally returned home to Newport, Rhode Island just before the Holidays. As you can well imagine, I will never forget that cruise.

After my two year Navy enlistment, I enlisted in the Navy reserves. While in the reserves I was in Navy Intelligence and retired twenty years later as a First Class Intelligence Specialists (IS1). I also served three years in the National Guard with the 42nd Rainbow Division.

JICPAC 0819 Sailor Non-Stop Adventurer

Editor's note: This story appeared in "The Triad Navaires San Diego" magazine, June 1992

OK, you've finally decided that Tom Clancy shouldn't have all the fun. You're going to write your own Navy adventure book and make a fortune. First thing you'll need is a hero, a cool dude who's been everywhere and done everything. It goes without saying that this hero will be in Naval Reserve Intelligence. Now let's add an action background: how about a former policeman who worked undercover in New York? That's a good beginning,  but we need a glamorous current career for interest. Maybe a flight attendant based in Las Vegas, travelling throughout the country, returning periodically for a well-earned rest by his pool?

Oops! Is it a little tough to think like a guy who just stepped out of ***Lifestyles of the Rich and Famous?*** OK, let's just step over to JICPAC 0819 and ask IS2 Robert Nava – because the hero we've described **is** Nava.

Nava, a 14-year Naval Reserve veteran drilling with JICPAC 0819 in Las Vegas, moved to Las Vegas in 1988 and affiliated with the then – IPAC 0319. He is currently an analyst with the Mutual Support division of JICPAC 0819.

In his first civilian career, Nava was an officer with the New York City Sanitation Police Department, retiring after 23 years as a Lieutenant, supervising 40 police officers. Does the Sanitation Police seem like a dull detail? This seemingly dull assignment is actually very dangerous, since illegal dumping means big profits to unscrupulous tank truck drivers. Then you have to actually catch the person in the act to get a conviction. Nava describes stake-outs in the early morning or late at night, knowing that, if you actually catch the perpetrator, he could very well shoot first. In one case, he and his partner went to the office of a suspected Mafioso, who attacked Nava by jumping across his desk.

"We had to subdue him. Later on, somebody else decided he needed more subduing, since he was executed gang-style and dumped in the river." said Nava.

OK, you're saying, what about the glamorous new career? How many retired New York cops become flight attendants based in Las Vegas? Probably not too many, but Nava did. Nava has been a flight attendant for America West Airlines for over three years, beginning at age 52. He has flown everywhere American West flies, including Baltimore, New York, and Hawaii.

So there's your hero, all you Tom Clancy wanabees – you just better hope that Nava doesn't decide to write a book before you finish yours!

Editor's Note: While at the Airline, Bob became the Corporate Security Regional Manager – LAS which covered the entire West Coast from San Diego to Alaska and had about 20 stations.

Bio - IS1 Bob Nava

I was born in Brooklyn, New York a long time ago. After high school I enlisted in the United States navy and served aboard the USS Johnston DD-821. After separation from the Johnston I went into the reserves and served another 20 years and retired as an IS1.

In my civilian career I worked for the New York City Police Department. I retired after 23 years on the force as a Lieutenant. After retiring from the police force we moved to Las Vegas and I went back to work, this time for America West Airlines. I worked in just about every department including as a Flight Attendant, customer service and baggage claim. After four years working those different jobs, I went into Corporate Security which turned out to be one of the most interesting jobs I ever had. As a liaison between the Airline and Law Enforcement Departments I had a lot of VIP assignments and a lot of one on one contact with former Presidents such as Ford, Bush #1 and Clinton. I also met Congressman Harry Reed and Governor Mitt Romney. Some of the celebrities that I have met and had my picture taken with include: Frankie Avalon, Bobby

Riddell, Fabian and The Righteous Brothers. I'm personal friends with Steve Shirripa who played Bobby Bacala on the "Soprano" TV show. Most of these guys are just down to earth when you talk to them. I was also the corporate liaison with the Secret Service, FBI, CIA and the TSA. It was a great experience talking to all these people. I retired from the Airline after 20 years. I figured after three, 20-year jobs including the military it was time to retire. I believe I was truly blessed to have worked in jobs that I truly loved and it was finally time to call it quits!

My wife Pat was born in Northern Ireland and came to New York when she was 20 years old. She worked in a Physical Therapy office in New York doing clerical work. We met in Long Island, New York in 1974 and we were married a year later in 1975. We have six children between us, seven grandchildren and two great grandchildren.

Bob Nava with Frankie Avalon

We moved to Las Vegas in 1988 and have been here ever since. We love the weather here and there is always something interesting to do.

Editor's Note: At the time of this book's publishing, Bob was serving as President of the USS Johnston DD-821 Association.

Bio – Commander Herman O. Sudholz

Served on USS Johnston: 1959 to 1963

CDR Sudholz was born in Glen Cove, Long island, NY on June 22, 1934 of German immigrant parents. He graduated from Glen Cove High School and then from Lehigh University with a degree in Civil Engineering. Six months after graduation he reported to the Navy Officer Candidate School (OCS) in Newport, RI.

His first assignment after OCS was the USS Johnston (DD-821). During his almost 4 years onboard Johnston he served as Damage Control Assistant, First Lieutenant and finally Weapons Officer. While on board, the ship made 2 deployments to the US Sixth Fleet in the Mediterranean Sea, a Red Sea patrol, NATO exercises in the North Atlantic, underwent a 10-month Fleet Rehabilitation and Modernization (FRAM) overhaul, participated in the Cuban blockade of 1962, and finally acted as range tracking ship for the Polaris submarine qualifications.

During his first Med. Deployment he met his future

wife, Cynthia Fletcher, in Naples, Italy and married her on his next Med. Deployment 18 months later.

His first tour ashore was as Head Research and Development at the naval Explosive Ordnance Disposal Facility, Indian Head, MD. He returned to sea as Executive Officer (XO) of the USS Brister (DER-327) spending two 9-month deployments on Operation Market-time as a part of TF-115, the Vietnam costal interdiction force.

He returned ashore as a member of the DX/DXG development team in the office of the Chief of Naval Operations. This developed into the DD-963 Spruance class destroyer.

LCDR Sudholz next reported as XO of the USS Richard S. Edwards (DD-950) which sailed on 24-hr notice in April 1972 for Vietnam in response to the North Vietnamese Easter offensive. That deployment resulted in RS Edwards being a part of Operation Linebacker II engaging targets along the North Vietnamese coast as well as shore batteries during the mining of Hyphong harbor.

Leaving the R.S. Edwards in the Gulf of Tonkin, he was temporarily assigned to the staff of Cruiser-Destroyer Group Seventh Fleet (CTF-75) on board USS Providence (CLG-6) as staff navigator and Assistant Intelligence Officer.

After leaving the western pacific he reported to the staff, Commander-in-Chief US Pacific Fleet. Four years later he was assigned as the Surface Operations Officer for the Commander Third Fleet, both in Hawaii.

Returning to sea once again, CDR Sudholz served as XO of the USS Dixie (AD-14). After a post overhaul workup Dixie sailed for the western Pacific only to be diverted to Diego Garcia in the Indian Ocean in response to the taking of American hostages in Iran. Dixie spent her 40th birthday tending ships in Diego Garcia and as a result of CDR Sudholz's proposal to the Secretary of the navy she hoisted the "Don't-Tread-on-Me' jack emblematic of the oldest active ship in the US Navy.

CDR Sudholz assumed command as the 60th Commanding Officer of USS Constitution, "Old ironsides", in September of 1980 and retired from that command in June 1985 having held command of that then 188-year-old national icon longer than any other commanding officer.

While in Boston he was active serving as President of the Wardroom Club, as an officer on the Board of the Copley Art Society, the oldest art society in the country, the Armed Forces YMCA, the USO, The Freedom Trail Foundation, and as an Overseer of the USS Constitution Museum Foundation and others.

After a year of full retirement, CDR Sudholz accepted the position of Project manager for the reconstruction of Boston's Copley Square the prominent park in Boston's famous Back Bay. Upon completion of that project he took the position of Project Manager of a multi-year National Science Foundation (NSF) project at Harvard University. He added the concurrent task of overseeing the construction of the monument to the 100th running of the Boston Marathon. Upon completion of the NSF project CDR Sudholz and his wife Cynthia finally fully retired to her ancestral home in Carmel, California.

CDR Sudholz holds two Navy Commendation medals, the Vietnamese Cross of Gallantry with Bronze star, Combat Action Medal, the navy Unit commendation, the Navy Meritorious Unit Commendation, Expeditionary Medal (Cuba), plus other service awards. He is a golden Shellback, a member of the Marines Memorial Association, U.S. Naval Institute, American Philatelic Society, Monterey History and Art Association and is a life member of the Military Officers Association of America.

He enjoys choral singing in German Mannerchoirs and is a member of the Aloha Barbershop Harmony Chorus. He is an avid collector of USS Constitution cancelled envelopes and other historical memorabilia.

Chapter 5

YEARS 1960 THROUGH 1969

WHAT CURED MY SEASICKNESS
By: John Engelien, Fire Control Technician (FTG-3)

Years on board the Johnston: 1960 to 1961

I joined the Navy on December 1, 1959 – two days after my seventeenth birthday and so I embarked on a "kitty cruise". We were sworn in at Whitehall Street in NYC and were whisked to Great Lake Naval Training Center for boot camp. After ten weeks of training, I returned home for two weeks of leave and then it was back to Great Lakes for Fire Control Technician "A" school and then "C" school. In November of that year, I completed my training and was a full-fledged FTSN. I was heading back home for leave and was looking forward to my first assignment aboard the USS Johnston DD-821 in Charleston, South Carolina. As I said goodbye to my family and friends, some said "Good Luck", some said "Stay Well" and some said "Keep in touch" but they ALL said "Don't get seasick!. With those words of wisdom, I was on my way to Charleston.

When I arrived at the naval base, I was told I would find the Johnston at "Hotel" pier and that is where I headed. After a long walk down the pier, I saw four destroyers nested together. I could tell by the number on the bow that my ship was the furthest one from the pier. I remember thinking back to my boot camp days and trying to remember the correct protocol for approaching a ship's quarterdeck. Was it to salute the officer of the deck and then the ensign on the fantail or vice-versa? Luck was on my side because another sailor - more experienced then me (at this point they were ALL more experienced then me) walked up the gangway and saluted the ensign and then the Officer of the Deck. I did what I had seen the previous boarder do and told the OOD that I was headed for the Johnston and he pointed me in the right direction. After crossing over the next two ships, I had my routine down pretty well and as I boarded the Johnston, I gave my order forms to the OOD. The OOD summoned another fire control technician and after a brief introduction I was taken to my rack. I learned that I was in Fox Division and our compartment was right down below the mess deck.

The next few days were full of orientation sessions as there were many new members of the crew who were as green as me. The "fire control gang" seemed friendly and helpful and I learned my main responsibility would be the Mark 25 Fire Control radar system which was mainly located on the 01 level across from the radio room. What stands out in my memory about that room is that it was very small and very warm because of all the equipment. Lots and lots of vacuum tubes as there were no transistors in that radar. Those tubes when powered on made for a toasty environment.

I was in that room with my 1st and 2nd class petty officers (Bill Wheaton and John Holt) discussing a major change we had installed on the radar system when the ship left the dock for the first time since I came aboard and we were heading out to sea for exercises. We were still in the Cooper River when I felt the motion of the ship for the first time. Now I don't know if I was being affected by the power of suggestion "Don't get seasick" or just plain prone to seasickness but all of a sudden I was glad there was a plastic wastepaper basket in the room and I sure made good use of it. Bill and John beat a hasty retreat and left me alone in my misery. I found that by lying on my back I could keep things down but I still felt terrible. For the next few days I stayed that way and John stood my bridge watches for me. Finally he lost his patience and told me it was time to start standing my own watches. I didn't blame him at all and was thankful for all he'd done. So, with my bucket by my side, I stood my watches and wondered how in the world I'd be able to take three more years of this.

After a day or so, I was asleep in my rack one night and we heard a loud bump and the ship leaned over several degrees. This was followed by a second and harder bump and another more severe roll to the side. Then, the collision alarm sounded and the words over the PA system "This is not a drill! Man your battle stations!" Wow! Everyone jumped out of their rack and started leaving the compartment. My rack was on the bottom so once there was room for me to get out of it I did and started getting dressed. My battle station was in the main battery director which meant I had a lot of ladders to climb and I wanted to have my pants and shoes on. As I was leaving the compartment I realized that everyone else had already left and there was someone on the mess deck trying to secure the hatch I needed to go through. He finally realized I was still down there so he opened it and told me to secure it before leaving the area as he ran off. As I was securing the hatch, I felt cold water swirling around my ankles and I thought for sure we were sinking. I quickly made my way up to the director and got into position in front of the radar console. I plugged in my sound powered phones and heard that while the ship had been damaged, we were still maintaining water tight integrity - and not sinking. It was couple minutes after this that I realized I was sitting upright and no longer felt sick.

We learned over the course of the next several hours that we had been hit by another destroyer, the USS Keppler DD-765 out of Newport, Rhode Island. We were in formation with several other ships under the flagship USS Canberra and we had been sailing under simulated war-time conditions - no lights or radio or radar emissions. Apparently the Keppler was also in simulated war-time conditions so they didn't see us and we didn't see them. They were heading out to meet their own formation and had cut right through the middle of ours. They had come up on our port side and were passing us when was saw them and turned hard to port. Her stern swiped our bow and ripped it open well above the waterline. The next day the Canberra sent over an inspection team in their motor whaleboat to assess the damage. Luckily it wasn't severe enough to jeopardize our safety but we did have to make a trip to dry dock in Norfolk to have the bow replaced. We were there for over six weeks. Scuttlebutt had it that hours after the incident the Keppler had reported hitting an unidentified object in the North Atlantic!

To this day I'm not sure what caused my seasickness but I know what ended it. Once my mind was off my problem I was fine. I will never ever tell anyone "Don't get seasick!"

Oh, and the water that was sloshing around my ankles on the mess deck? It seems the ice maker had just finished its cycle of making ice and was full of water for the next load. When the ship took such heavy rolls, the water spilled out and had flooded the deck.

IN THE BEGINNING......
By: Dave Batsche, Fire Control Technician (FTG-2)

Years on board the Johnston: 1960 to 1963

After reading "The Real Story of the USS Johnston DD-821" 1st edition, I realized that we could indeed tell it "like it was". So:

To tell my whole story, I must start at the beginning. I arrived at Great Lakes for boot camp in March 1959; our Company Commander was Patrick B. Boyland, RD1 with three hash-marks. He had already extended his shore duty by claiming he needed more time to achieve "Hall of Fame Company Status". That which was done by winning Flags during weekly competition in athletics, military drills and academic achievement and weekly tests. Well he cheated on the athletic ones by borrowing good athletes from other companies, borrowing smart recruits who had taken the tests in prior weeks and finding places to hide our own company's lamebrains who were still learning to tie their first pair of shoes. We won 49 flags, one short so he got his extension.

If there ever was another Patton, as portrayed by George C. Scott in the movie, it was Boyland. Within the first week he had established himself as our supreme commander. We all took the battery of intelligence tests to determine our career paths for the rest of our naval enlistment. Boyland strongly suggested we all enter our selected choice, fill in the blank and request to become Radarmen – believe me, we all did. However I was sent to Key West, Florida for 24 weeks of Fleet Sonar School. All went well until the 16th week when I fell asleep in class. When it happened two days later in the same week, I had a verbal disagreement with the instructor and was expelled. I spent the following three weeks scrubbing the stairs with a toothbrush (ala, a West Point plebe) which was a prime example for the entire student body and it did wonders for my reputation. Every so often one of my previous instructors, Mellon SO2 would pass me in the hallway and ask; "How's it going Batsche, you deck amp?" Well, did I mention that he was slightly cross-eyed? One fine day I replied; "Mellon, you cross-eyed cantaloupe where are my orders to ship out?" After a short back and forth encounter of verbs he suggested that I go see our division officer who was a Chief Warrant Officer who had access to the school fishing boat which is similar to the commercial vessels used for sport fishing in exotic vacation areas today. Well, I had been a member of several small group fishing parties (5 or 6 who pay $5.00 to cover bait, beer and sandwiches) which meant he knew me. I knocked on his door, entered and respectfully requested a chance to complete the school. The instant response was; "Get your books and get through week 16." Week 16 was the test I had previously failed. All went well through the final eight weeks of which sea phase was the real fun part as we went out on a DE and hunted a mini sub that was part of the program. We killed the sub with depth charges which were dye packets taped to hand grenades and matched the dye packets released from the sub at the "Fire Three" command over "Gertrude" the underwater telephone. The school had shut down over Christmas and those of us not taking leave just remained and did maintenance. We tiled a couple of classrooms during that time. The delay of my own doings and the Christmas break made my 24 weeks almost 9 months. I received orders to the USS Johnston DD821, but it was in the Med. As a result, they put me TAD to the USS Cascade AD16 in Newport, Rhode Island. Pretty dull life there, tied up all the time with coffee grounds a foot deep between the ship and the pier.

Finally in April 1960, the Johnston returned and I reported for duty. Little did I know that my infamous reputation had preceded my arrival. Several of the sonar school graduates who had been there at the same time as me had already enlightened the sonar gang to wait until you see this guy. They had been flown over to the Med right out of school! All was great and good standing watches underway in sonar and as messenger in port. We all took the test for 3rd class and were all informed that we had passed and would be promoted.

When I had first reported aboard, I was greeted by Fannin GM2, the ships permanent Master at Arms. He got me a fart sack and pillow and assigned my berthing area, Fox Division just below the Mess Deck. He also assigned me to the starboard 3 inch gun crew (he was a GM remember) for GQ. I was on that gun crew for one shoot when someone said get that Sonarman off that gun crew. You can't have a Sonarman on a gun crew. I hadn't thought much about it but the noise from the shoot had left my ears ringing for a time but all seemed OK after a while. Well just before the promotions were to be, the XO Stanley Fini sent the entire sonar gang to the base infirmary to have their ears tested. After repeated attempts I could not pass the audiometer test. The Doc really tried and so did I, I wanted that Crow! When the report got back to the ship, I met with the XO to determine my future. What rate would I like to pursue? I wanted to be a Sonarman! You can't be one unless you go to Sub School where the hearing requirement doesn't include the ability to assess Doppler Effect, but you have to extend your enlistment two years for the sub school and additional training. I declined that proposition quickly! Stanley then played his hidden trump card and offered 12 weeks of FT school in Bainbridge, Maryland which I accepted. What a deal, I'm a SOGSN with a ship's patch on my shoulder which makes me an old salt at 19 years of age amidst all of these FT students right out of boot camp. I was a celebrity, didn't have to march to class and went to chow with the instructors – cool, very cool. Bainbridge was home for WAVE Boot Camp and the best EM Club ever. In their third week of boot, the WAVES were allowed their first visit to the EM Club. They typically would enter wide eyed and bewildered as to what to do. Having the most advantageous seats near the entrance meant that waving over to a desirable acquaintance to join us was usually very successful. I met some really nice girls and also some real air-heads. There were usually a few good men in the club, by that of course I mean jar-heads and brave as we know they are, they couldn't pass on a challenge for a chug-a-glass for a pitcher. Well I had a friend named Holland who never ever lost so we drank free nearly every night!

    Now back to the Johnston and reality. I was the only SOSN among all those new Third-Class PO's and I had to take the test for FT3 and get this: I still stood my underway watches in Sonar until I made Third. Then it was to the Bridge for underway watches, the routine was broken down to four stations one-hour each for the four-hour watch. It began at lookout on the flying bridge outside and sometimes cold and/or wet. Spotting an old freighter with binoculars somehow couldn't compare with finding a sonar contact. The next station was to take the helm and what an experience that was - especially when it was an extremely stormy and heavy sea. When yawning in a following sea and the rudder and the screws are both out of the water, the wheel does nothing. Then when they go down in the water, you try to catch up and get back to the course heading. I got to steer during sea trials and ASW maneuvers where you go from left full rudder to right full, back and forth to zigzag to avoid torpedoes all while at "All Ahead Full Speed". After that, I did the Engine Order Telegraph, the machine that tells the Engine Room how many turns to make for the Knots of speed order given by the OD.

Another major thrill and again at sea trials while running at "All Ahead Flank", something over 30 knots and then being given the "All Back Full" command. You take those two handles and slam them from the forward position to all the way back and down. It is like putting on antiskid brakes. The ship just shudders and groans and I think the Snipes have to change their skivvies. What a ride!

One more ride you can't buy is to get into the main battery director during extra heavy weather when the bow goes under and the main deck disappears and the bridge gets battered so you can't see out the windows. I would get on the stool in the Director, crank open the hatch and catch another thrill no civilian can buy at any amusement park!

The SAND PEBBLES – Part Deux
By: Dave Batsche, Fire Control Technician (FTG-2)

On the 1961 Med. Cruise our Mighty ship was docked in Catania, Sicily for some R&R and of course as a "Good-Will" ambassador ship. We were to be there for several days and somehow the local men knew that and they solicited work from the ship. They were allowed to scrub the sides of the ship from the hull to the fantail and paint a fresh coat of grey from the water line to the main deck. There were about eight of them and they were allowed to eat our leftover chow after the crew was finished with each meal. They appreciated the food and did a very nice job with the painting. Then came the time for compensation, it was realized that there was no provision for monetary funds to be paid to civilian workers. It was negotiated for these workers to accept a number of five-gallon cans of paint and a quantity of line or what we know as "used rope" instead of money. However somewhere down the line someone went one better and substituted white canvas preservative instead of paint. The line was some old rotten manila hemp not any of our nylon line. Soon after this skullduggery was discovered, word got back to the ship that the natives were becoming hostile. It seems several of our boys had the rear pockets of their trousers cut with razors and their wallets had gone missing. Shore Patrol was dispatched ashore to immediately return all those on liberty as the ship was to get underway. As soon as all were present and accounted for, we began casting off all lines. Before this was accomplished, a small mob appeared to be coming down the pier, fires hoses were broken out to prevent any unwanted boarding and our mighty ship escaped without further incident. The Steve McQueen movie "The Sand Pebbles" always reminds me of that incident.

Please don't get the wrong impression, I most thoroughly enjoyed my experience on board and the vivid memories still enter my dreams. The crew and most of the officers were diligent and dedicated to make the Johnston the best ship it could be. The Sonar gang was extremely well qualified as was evidenced by their winning the very rare ASW "A" which was proudly displayed on the superstructure and also was allowed on our jumpers above the striker's badge. It also earned me a commendation in my service record, one of the few plusses in that document. The Engineering department, from boilers to electrical through damage control was outstanding as well as evidenced by the red "E" on the stack. The Gunnery division, not to be outdone, had its own share of diligence. FT 1st Class Buddy Wheaton dug out the old construction books, found the old benchmarks to survey the correct alignment of the ship's guns with the Fire Control systems. In our subsequent shoots, we literally knocked the target sleeves pulled behind the plane out of the sky. We also hit the surface sleds that were towed by another vessel. Result: Battle Efficiency "E" on the bridge.

Yes I'm leading up to something. Obviously we had an outstanding crew and most assuredly a fine XO who in the years to follow his position on "our" ship had been seen in San Diego wearing Captain Bars, and as has been reported lately was promoted to Rear Admiral.

Well I just wonder if the Catania incident can be found in any of the old Ship's Log Books, or possibly if BUPERS knew or if it's in the old XO's service record?

"THANK YOU SUDS!"
By: Dave Batsche, Fire Control Technician (FTG-2)

One of the most anxious periods aboard the Jolly J occurred just weeks prior to my discharge. We were docked at a pier at Cape Canaveral, Florida. Jim Legs, Ely and I hitch hiked to Daytona in February to watch the time trials for the Daytona 500. They let us in for free while in uniform. We were late getting there but they let us go through the tunnel under the track to the pits.

All was fun and good until the trip back to the ship on Sunday.

Legs and I had stopped at what had become our home bar while in Daytona and had a few to fortify ourselves for the return trip. The local Police stopped where we were hitch hiking and my mouth got me in trouble so they took me in for public intoxication. Ely returned to the ship and woke up enough mates to round up enough money for bail, but the OD wouldn't let him go back to Daytona as time may run out before we were to get underway in the morning. I went to Court the next day (Monday) and our Shore Patrol picked me up Tuesday. We stopped for a hamburger and then returned to the ship. Our XO Stan was absolutely thrilled to have a pre-Captain's meeting. I was on a suspended bust, potentially all the way to the E1 and he had me. However my Division officer accompanied me and his description of my diligence on the job and all my other virtues never will cease to astound even me. After all the accolades, Stan still had the look of major satisfaction in his demeanor. However, then came the most unexpected outcome, the remembrance of a lifetime. My Division officer explained to Stan that he had given me verbal extra days of liberty and therefore I hadn't missed movement or been AWOL. Since I had 54 days leave saved up it also saved a lot of cash. "Thank you SUDS!"

WHAT A LIFE
By: Dave Batsche, Fire Control Technician (FTG-2)

We were tied up in Portsmouth, England and one of the British Carrier's crew came aboard to solicit a potential boxing match. It seems the Carrier also in port had a boxing team looking for a workout. Word went out around our ship and a few of our tough and bad guys who were willing to give it a go came forward. Let me introduce Louie Bishop FT3, 185 pounds, six feet, one inch tall, solid and the undisputed baddest man on the ship. Well Louie and all the other brave guys were defeated by the Limeys, but their coach was disappointed as none of our guys were close to his weight class.

Enter Johnnie Cortez, he came aboard as a 3rd class GM after spending a first hitch in special services on the Navy Boxing team. Johnnie had a scrap book with pictures and autographs with good wishes for a great future in boxing. Signatures by Willie Pep, Sugar Ray Robinson, Del Flanagan, Archie Moore and many more of the best at that time. Cortez made the finals of the All Service Boxing Championships but lost in a split decision to a jarhead. He weighs 135 pounds and was about five feet, six inches, fast as lightning, ala, Manny Pacquaio, got in the ring with the carrier's coach who begged for a work-out. In three rounds he never got hit once; literally beat the pants off the Limey. Cortez was also the undisputed best Helmsman, as steering through the Suez Canal required steering by ½ degrees. He was on the Helm almost the whole trip.

I never met anyone who could play whist or tonk and talk cards like John. I know some of you on board after I left knew him and also Merle Buddha Brown, another gunner's mate from the Air Force. He used to wake me at all hours upon returning from the beach usually with a hamburger, like I was starving to death in my sleep. What a life!

Back in Time; 1962, The Story of Our Charlie Brown

By: Dave Batsche, Fire Control Technician (FTG-2)

John B. Holt FT-2 was an easy going, very well liked member of our FT gang. Some time in '62, John was due to be discharged. He had his plane tickets purchased for his trip home and had his bags packed. He had given me all of his uniforms except the ones on his back. Well you better believe it was a sad day when he was informed that he had been extended for up to one year. Remember how we all wore our short-timers chains and anticipated our release from what was then "Hell" but now is remembered as some of our best days or years ever? John took a few days leave and went home somewhere on the upper East Coast. His ancestors were from Norway so he had talked about ski jumping and was going to compete in that event at home. "Ya sure John?" we all said. By golly he came back with a second place trophy with John Holt engraved on it. He also came back with a guitar and no idea how to play it. Well we all know that in the "Peanuts" comic strip Linus is the guy with the blanket. However, somehow John picked up the name Charley Brown since after morning muster at quarters Charley and his blanket would vanish. Our first class leader Buddy Wheaton would search our spaces daily constantly asking "Where's Brown? Anybody seen Brown?" Well he could be found at all hours of the night in the I-C room watching any and all of the ship's movies. The projector and movies were in there and the IC guys had shown us how to thread the film, and we just projected them on the wall.

Charlie also learned to play his guitar, first some chords – over and over and eventually "Ghost Riders In The Sky", again – over and over. The reason for his extension by President Kennedy was probably the "Bay of Pigs" ordeal that happened around that time and FT was deemed a critical rate.

Well John finally got out before we went to Boston for FRAM. Last heard about; he roomed with Dale Billings SO-2 from the same crew. Billings moved to the San Diego area and went to work for a defense contractor. Charlie Brown, where are you?

A Short Tale from the Boston Shipyards

By: Dave Batsche, Fire Control Technician (FTG-2)

We were moved off the ship into barracks as the entire superstructure was removed and the yard birds "worked" around the clock. We stood Fire Watches for the guys cutting and welding on the vessel we called home. We also did tours of the shipyard, visiting various shops to check on our gear, i.e.: radar and gun fire control components which had been removed for overhaul. We did this with occasional stops for coffee and the library of course. Pretty tough duty!

Well down the back stairs of the barracks and across the street in the basement of one of the buildings the USMC had a small bar. These were the friendliest Jar-Heads anywhere, as they allowed us to patronize their establishment. A pitcher of beer was cheaper than at the gedunk and they would flip a coin double or nothing so you always got a couple of pitchers for nothing. Business got so good for them that the place got over-crowded and they restricted patronage to Second Class & above. No problem for Batman, he borrowed a 2nd class jumper from his SD friend and became probably the only Caucasian steward in the whole dang Navy. By the time we left Bean Town they had made enough extra money (non-profit of course) so that they purchased all new bar stools, a new TV set, new toaster for chuck-wagon sandwiches and a brand new Whirlitzer Juke Box which played two songs continuously; "Patches" and "Silver Threads and Golden Needles".

THE END OF THE JOURNEY!
By: Dave Batsche, Fire Control Technician (FTG-2)

The end of my journey brought the ship to port at Cape Canaveral, Florida. We tied up next to the new nuclear sub, Thomas Jefferson. Due to my previous misdeeds, I had to decline an invitation to take a ride on the sub including a dive. Harry Lee Williams was then selected to go. He was given a ship's tour, a very fine lunch (he said they really eat well) and was given a card to remember the ride. This was truly one experience I regret missing. We had about two hours till getting underway, a rare deal in the afternoon. I then got word that if I wanted to get discharged two days early here at Canaveral rather than ride the ship back to Charleston, I could get my gear together and personnel would do the paperwork! Boy at that point you start shaking hands, saying farewell and time just flies by. I had what I considered a lot of friends and I know I missed some farewells. All went OK until I tried to return my foul-weather jacket at the Bosun's locker where my least friendly comrade was in charge - namely BM2 Larimore. We had some discussions as to who could go to hell and stay there. The number on the jacket didn't match the record book. Once again, Williams saved the day. He searched the racks in all compartments starting in the Aft most. He found the right jacket and saved me the $75.00 that Larimore was holding me responsible for. You can ask almost anyone who came back from liberty with the most black eyes and the answer will always be BM2 Larimore. I dragged myself and stuff off the ship and they immediately pulled the gangway and casted off the lines. The crew was manning the rails as the special sea detail does for getting underway. My lasting final memory of my fantastic adventure was the sight of the guys on the rail waving and yelling curse words and good luck to me.

SPECIAL MEMORIES
By: Dave Batsche, Fire Control Technician (FTG-2)

I remember TM2 "Tubes" Lambert who just knew someone was messing with his wife, returned to the ship and asked for volunteers to tip over the car in his driveway. They did it and then he found out his wife had granted the neighbors permission to park in their driveway for a party.

I remember SOG2 Lenny Kapala who said he'd suck a _ _ _ _ if he shipped over. We bought him a case of Lavoris after he shipped over.

I remember Vern Hjorth whose mother wrote him and referred to him as "Vern Dear". He was almost driven nuts by Bill Hudson's continuous reference to him as Vern Dear.

I remember SO3 Wesley P. Alloway who had both a Bass Guitar and a Slide Trombone, both of which he slept with.

I remember Captain Smith shooting "Flying Fish" with a 30-30 carbine from the Bridge.

I remember skipping the pudding desert just because the server had a vomit bucket tied around his sea-sick neck.

It wasn't just a job, it truly was an ADVENTURE!!!!
THANK YOU JOHNSTON.

MED MIDWATCH - DEPARTING
By: Jack Hughes, LTJG

Years on board the Johnston: 1962 to 1965

"This is Tampico. I am backing." The stern of the USS Strong (DD-758) was ominously close and I was notifying the ships astern.

In the first installment of "The Real Story of the USS Johnston DD-821" I described the activities of my actual first midwatch as a real live OODF. I also mentioned that there were no more nocturnal exercises from our DESRON 4 Operations Officer until we started heading west. We were now, toward the end of August, 1954, steaming west toward the Straits of Gibraltar where, after the transit, we and the squadron were to put into Rota, Spain for fuel, provisions, and have a new officer commissioned by his father, the U.S. Ambassador to Portugal and the former Commander of the Sixth Fleet, Admiral Anderson. Just as important, it was to have that final beer before crossing the Atlantic.

After distributing our remaining midshipmen around the squadron, except for one, DESRON 4 sortied Naples as around 0800 with the intent of arriving USNS Rota at about the same time the second day, or Saturday. I had the evening watch our first day out and the forenoon watch the next morning. This rotation leads to the midwatch for transiting the Straits, arguably the busiest waterway in the world at the time.

Because of the large amount of visible traffic, I clambered up to the bridge early as I expected a rather complex relief briefing. I was not surprised, the coastal traffic was fierce. I relieved the deck and conn at about 2355. Though this was my fourth trip through the Straits, it was my first at night and first as OODF. The number of lights and the near constant contact designations from CIC was a bit unnerving.

For reasons unknown, we had been formed into a column with a 1,000 yard separation. Recognizing that a Gearing class destroyer is roughly 130 yards long, which amounts to an actual separation of 870 yards, but a 4 nautical mile long formation.

The first few minutes were relatively calm as I settled into what I now knew was to be a very busy night. We passed a number of fishing and other craft abnormally close aboard but not dangerously so, a few at 100 yards or so. I wondered just how much disturbance our 9 consecutive 20 knot wakes caused on those boats. I also figured that this was to be the norm until we cleared the narrows.

Then came the first maneuvering order with an "immediate" execute. We were to come left 7 degrees. The entire formation was cutting 4-mile swath 7 degrees off our intended heading. After 10 minutes or so, we were ordered right 7 degrees. We were back on our original heading but about one mile south of the center of the channel. None of us had been granted any independent operating authority. The bridge radar repeater indicated some of the ships forward of us (in position 7) were taking the unilateral responsibility of protecting themselves. Over the course of the next 3.5 hours, we made multiple formation and course changes and all ships were forced to take independent action, including DD-821. Ultimately, independent activity was authorized long after it was a fact. The net result of all this was a pretty ragged looking formation; offset about 10 degrees from our base heading of 270 making our formation something over a mile wide. This placed the final ship just about a mile or so off the Moroccan coast. We had long passed the point where bridge to bridge communications were not only common, but necessary. Since we were spread out to port, contacts on our starboard side were not important unless they changed course to port. In other words, once a contact had passed the Manley and did not change course, it was deemed to probably not be a problem, but was watched. Contacts to the port side of the Manley, on the other hand, were deemed inside the formation. Depending on where you were in the somewhat lopsided formation, you would take the contact on whichever side was the more safe and advise the following ships of your decision so they could make their own, always passing on any relevant data on the contact. Clearly, some of the small craft started out to the starboard side of the Manley and depending on course and speed, wound up on the port side of the formation, trying to get through. Many more started on the port side and wound up on the starboard side soon to be forgotten. Some ships were 200 – 400 yards or so to port or starboard of their intended positions; others were roughly the same distance ahead of or astern of their intended positions. A few were both. Hence, the opening comments to this essay. There were multiple near misses (near collisions) and many similar bridge to bridge radio messages.

While small craft on parallel or reciprocal courses were something of a nuisance as described above, those on tangential courses were something else. While we were all in "see and avoid" mode, remember that this was the Med, home of the Tripoli and other less violent, pirates. None of them were trying to commit suicide, but their mindset seemed to be that getting bumped by a big, bad

American destroyer would at least bring them a new boat, particularly in a European court, which of course, put us on the defensive, with our 3250 to 3450 ton destroyers trying desperately to avoid even grazing one of these bumboats. Talk about modifying the Rules of the road to suit the circumstances, but we got through without incident. The fact about the Rules of the Road is that they are only effective if both ships are following them.

At about 0100, CIC ceased designating contacts unless they had a 100 yard or less CPA. Even so, by the time we squirted through the Straits and had open ocean, we still had around 200 designated contacts on the board. OODFs will have a good idea of how far we were into the alphabet.

I cannot even begin to describe these vessels by type, but the one that cracked me up was a 16 to 18 foot blue sailboat that a young couple had decided to take out on a pleasure cruise in the sea lanes at 0300. They were on a starboard tack as they ghosted past on our starboard side. Yes, you sailors know that we were blanking their sails, but only for the few moments they were in the lee of the tallest part of the ship. I stepped out on the wing with glasses to see if I could tell whether they were drunk or drugged. They both seemed to be having a great time as though it was a normal event for them. As they swept by the bridge, the young man at the tiller stood, faced me and rendered a pretty good salute. Just for the hell of it, I returned and left the wing. As we went through the narrows between Gibraltar and Casablanca, the transverse traffic dwindled to near nothing and I began to breathe easier.

One of the very odd happenings of that watch began with a warning from the USS Manley (DD-940) at about 0240 that a large ship was on a reciprocal heading passing to port. I asked CIC if it painted on their radar as the bridge repeater did not show it. Each chip in order of position reported a visual sighting on what turned out to be a Japanese tanker in ballast. That ship had not painted on any of the 9 surface search radars. I cannot say that I was totally surprised because the amount of traffic and the very confined quarters pretty much overwhelmed the radar.

My relief appeared right on time at 0345, just as we were clearing the Straits and moving into the Atlantic, but the situation was far from resolved. There were still a lot of contacts, but we were led offshore to get away from the coastal traffic. It should probably be noted that my somewhat shaky relief accepted the deck and conn at about 0430 when we were about 15 miles into the Atlantic at that point and had reformed the column. We were ordered a sharp right turn and into a bent screen toward Rota. I went below!

Though emotionally and physically exhausted, I actually felt pretty good about one thing: nobody, Navy or civilian, was hurt; the U.S. Navy was not on the hook for any small craft damages, and there was no contact between ships.

I went to bed, shoes and all, and did not make quarters the next day. LCDR Beaulieu sent a steward to see if I was all right. I told him, no, I was not all right but to bring me a POD so I would know when to muster and where in what uniform. About 0900, I staggered to the wardroom, got a cup of (miraculously) fresh coffee and asked the steward on duty if he could make me a double fried egg sandwich. About 20 minutes, the sandwich, and two coffees later, I was feeling as good as sub human and went to prepare for our big day. I showered, shaved, took 3 APCs, found one still more or less presentable set of whites, whitewashed my shoes, changed the cover of my combination cap and even remembered the white belt. I stepped out to meet the day; the steely eyed naval officer eager to do his duty. Not quite! How about the bleary eyed naval officer trying to stay out of the way.

We had moored at the U.S. Navy base in Rota at about 0815 and began preparations for the commissioning ceremony. The ambassador and wife arrived about 1030 and were entertained in the wardroom by the skipper and exec while the rest of us were taking care of business. At the appointed hour of 1100, Midshipman Anderson appeared on the fantail in Ensign's Dress White uniform. All of the rest of the officers and crew were in Service Dress Whites. The skipper escorted Ambassador and Mrs.

Anderson out and made a short address commending the almost officer on his performance while aboard. There was not a man present who privately disagreed. We were all convinced that he was destined to be a credit to the Navy and a standout officer. His father commenced the commissioning ceremony; we all clapped and cheered, as did the squadron ships around us. His mother cried, the family hugged and the Navy's newest Ensign disappeared forward to the CPO quarters where he had been living. After a few minutes, he reappeared dressed in shorts and a skivvy shirt and in the hands of about half of the ship's Chiefs who strode purposefully to the stern and unceremoniously tossed him into Rota Bay.

Evidently, his parents had been prepared and cheered along with the rest of us. This got the other ships wound up and they really hooted. He swam around to the starboard screw guard and climbed back aboard with the help of many hands and a line that had been conveniently tied to a lifeline stanchion. The family returned to the wardroom to await their new Ensign. I and a couple of other junior officers joined them in small talk, mostly about Lisbon where few, if any of us, had been. After a suitable interval, they collected their son, now in traveling civvies and returned to the fantail where ships company was still loosely assembled. Now Ensign Anderson thanked the crew collectively and turned the four OODFs with whom he has spent many hours on the bridge soaking up knowledge. He walked to each of us in turn with hand extended in thanks. Then, to our collective astonishment, he hugged each of us. He turned to the skipper and offered his hand. They shook and CAPT Pringle stepped back, opened his arms and said, "What? No hug?" The sight of our 6'6", 255 lb. CO gathering up the 5'8", 145 lb. Ensign was memorable, to say the least.

The family thanked the entire ship and departed for a vacation in France.

During the transit from Naples, or maybe before, the Chiefs had issued a sort of formal challenge to the wardroom: SOFTBALL. Losers to stand the winners for pizza and beer at the CPO Club. At this point, it should be noted that Captain Pringle was a former Chief Boatswains Mate. He appointed himself as umpire and the wardroom team knew that every close call would go to the Chiefs. He also declared that the CPOs would be the visiting team and bat first. Well, all the competing officers were in their early to mid 20's and almost all of the CPOs were over 35. We soon learned that we were not taking them seriously enough. By the time we closed out the top of the first, the wardroom was behind 1-0, partly because of the Skipper's obvious favoritism and equally our failure to buckle down. However, the wardroom team regrouped, gritted our teeth and proceeded to play ball. By the end of the third inning the score was something like Wardroom 21, Chiefs 3. We decided as a group that the issue was no longer in doubt and noted the cocktail hour was approaching. We packed up the gear and returned to the CPO Club. Even though my ass was dragging, I did hit 3 home runs and drove in 4-5 more.

As we stood in line to order pizza, Captain Pringle, with pizza and mug in hand, told me he wanted me to sit with him. Needless to say, I agreed, but was curious. After a few minutes, I had pie and beer and found him sitting at a table for two. He motioned me into the other chair. After a couple of minutes of small talk, mostly about the game, he said "You know I attended the skipper's meeting this morning with the Commodore?"

"Yes sir."

"I'm wondering why I was the only one who slept soundly through the Straits? All the rest were on their bridges. All I could do was nod sagely and hope I looked tired. Why didn't you call me?"

"Well Skipper, it was busy as hell but it never got scary or to the point where I felt over my head. I did start to call you a couple of times but the issue resolved itself before I could get to it."

"Did anyone ask if your CO was on the bridge?"

"No, Sir."

"Well, I am pleased that you judged the situation within your capabilities and evidently you were right. The Commodore complimented mo on how well we handled a difficult transit. If something similar arises, please let me know, even if I just sleep in my chair. At least that lets me honestly say that I was on the bridge and implies I was on top of things. That having been said, let me toast you for a job well done." We clinked steins, ate our pizza, chatted about shipboard stuff and that was the last I ever heard of it.

At 0800 the next morning, we thanked our Navy hosts for their hospitality, full water and fuel tanks, cast off and went to blue water for a comfortable crossing.

Not counting the hurricane roaring up from Florida!

THE GREAT TWO BOILER RACE
By: Jack Hughes, LTJG

Before leaving Naples, somebody presented the Commodore and the Captains of the USS Johnston, the USS Laffey and the USS Strong with the idea of a two boiler, three hour race between the three destroyers. The thinking, or at least the justification, was that it would be a good measure of the readiness of the ship's engineering plants and crews. The six destroyers making up the rest of Destroyer Squadron Four were already about half way across the Atlantic.

We in the Engineering Department of the Johnston began planning (scheming and plotting) about how we could gain the upper hand and win as convincingly as possible. At this point, if only for the purpose of setting the stage, it should be mentioned that there was a fairly significant sum of money being wagered among the various groups on the ships, i.e. Officers, Chief's Quarters, Engineering personnel and so forth. The winner would win the entire purse, distributed according to the size of the wagers. The Executive officers on the three ships were responsible for record keeping and money holding. Our engineering Department, including myself, placed the largest amount by far. In the event of a tie or near tie, the Commodore would decide. The Johnston Engineering department had already decided that there was not going to be a tie or anything resembling it.

Our Chief Engineer (Engineering Officer) was LT. Bill Griffis, who joined the ship just before we left Charleston. He had completed the Engineer Officer Replacement course as I had, but had no experience. The responsibility of the Fire Rooms (boilers or steam generators) and the Engine Rooms was that of the MPA or Main Propulsion Assistant: me, recently promoted LTJG J. W. Hughes. I had had the job for 15 months.

Any ship's speed is limited by the maximum calculated hull speed and the RPM of the propeller(s). The longer the hull, the higher the theoretical speed. The formula is: the square root of the length of the waterline (not overall length) times 1.34. We were a Gearing Class at 390' 6" while our competitors were Sumner Class at 376' 3" but carrying the same engineering plants. The crews of the other two thought their somewhat lighter weight coupled with the same available power should give them an edge. Our maximum prop speed was about 360 RPM under maximum power, i.e. using all four available boilers. If we tried to exceed that, the props would cavitate and actually reduce our speed.

Knowing that with two boilers we would have about 250 RPM to work with, we figured that an additional 2-3 RPM at the propellers would give us about a one mile advantage after the three hours. All we had to do was determine how to get that 2-3 RPM over and above what our competitors could muster.

We knew that all three ships had filled their feed and potable water tanks at Rota and it was pretty much a given that they would secure the evaporators during the race to conserve steam. We knew we had to do better. LT. Griffis, myself and the two leading chief petty officers from both boiler and engine rooms conceived a plan that we would present to Captain Pringle.

In normal steaming operations, each of all the assorted pumps that fed the boilers and the steam turbine engines had a standby that was turning slowly and ready to go on line almost instantly if the primary failed. Keeping all of those pumps turning used a lot of steam. None of the senior petty officers had remembered an auxiliary failure without a great deal of warning in many years. Except for the lubricating oil pumps serving the engines, we decided to shut the auxiliaries down for the duration of the race. Normally, we maintained one of our two electric power generators on line and the other in standby.

We did have an emergency diesel generator which would keep the lights on, but then we also had battery driven battle lanterns which provided adequate light for the few we felt would be moving around the ship. So, we decided to simply shut down the generators, leaving a steam blanket on one should we need it. We elected to man the machinery spaces during the race with the more experienced and most senior members of our engineering crew and suggested everybody not involved move around as little as possible. We secured the laundry and the galley, both of which used steam for heat. During the transit from Naples to Rota, we attempted to determine if any combination of two of our four boilers offered any advantage over the others, eventually deducing that if there was, we were unable to determine it. We did decide to use boilers 2 and 4 for the simple reason that they were closer to the engines they would be powering than were numbers 1 and 3 and would lose slightly less steam in the transfer. We later learned that the other two ships reached the same conclusion. We also decided to run the plant as two completely independent operations rather than cross connected which would jointly power both engines from both boilers. We felt the latter to be nominally less efficient.

As the hour approached to begin the race, I went down to the forward engine room, also known as Main Control, to supervise the securing of those auxiliary pumps we felt were appropriate throughout the plant. We had carefully identified each machine and provided a list for each machinery space to the senior petty officer responsible for that space. As they were secured, I could see the Throttleman slowly reducing the steam flow into the engine to maintain constant propeller RPM as the machines were taken off line and secured.

About 5-10 minutes before the official start we were formed into the now familiar column and 1000 yard separation steaming due north at about 20 knots. The actual race was triggered by a radio message from the commodore himself as he ordered the three ships into a left turn to settle on a homeward bound course of 270 degrees and maximum two boiler speed. All three accelerated at about the same speed as we settled onto 270. At this point, I was on the bridge as the official engineering observer and noticed that while our forward stack was exhausting near clear gasses, the after stack was showing a medium brown haze. Over the 1MC, I requested our senior boilerman, BTCM Cochrane, to meet me in the after fire room, only to be advised he was already there. I scrambled down the four levels and arrived just in time to see Chief Cochrane peering through the periscope to observe the stack gasses and judge whether we were running the boiler too rich or lean. After a minute of study, he made a minute adjustment to the fuel flow, waited a couple of minutes and used the periscope again, smiled and said to me, in effect, that we were getting all we were going to get. I returned to the bridge and reported to the Captain that we were running with maximum efficiency and speed. I also reported to the four engineering spaces that we were gaining a couple of feet on the competition every minute. We were making roughly 27.8 knots and about 254 RPM.

The only excitement in the first hour was that the Johnston was steadily pulling ahead of the Laffey and the Strong until we picked up a large surface contact on our starboard bow at a distance of about 20,000 yards on a course and speed to pass very close aboard ahead of us, the lead ship. The International Rules of the road made us the "burdened" ship and we were obligated to defer to what turned out to be a Dutch passenger vessel of about 25,000 tons. In retrospect, we figured there was much consternation on that bridge as there was on ours as to what to do. The Dutch ship was the "privileged" vessel and as such was required to maintain course and speed so that we could "see and avoid."

About the time the Commodore seemed to be leaning toward a recommendation to change course to pass astern, the Dutchman apparently decided that tangling with three U.S. Navy destroyers who were very obviously in a hurry was possibly not in his best interests and came left to pass us starboard to starboard at about 4000 yards and we put up the international flag signal for "Thank You." After passing us, he returned to his previous course aiming, we guessed, for a Caribbean cruise.

This took the race into the third hour and it was clear that the USS Johnston was running away with the race and the prize money. We were far enough ahead that we felt we could ease off a little without losing any ground. So we eased the throttles just enough to keep our roughly 2000 yard lead and were still a mile ahead of the other two when the Commodore declared it over. The Laffey transferred our winnings to the Strong by high wire and then after adding theirs, to us. I made about $600 which at the time was nearly 150% of my monthly Navy pay. It was widely rumored that Lt. Griffis bet heavily and won several thousand dollars. We never knew for sure.

The remaining three days at sea went relatively smoothly. We returned to normal plant operations, moored at our usual pier in Charleston, SC and married officers and crew were reunited with spouses and family. In port watches were set and being Saturday, those without the duty retired to homes or base housing. Most junior officers hit the sack in preparation for the planned celebration at the "O" club that evening. At sea, most junior line officer's work days averaged about 20 hours, spread out around the clock, so our first desire on returning to port was rest.

The great Two Boiler Race was history.

Bio - Robert Charles Pringle

Captain of USS Johnston: 1964 to 1965

Robert Charles Pringle was born in Honolulu, Hawaii, on 14 May 1920. He enlisted in the Navy in March 1939, advanced through the enlisted ranks, graduated from the

University of Minnesota, NROTC and received his commission as Ensign in October, 1945. He served aboard the USS Earle (DMS-42) with the Pacific Fleet until 1947. During the period 1947 - 1949, Commander Pringle was Executive officer aboard the USS Gull (AMS-16) which was assigned to WestPac for minesweeping operations. Subsequent sea duty included tours aboard the USS Macomb (DMG-23) and USS Bache (DDE-470).

Upon returning to the continental United States in 1952, he reported for duty under instruction at Guided Missile School, Ft. Bliss, Texas. From there he was assigned for duty to the U.S. Naval Guided missiles School, Pomona, California, where he served as Executive officer and later Commanding Officer. Between 1955 and 1957, Commander Pringle was in command of the USS San Bernardino County (LST-1110). From there, future assignments included duty as Administrative Assistant in the Technical Staff of the Special Projects Office in Washington, D.D., and Executive Officer aboard the USS Stribling (DD-867). It was from this latter assignment that Commander Pringle reported aboard the USS Harry E. Yarnell (DLG-17) as Executive Officer.

Commander Pringle is married to former Florence Probst of Northfield, New Jersey. They have three children, Jeffery, Robert and Robert.

The Real Story of Eli Takesian
By: Eli Takesian, Chaplain (USN & USMC)

Years on board the Johnston: 1964 to 1967

Official USMC photograph

Editor's Note: Captain Takesian is obviously a humble man as you will see after reading the next several stories. It is also easy to understand why a Monument was created in honor of Captain Takesian, USS Johnston's Chaplain. There is no question he is a hero and is respected by all whom served with him!

INTERVIEW OF ELI TAKESIAN
WILMINGTON, NORTH CAROLINA HISTORY
UNIVERSITY OF NORTH CAROLINA AT WILMINGTON
MILITARY CHAPLAIN ORAL HISTORY PROJECT
DECEMBER 13, 2002

INTRODUCTION: Good morning. My name is Paul Zarbock. I'm a staff person of the Randall Library at the University of North Carolina, Wilmington. Today is the 13 of December in the year 2002 and we're at Fort Myer, Virginia. I'm with Rear Admiral David White, United States Navy (Retired). Today we're interviewing Eli Takesian.

(Time & Place: TET Offensive, 1968, Citadel of Hue', Vietnam ... Marines an NVA (North Vietnamese Army) are fighting fiercely ... USS JOHNSTON (DD-821) is off the coast of Vietnam, close to Hue')

Excerpt of interview:

Takesian: That night the situation became worse. Our own casualty figures had caught up with us. An ARVN (South Vietnamese Army) unit was supposed to cover our left flank … but never showed up. Because of attrition, we the pursuers were becoming the pursued, as fresh NVA troops, attempting to enter the fray, were climbing over the Citadel walls, to trap us. Our artillery support was insufficient. So we radioed US Navy ships, requesting H&I (Harassment and Interdiction) fire support to prevent the enemy from breaking through. Two ships assisted a cruiser and the destroyer USS JOHNSTON (DD-821). I detached from JOHNSTON a year earlier, almost to the day. I had once been present for her crew when they needed me ... now they were present in Hue' for my Marines and me when we needed them. The entire night was boom-boom-boom, all around us, rounds accurately placed, providing needed protection, thanks to superb firing from the cruiser and USS JOHNSTON (DD-821). A small world!

THE BRAVEST MAN I HAVE EVER KNOWN
By: Vinny Rawlins, USMC

Corpsman Hubert, another sea story for your collection from us old Jarheads: A few years ago some of us enlisted men were asked to meet with some members of the enlisted crew of the USS Hue City during the annual Memorial service honoring those who served in that battle. The keynote speaker that year was the chaplain who had volunteered to go with us when he became aware we were entering the captured city without a chaplain. Father Eli Takesian is by far the bravest man I have ever known. After one of us had given a short summary of the challenges facing us during the battle, each of us was asked to give some comment on our individual perspective of our time in Hue City. My comment was that the bravest men on the battle field were not Marines, but Navy Corpsman and Father Eli!!! All of who served in Delta Company agree that nothing anyone can imagine will come close to the courage and devotion to duty displayed by our Corpsmen and Chaplain. Only someone who has been engaged in a fierce firefight and heard "Corpsman up" and seen that individual get up and go to the wounded time and again can really know what true courage is. Please pass on to your Brothers and Sisters in uniform how much we appreciate their service and dedication in carrying on the traditions that make use proud to have served and that make us proud of those of you serving today!!!

Saepe Expertus, Semper Fidelis, Frates Aeterni,

"Often Tested; Always Faithful; Brothers Forever"

DEDICATION OF A MONUMENT TO CAPTAIN ELI TAKESIAN, CHC, USN (Ret)
Pleasant Valley Street and Merrimack Street
Methuen, Massachusetts
October 24, 2007

Preface

These remarks were prepared by the then-SSGT (later 2nd Lieutenant) Robert Thoms, USMC, ("Cajun Bob"), a Delta Company Platoon Commander of the First Battalion, Fifth Marines at the time of the Battle of Hue' City during the Tet Offensive of 1968. It was SSGT Thoms who nominated Chaplain Takesian for the Navy Cross. Regrettably, the paper work never found its way to the proper authorities. So, suitable recognition of Chaplain Takesian's heroic ministry on the battlefield had to wait another thirty-nine years.

The Dedication

The purpose of this dedication ceremony is to honor a home-grown Methuen hero: a combat Marine who served in 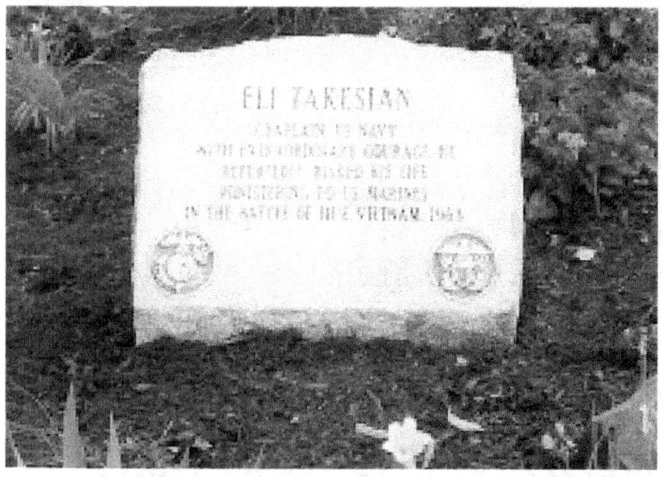 Korea, a Navy Chaplain who served in Vietnam, and a man who later became the 8th Chaplain of the United States Marine Corps, hand-picked by Marine Commandant, General P. X. Kelley. Beyond his many titles, duties, acclamations and medals, are the personal stories of inspiration, incalculable acts of heroism, spirituality, moral courage, and leadership this man has provided to others. Today, Eli Takesian is especially being honored for his extraordinary courage in which he repeatedly risked his life while ministering to US Marines during what was universally called by the media "the bloodiest battle of the Vietnam War." The Battle of Hue' City occurred during January and February of 1968.

When the Tet Offensive began at the end of January 1968, the North Vietnamese Army, in a massive, surprise invasion, captured and took control of nearly every major city and strategic geographical area throughout South Vietnam. Thousands upon thousands of South Vietnamese citizens and soldiers were killed, while the North

Vietnamese Army dug in to maintain their control. Hue' City was the cultural and educational Capitol of South Vietnam with its universities, palaces, religious monuments and plush gardens.

The North Vietnamese invaded Hue' and took control of 99% of the city. With elements of the South Vietnamese Army holed up in the Citadel, the most palatial and beautiful area in the innermost part of Hue' City, and with innocent civilians being killed or running for their lives, elements of the 5th Marine Regiment along with other units - less than 2,400 Marines in all - were assigned to retake the city of Hue' from the entrenched, heavily-fortified North Vietnamese Army who in retrospect, was estimated to number between 10,000 and 15,000 troops.

It was during this long, horrendous, street-by-street, house-by-house, battle that Chaplain Eli Takesian selflessly interjected himself into the front lines of battle to help the injured and dying Marines as they fell in the streets. When the Tet Offensive began, Eli Takesian was serving as the Regimental Chaplain of the 5th Marines, overseeing other Chaplains who were assigned to the Battalions. Upon learning that the 1st Battalion, 5th Marines, who were heading for the fight in Hue', had no Chaplain, Eli went to serve the men himself, rather than sending someone else. He knew Hue' was a hot area and very, very dangerous.

He could have stayed in the Regimental Command Post,

some ten miles away from the intense battle, but he didn't. He went himself. He could have gone to Hue' and stayed in safer Command Posts there, but he didn't. He could have stayed near the Battalion aid station that was somewhat better protected from enemy fire, but he didn't. During the period of some of the heaviest fighting of this battle, Chaplain Eli Takesian dispatched himself personally, selflessly, to the front lines, out in the midst of the house-to-house fighting, unarmed and defenseless, to comfort and minister to those Marines who fell.

Staff Sergeant Robert Thoms (Cajun Bob), the only Delta Company Platoon Commander left at that time in Hue' City, describes Eli's actions in the Citadel as the most incredible feat of courage he's ever witnessed. He says:

"Eli's actions took extra-ordinary heroism to another level. We were under withering enemy fire in a fierce gunfight in front of us and to our right flank. We were attempting to take the Dong Ba Tower which was perched atop a hill of rubble above us. We were along a 12-foot stone wall, with the enemy behind it and on top of the Tower. The North Vietnamese were also in the houses along "Rocket Alley", the name the Marines called the street beside us. There was little cover or concealment from the mortars, the RPGs, the machine guns, and sniper fire. It's difficult to describe the chaos

that surrounded us. We were in the midst of a vision of hell: the smoke, the fire, the noise, the screams of the wounded, and the suddenness of death could be likened to Dante's Inferno.

In the middle of all of this, we see the Regimental Chaplain, Eli, right behind us, helping Marines and Corpsmen who were wounded and dying. It was the most incredible thing to watch. Eli was unarmed - the only person on that battlefield who didn't have a weapon to even defend himself - running back and forth across Rocket Alley, comforting and aiding all who were down. In the midst of this hell, we watched this small-statured guy comforting the wounded. He was unfazed, seemingly oblivious to the mortars, the RPGs and gunfire around him; he didn't even flinch as he cared for these men. He looked completely unconcerned about his own safety and well being, as he ministered to them. The entire time while he was exposing himself to - and even drawing - enemy fire upon himself, he was kneeling beside, touching, praying, and reassuring these guys as they waited for medical help. We watched Eli do this over and over, with many casualties. We saw him drag Marines and civilian bodies from the center of Rocket Alley, so their bodies wouldn't be further mutilated by tanks or enemy fire. As we watched these extraordinary acts of bravery, we were inspired to

> *accomplish things in that battle we didn't believe were possible. His courage, faithfulness and unwavering commitment to duty filled all of us with a sense of confidence that had been sorely tested up to that point, and gave us a renewed sense of purpose in accomplishing our mission."*

About two years ago, Cajun Bob was counseling Jim Walsh, one of the wounded men to whom Eli attended in Hue'. When Cajun Bob told Jim that Eli was alive, Jim was overjoyed. He said, "Eli looked at my wounds and said he had seen a lot worse and I was going to be okay. He knelt down, and put his hand on my chest, and when he looked me straight in the eyes, there was no fear in his eyes as he talked to me. I knew then that he was telling the truth and I believed him. I relaxed instantly. I thought about that a lot afterwards over the years, and I've been thinking about that a lot lately," Jim said. Three weeks later, after sharing this story about Eli, Jim Walsh died of cancer. The comfort and confidence that Eli provided to Jim in Hue', continued to comfort him during his approaching death, 38 years later.

Cajun Bob explains there are about a dozen Marines he knows who are alive today from Delta Company who served in the Battle of Hue' City. For 32 years, these men thought Eli had died on the streets in Hue. About three years ago, Brian McCabe, another Methuen-raised Marine, who served during the Korean era, and who reenlisted when he was in his 30s, to serve in Vietnam with Delta Company, began a search to locate Eli's gravesite so that the Delta Company brotherhood could pay their respects and honor his memory. Through a series of contacts, Brian spoke to Eli's sister who, to everyone's joy and amazement, told him that Eli was alive and well! Brian McCabe suggested honoring Eli in their hometown of Methuen by erecting this monument that is being dedicated today.

The men of Delta Company wish to express their gratitude to all of you here and to all who helped make this tribute possible. Thank you, and Semper Fidelis!

Bio – Eli Takesian

Chaplain of USS Johnston: 1964 to 1967

Feb 28, 1932 Born in Methuen, MA

1949-1953   U.S. Marine Corps, Sergeant, 1st Marine Division, Korean War

1953-1960   Education

   Baylor University (Bachelor of Arts, 1957)
   Mexico City College, Mexico
   University of Edinburgh, Scotland
   Princeton Theological Seminary (Master of Theology, 1960)

1960   Ordained a Presbyterian minister (Northern New England Presbytery)

1960-1962   U.S. Navy Chaplain

                1960-1961 1st Battalion, 6th Marines, Bay of Pigs, Cuba (Apr1961)
                1961-1962 USNS BUCKNER (TAP-123)

1962-1964   Pastor, Amsterdam Presbyterian/Methodist Churches, Amsterdam, Ohio

1964-1987   U.S. Navy Chaplain
                1964-1967 Destroyer Division Four-Two, Charleston, SC
                1967-1968 3rd Battalion, 5th Marines; & Regimental Chaplain, 5th Marines, Vietnam, Citadel of Hue' (TET '68)
                1968-1969 Naval Air Station, Lakehurst, NJ
                1969-1970 3rd Battalion, 1st Marines; & Regimental Chaplain, 1st Marines, Vietnam
                1971-1974 National Naval Medical Center, Bethesda, MD
                1974-1975 Senior Chaplain, Naval Station, Adak, AK
                1976-1979 Senior Chaplain, Coast Guard Support Center, Governors Island, NY; & Chaplain Coordinator, USCG
                1979-1982 Senior Chaplain, Naval Station, Subic Bay, Philippines
                1982-1986 The Chaplain, U.S. Marine Corps, Washington, DC (Chaplain to the Commandant of the Marine Corps & Chief of Chaplains to chaplains serving Marine Corps)
                1986-1987 Naval Medical Command, Washington, DC
                1987 Retired from active naval service

1987-1995   Associate Pastor, Vienna Presbyterian Church, Vienna, VA

1995   Retired from active parish ministry

Married Margaret Broderson, 6 May 1978. Margaret was born in Lyndon, KA.

Margaret's education: University of Kansas City; Juilliard School of Music, NYC.
Retired professional singer: <u>Voice of Firestone</u> (Firestone Hour), ABC Television, 1955-60; original Broadway production of <u>My Fair Lady</u>; etc.

Recollections of Service Onboard USS Johnston DD-821

By: Paul K. Johnston, Machinist Mate (MM-3)

Years on board the Johnston: 1965 to 1967

I joined the Navy in May 1964, just prior to graduating high school on the outskirts of Pittsburgh, Pennsylvania. One week after graduating I was headed off to Boot Camp in Great Lakes, Illinois. After completing Boot Camp and Machinist Mate Class "A" school, I reported to the Johnston on January 3' 1965. Three days later we departed Charleston, South Carolina for a Med Cruise.

My first experience onboard the Johnston came in a very unique way. After reporting aboard in the early evening of January 3rd, I was just in the beginnings of falling asleep when I heard my name announced over the 1MC. I went up to the Quarterdeck and asked the Petty

Officer of the Watch what he wanted. He said he didn't even know me, who was I? I replied I just reported onboard that afternoon and my name was Paul Johnston. He burst out laughing along with the Messenger of the Watch. In my naivety of Navy protocol aboard ship, I learned that whenever the Commanding Officer of a ship arrived or departed the Quarterdeck Watch was required to announce the name of the ship and whether or not he was arriving or departing. What I had heard was "Johnston departing." I thought I was being summoned to the Quarterdeck. It took some time to live that one down.

The next day I was assigned to the After Engine Room. One day prior to our departure for the Med Cruise I was instructed to clean up the lower level in the Engine Room. Upon seeing a bucket with dirty rags, I did what I was instructed to do; I dumped the bucket in the dipsty-dumpster on the pier. Unknown to me, the bucket contained small parts for the pilot valve to the Fire and Bilge Pump. Once the First Class in charge of the Engine Room found out what I had done, I was in for it. He had me climbing into that dipsty-dumpster and searching through all that trash for the small parts to the Pilot Valve. I was in that dumpster for most of the day; I never did find all of the parts.

On our way to the Med, we stopped at Key West, Florida for Sonar training. There I met a nice looking red head that would become my wife two years later. I also remember the unusual site I saw there, people swimming in the middle of winter! I'd heard of such things, but I had never seen it - in the middle of winter - WOW!

We made another stop at Guantanamo Bay "GITMO", Cuba. There, we enjoyed the warm weather and unexpectedly got into an altercation between the Navy and the Coast Guard (USCG Half Moon). As clearly as I can remember, both Johnston and Half Moon sailors were being thrown off the "cattle car" trailer on the way back to our respective ships. Both ships were "kindly" asked to leave "GITMO" in the morning. Continuing our trip to the Med, my cleaning station was the Main Turbine. During "field day" my job was to clean the insulating material on the turbine. I used two buckets; one to use to clean the insulation and the other to puke in. I think I had to empty my puke bucket more often than replacing the cleaning water. What a trip! I thought at the time I'd never become a "real" sailor. Getting "sea-sick" was not a fun thing!

At another time, after I was qualified to stand "Throttleman of the Watch", I was on watch on the Throttles during a practice "emergency breakaway" drill. During our evolution I remember hearing the words "emergency breakaway - this is not a drill." As I recall, we received numerous bell orders from the Bridge in quick succession. In this instance, the lead watchstander in the Engine Room (called the Top Watch) assisted me in answering all the bells by recording them on the Bell Sheet as I operated the throttles. I felt a strong thump against the hull. Ugh- oh! What happened? Next thing I remember happening was the First Class from the Forward Engine Room came rushing to our Engine Room and made both myself and the Top Watch sign our Bell Sheet. He then smeared the page we had just signed with butter. Yeah, butter. Not knowing what was going on, I remember him (I believe his name was MM1 Nix) saying that by smearing the page with butter, no changes, erases, or any marks of any sort can be made without messing up the page. I found out later that the Engine Order Telegraph Bell Sheet is one of only two official logs that can be used in legal proceedings in court, by the Navy or a civilian court. By smearing the bell sheet with butter, it protected us, the Throttlemen in both engine rooms and our respective Top Watches from accusations of improperly answering the bells. What I heard later was that we, the Throttlemen, were accused of such improper actions. However, with the bells sheets smeared with butter, we could not be found guilty. I don't recall what the outcome of the incident was, but I'll never forget that First Class coming into the Engine Room with butter!

It seems that so many things happened in my three and one-half years on the Johnston that I can't remember them all. I do remember the Myrtle Bank Hotel fire in Kingston, Jamaica. Unfortunately, I had gotten into some kind of trouble (I don't remember what now) but, as punishment I was assigned to an additional four hour watch on the Fresh Water Evaporator in the Forward Engine Room during the time of the fire. The Johnston crew helped to put out the fire and saved the major portion of the waterfront. I do remember there was a lot of missing damage control/fire-fighting equipment afterwards. Where did it go? In a town like Kingston with all of its "attractions", on can only imagine!

While onboard the Johnston, two of my best friends for my entire tour was MMFN Dennis Monaghan and MM3 Tom Mack. Dennis was assigned to the After Engine Room with me and Tom was assigned to the Forward Engine Room. Later (September 1967), I married that girl I met in Key West who was now working for the FBI in Washington, DC. Tom was my best man and Dennis stood up for me.

In May of 1967 we were notified that the Johnston was scheduled to go to Viet Nam. I was also informed that I'd made Second Class Machinist Mate (MM2) but that I'd have to extend my enlistment for one year to accept the promotion. I said OK, but I wanted to go to Second Class Divers School as a signing bonus. We had an opening onboard for two diver's billets, one of which was empty. I wanted that second billet. I was told that I would not be permitted to go, that I was needed onboard to get ready to go to Viet Nam. I only wanted to go to diver's school for five weeks (at that time) and I would return to the ship and extend my enlistment to go with the ship to Viet Nam. Again, I was told I could not go, I was needed! Some need! I was due to be separated in

November of 1967, just before the boat was to leave for Viet Nam. My offer to extend my enlistment to go to Viet Nam with the ship seemed to fall on deaf ears. If I could not go to divers training, I told them I would not extend my enlistment even for the promotion to Second Class MM. In denying me five weeks of training, they lost a good sailor. And I was a good sailor. I was young and brash as was the majority of the crew and did some dumb things (what young sailor didn't), but I had always wanted to be a sailor. My father was one during the Second World War. Ever since I could remember, I wanted to be a sailor like him. Now that I was a "real" sailor, I was proud; proud of being a "tin can" sailor, and extremely proud of my ship. After all, it had my name. How many sailors can say that?

To make a long story short, I was denied the training. I therefore, separated from the Navy November 10, 1967. After being separated for a short two years, I realized that I still wanted to be a sailor. I reenlisted in June of 1970 as a Third Class Machinist Mate and eventually went on to Submarine duty, qualifying in several classes of submarines, retiring in 1986 as a Chief Machinist Mate.

Regardless of my duty stations after my tour on Johnston, I will always remember the shipmates, the times and the pride I had while serving on her. When I found out her inglorious end, I felt a sad loss of this proud ship. But, the memories she gave me will never be forgotten, shaded maybe by age, but never totally forgotten!

Bio – John & Donna Argonti
By: John Argonti, Fire Control Technician (FTG-2)

Years on board the Johnston: 1966 to 1968

John & Donna (Hoogerhyde) Argonti

Born: John, August 10, 1947, Pittsburgh, Pa.
Donna, November 11, 1947, Pittsburgh, Pa.
Married: June 23, 1973
Family: Two children, Jennifer and Steven. Three grandchildren, Cory, Jonathan, and Kaylene.

John graduated Brentwood High School (Pittsburgh) in June 1965 then joined the Navy, reporting for boot camp (San Diego) in October 1965. After boot camp, he was assigned to "A" school for Fire Control Technician (FTG) at Bainbridge MD. Upon completion, he was assigned to the USS Johnston DD-821 at Charleston SC. Just prior to the Johnston going into dry dock in 1968, he was transferred to the USS Richard E. Kraus DD-849 where he served as an FTG2 until he was discharged in September 1969. He then attended The Pennsylvania State University, graduating in 1973 with a degree in Electrical Engineering.

In 1970, he met Donna Hoogerhyde and they were wed in June 1973. Donna graduated from Fox Chapel High

School (Pittsburgh) in 1965 then attended Thiel College and DT Watson School of Physiatrics, graduating in 1969 as a Physical Therapist. She worked at Presbyterian University Hospital (Pittsburgh) until John and Donna departed Pittsburgh in late 1973.

After John and Donna were married, John joined the Air Force to become a pilot. He first went to the Navy but the Navy had no available pilot training positions, so it was off to the Air Force. John went to OTS in July 1973 and was commissioned in November. They were sent to Reese AFB, Lubbock Texas for pilot training, where he graduated in February 1975. During this time, Donna worked as a physical therapist at Texas Tech Medical Center, until Jennifer was born in January 1975.

Their 1st assignment was a KC-135 tanker at Kadena AB, Okinawa Japan. During this assignment, Steven was born in November 1976 at the Army Hospital. After departing Kadena in 1978, they were assigned to Travis AFB California flying the KC-135. In 1981, John was selected as one of the first pilots to fly the new KC-10 Tanker at Barksdale AFB Shreveport La. In 1982, they moved to March AFB, Riverside Ca. to open the 2nd KC-10 base. Donna resumed her PT career and worked at Riverside Community Hospital and Riverside Medical Clinic until she retired in 1998. John transferred from active duty to the Air Force Reserves in 1987 and was hired as a pilot at United Parcel Service where he flew the DC-8, B-757, and the B-767.

John retired from the Air Force Reserves in 1996 as a LT. Colonel and from United Parcel Service in 2007. After retirement, they moved out of the southern California rat race to Cambria, a small community on the California central coast.

John and Donna during a recent visit to Sicily

Editor's Note: John and Donna have been attending the USS Johnston reunions since 1998 in Las Vegas. In all these years they have only missed a couple due to work restraints. At the time of writing this bio, John is serving as Secretary for the USS Johnston DD-821 Association.

Many Years of Service

By: Billy Cook, Fire Control Technician (FTG-3)

Years on board the Johnston: 1965 to 1968

The USS Johnston (DD 821) was a Gearing class destroyer laid down in March 1945 and commissioned in August 1946. She was named for her fallen predecessor USS Johnston (DD-557), sunk on October 25, 1944 in the incredibly heroic battle against a much more heavily armed Japanese Task Force at the Battle of Leyte Gulf.

For most of her career Johnston was a Cold Warrior, making many deployments to the Mediterranean and operating in the Atlantic and Caribbean out of Newport, Rhode Island and Charleston, South Carolina, but in late 1967 she deployed to the Western Pacific for the Vietnam gun line and Tonkin Gulf escort duties. After surviving a typhoon in the mid-Pacific in late 1967 and doing escort duty with USS Ranger in the Gulf of Tonkin during January 1968, Johnston finally arrived off Hue City on 6 February and immediately engaged in intense gunfire support during the height of the Battle of Hue City and the TET offensive. Thru successful evasive maneuvering the Johnston avoided direct hits on two separate occasions from a total of seven rounds of enemy incoming counter-battery fire. On one of the attacks the Johnston returned fire and destroyed the counter-battery causing additional damage to the enemy as a result of subsequent secondary explosions. The Johnston remained in a continuous gunfire support role until mid-March of 1968, the ship then returned to Charleston having expended over 10,000 5-inch rounds.

The Johnston remained in commission until 1980 and was then transferred to the Taiwanese Navy and served there until 2004 – an incredible 58 years of continuous service.

Another Pretty Good Lesson
By: Billy Cook, Fire Control Technician (FTG-3)

In May of 1965, upon completion of FT-A school, I was assigned to the destroyer USS Johnston. I was one of a compliment of about eight Gun Fire Control Technicians (FTs) aboard the destroyer at any given time. During this period, four junior FTs right out of A-school (Cook, Hogan, Manning, & Reed – names changed to protect the guilty), were assigned to the ship's 2nd division within a year's time of each other. We were all single and about the same age. It did not take long for us to become very good buddies. We did a lot together on and off the ship. During our leisure time, if we weren't on liberty together, you could usually find most of us hanging out in the IC Room. The IC Room was forward of amidships, beneath the main deck, just aft of the mess deck on the port side, across from the scullery. FTs bunks and lockers were in 2nd Division which was just below the mess deck and therefore very close to the IC Room. The IC Room contained the Mk-1A Gunfire Control Computer and was the control center for the ships two twin 5 inch 38 gun mounts, that were located both fore and aft on the ships main deck. In addition to the Gun Fire Control Computer, a Star Shell Computer, a Stable Element and the Fire Control Switchboard were contained in this space. The old gun fire control computer was ANALOG, not digital, and about the size of four washing machines, and just as noisy when it was cranking data. The ship's Gyro was also located in the IC Room; however it was maintained by IC Men who also occupied this compartment when the ship was underway. The stable element and ships gyro were each about the size and height of a washing machine. Both were flat on top, with a thick clear glass for viewing and they each made excellent card tables that four men could stand at while dealing and playing cards. There were three IC men aboard the ship, one of which was a Chief Petty Officer. The IC Room was a watertight compartment because of the necessity for the ship's gyro

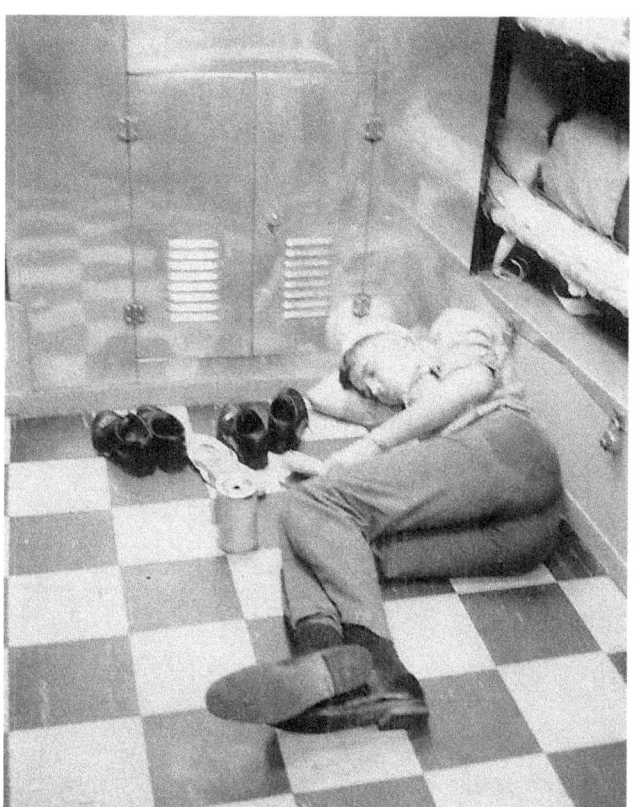

172

and gun fire control to help ensure the ships survivability during combat. You had to enter the IC Room through a watertight compartment door that once closed could have been locked from the inside. It was always kept closed although it was seldom locked. The IC Room WAS the FT's HANGOUT because it was private, air conditioned, and generally not visited by most of the ship's company unless you were friends with one or more of the FTs or IC Men. However, the IC men's bunks and lockers were far back in the aft part of the ship, so unless they were working or on duty, they generally hung out with the snipes back aft. The Chief IC Man, of course, slept in the Chiefs Quarters. The Chiefs Quarters were relatively close to the IC Room as it was just

forward of, and one deck below the mess deck. However, the Chief was married with a family and whenever we were in port he was at home with his family unless he had duty. So he rarely frequented the IC room when we were in our homeport.

Whenever the ship was in any port, if not on liberty, you could find most FTs hanging out in the IC Room. Generally we were either playing cards, goofing off or covertly watching movies. Several of the FTs were certified to operate the ships movie projector and we would frequently lock the door and preview movies transferred to the ship. However most of our leisure time, if we were aboard the ship, was spent playing cards. We either used the ships gyro or stable element as our card table. And for these sessions we never felt the need or bother to lock the door. In our home port, the Chief was always at home with his family so we weren't concerned he would be around to catch us. Occasionally during the day or early evening a couple of the ship's officers would drop by and join us in a game of "Whist", "Pinochle" or "Hearts", but they never stayed much past lights out. Because the IC room was fairly isolated we would play cards well into the night or early morning. After playing cards or watching movies, we sometimes just hung out shooting the bull, not ready to go to bed, proving the old English proverb that "Idle hands is the Devil's workshop" It was on one of those nights that I regret…

Late, late one night Hogan, Manning, Reed and I, after playing cards, were sitting around twiddling our thumbs with nothing to do. It was well past midnight we had not eaten in quite a while. Being hungry started us to thinking about food and we began discussing our options. Back then, aboard the Johnston at least, we didn't have any Gee Dunk machines or anything like that. So if you were hungry you were just out of luck, unless of course you were a resourceful FT. We knew there was the possibility that there might be bread or crackers, or something like that in the ship's galley, and if we were real lucky we might even find something like a desert prepared in advance for the next day's meals. The problem and concern of course was what if you got caught? We discussed this and decided so what would be the big deal? Nobody would really care. And, it had to be safe, because everyone else on the ship, with the exception of the crewmen "on Watch" at the Quarterdeck, were fast asleep. The Quarterdeck was on the port side main deck aft of amidships and pretty far away from the IC Room and the Galley. As I recall, Hogan was the first to leave the IC room on a reconnaissance mission to check it out. After about twenty minutes the door to the IC room opened and in stepped Hogan with a slice of double layered Devils Food chocolate cake, are you kidding me! Cakes cooked by the ships cook were always single layer flat pan cakes… This Was A Find… and it should have raised a big red flag… but it didn't. We were just overcome with excitement at the prospect of eating Chocolate cake at two in the morning… and where in the hell did you get that cake! He told us the Chief's quarters… another red flag! That concerned me, but Hogan assured us that everyone was asleep and most were snoring. Manning then left for the Chiefs Quarters and soon returned with a slice of the cake. That was enough for Reed and he lit out to get his piece as I sat there drooling, watching

Hogan and Manning lick their fingers and smack their lips as they slowly savored the cake. Then Reed returned with his piece. That did it! I wasn't going to sit there watching them and let them brand me as a coward, so I bolted for the Chief's Quarters to get my piece. When I got to the Chief's Quarters, I saw a table with what was about a third of the original cake left setting on it. It was fairly dark but I was able to see that someone had lifted up one side of the cake and broken off a piece. I could tell this happened because a thumb print was embedded in the chocolate icing on top of the cake. I took out my knife and cut off about half of the cake that was left, leaving of course, the piece with the thumb print in it. Then I hurriedly made my way back to the IC room. Upon arrival I laughingly described what was left of the cake and asked "who was the moron that didn't bother to cut the cake." Hogan and Manning claimed they used their knives and that left Reed. He was smiling and said he was in a hurry to get out of there. Hogan and Manning finished their pieces. We were all smiling and laughing about our conquest. Reed was licking chocolate from his fingers and I was eating my piece of the cake as I was sitting directly across from the IC Room door as it opened…

"Holy Shit", I thought to myself as the Chief IC man stood at the door glaring in at us! Why is he here I thought? (Turns out he had been on watch and went to the chief's quarters to wake up his relief.) While Reed just continued to lick his fingers all the while and I was thinking to myself, why in the hell is Reed doing that! The Chief looked at each of us slowly as I recall he said, "In a controlled rage", something like "Cook, Reed, Hogan and Manning… I knew it. You @#%&*%%%%$, that cake was for my son's Birthday PARTY! We were celebrating tomorrow morning on this ship! You *&$#@^*^%$* are on report" as he loudly slammed shut the IC Room door.

Oh my god… what have I done!

Well he was true to his word and we went to XO' mast for theft. We were lucky that it wasn't Captains Mast and I do not know why it wasn't. I think we wound up getting about 20 hours of hard labor that had to be served after we knocked off ships work in the afternoon and in between any watches we still had to stand. The hard labor had to be performed in the bowels of Hell or so it seemed. I say that because we had to work lying, kneeling, and sitting on the steel plates that were the skin on the bottom of the ship. We were underneath the engine rooms soaking up water and wiping up grease and oil that had been collected from the time the ship was commissioned in 1946… or at least that's what I thought. I was miserable.

I know that at the time we took the cake, I personally was not thinking that the act was thievery in any form, or fashion, other than it was probably the wrong thing to do. And that was only because there might be some minor consequences if we got caught. However, when we were brought up on charges of theft, it became reality, and I was certainly guilty. I knew that I deserved the punishment I received for my actions. If truth be known we probably deserved more severe punishments because of what the impact may have had on others. I was very remorseful at the time because I knew that I was responsible for possibly spoiling a young child's birthday experience. To what extent I still don't know, because I never had the nerve to ask the Chief afterwards… I was too ashamed and full of guilt. I knew that I had lost any respect he had for me because he never talked to me after that and I could feel his disdain. I was fairly close to the Chief because he and I were taking a correspondence course at the same time from the Cleveland Institute of Electronics and he would help me occasionally if I questioned or did not understand something clearly. What I did to undermine that friendship and respect pained me.

Taking the cake, which seemed almost trivial at first and not such a big deal, turned into something far more important. This was one of those important life lessons for me; I am a better person for it. As a kid growing up, not having much, I took a few things here or there that were not mine. Never anything of real value… a candy bar from a store or coke bottles I could return to the store for a deposit that I took from a neighbor's garage. Nothing taken was a "big deal with no real harm done, or at least that was the way I thought. Today I am ashamed that I did it, but I did. I would not knowingly steal anything anymore. The thought of stealing is vile and repulsive to me. To me a thief is a lowlife bottom sucker that preys off innocents.

Seriously I would not take a dime that is not mine, even from my wife and that is supposed to be ours. I won't even open her mail without asking for her approval first. All in all that was just Another Pretty Good Lesson, I learned, while I was in the Navy! Go Navy!

The Mother of All Hangovers
By: Billy Cook, Fire Control Technician (FTG-3)

If you have ever really been drunk then you have probably experienced a hangover. Well I can tell you about an experience I had, that I think, was the mother of all hangovers. And the experience went something like this:

Assab Ethiopia (now Assab Eritrea) was near the horn of Africa and probably the most God forsaken liberty port the Johnston ever docked in. The city was extremely poor. I don't remember seeing any automobiles. But I do remember there were quite a few water buffaloes. The place was hot as hell, desolate and utterly miserable. I believe the reason the Johnston chose to stop there was for goodwill. I know that while we were there, we helped a local Catholic Church which at that time was the home for a boy's orphanage. The church had some maintenance issues, electrical problems; etc. that the ship's crew helped correct along with making some other needed repairs and such. That evening, after returning to the ship, and getting cleaned up, about half the ship's crew was allowed to go on liberty. A couple of my buddies and I left the ship in dress whites not knowing what to expect. There was nothing happening in this town. No shops, sidewalks or even paved roads. We went to the only bar we could find in town. Outside the bar were what appeared to me to be hitching posts. I remember we entered the bar walking on a dirt path. The bar wasn't much more than a barn and it had a dirt floor. But, at least it had a swamp cooler, so it was definitely better inside than outside. Back then when I drank, I like rum and coke or Seagram's 7 and Seven-Up (7 & 7's). Well this place didn't have cokes or seven-up; in fact they didn't even have soft drinks, because they did not have ICE! Even their beer was warm…. Oh my God. I can't take warm beer. However, you could get water, as a chaser for the whiskey, rum or vodka. I was not a hard core drinker, and did not like the taste of alcohol. The bartender took my buddies' orders and was waiting for me to order while my buddies, wanting their drinks, were giving me a hard time because I couldn't decide what to do. The bartender informed me, in broken English that they had Cognac that was somewhat sweet and it might be more to my liking. Me being the unrefined redneck kid from Texas did not know what Cognac was. I had heard of and tasted Pommac which was a soft drink made by Dr. Pepper in the early sixties that later went by the wayside as it failed to catch on. Pommac was somewhat sweet and did not taste that bad, so I figured that Cognac would probably be similar, and I could use it as a chaser for the rum or vodka. I think my buddies kind of egged me into this. So….I began to drink shots of vodka chased by shots of cognac….not smart. At some point during the evening it started to rain, and my buddies left me…drunk I might add…no, wasted is probably a better description because I was falling down drunk and I could not stand up. I remember being outside the bar on my hands and knees in the mud in my whites. I knew I had to get back to the ship, and fortunately for me, I could see the Johnston's med lights. Thank goodness the Johnston was the only ship in that god forsaken port at that time. Now med lights as most of you know, is a string of white lights that go from the fantail, up across the mast and down to the focsle. Because they are so high in the air, the ship can be seen from miles away at night. And that was exactly what I needed to make it back to the ship. I remember crawling along through the mud and I swear I think I crawled between the legs of a water buffalo, not to mention the buffalo shit, before I got back to the ship. I was a muddy stinking mess and still drunk as hell when I got to the Quarterdeck. I crawled across the ramp and the guys on watch did not want to touch me, but someone helped me up and I was able to make it to the stairwell that went down to the scullery. The watch asked me if I needed help getting down the stairs. I stated flatly that I did not need any help and could make it on my own. Well I took one step and boom…I was at the bottom of the stairwell. I'm sure that I must have broken the free fall to the deck by grasping the guard rail somehow on my way down. Being too drunk to feel the pain, at the time, I somehow managed to make it the stairwell in the mess deck that led down to my bunk in 2nd division. Again the watch asked if I needed help and again I refused his assistance and again I took one step…and boom, I was at the bottom again. From there I proceeded to my rack, and crawled in, and passed totally out. To my horror, the next morning, when I woke, the ship was underway, and I was STRAPPED into my rack. Some of the gunner's mates and probably a couple of my FT buddies, I'm sure, thought it would be fun to do that. They strapped me in with bunk straps. The straps were normally used to hold up the raised bunks that enable access to the foot lockers just beneath the lower bunk. I was sick. The air in the compartment was still. It was hot and the ship was pitching and rolling. I could not move my arms. I was in pain. The alcohol had worn off and I hurt everywhere. I was gagging trying not to throw up…Oh my God! Everyone was on sea detail and I was the only one in the compartment. I was flat on my back and could not move and OH NO!...ERUPTION…I was throwing up. All I could do was turn my head to either side and heave. I was hot. My head was pounding! All the while I was getting much sicker. I think I laid there for at least two hours. I smelled of vomit and SHIT and was incarcerated in my own puke. It was on my face and running down my neck. Oh God the embarrassment...AND THEY WERE MY BUDDIES! It was such an awful experience, that to this day, I firmly believe, that I had, what had to be, the "Mother Of All Hangovers".

Metamorphosis
By: Billy Cook, Fire Control Technician (FTG-3)

Growing up I had a troubled childhood. My mother was diagnosed a paranoid schizophrenic and was in and out of mental hospitals several times during my childhood. If not at work, my Dad was generally at home trying to manage my Mom or at the hospital with her. The stress caught up with my Dad and he eventually had a nervous breakdown. Through all of this I had little supervision or guidance, and was usually left a lot of free time to fend for myself. In the mornings my mother was always in bed so before school I usually had coffee that my Dad left, before going to work, and I would also have some toast I would make for breakfast. For lunch at school, my Dad would leave me six cents every morning to buy two half pints of chocolate milk. In addition, I would make myself a fried bologna sandwich with mustard for lunch to eat at school, unless we were out of bologna, and bread. It seems that more often than not it was just bread and mustard. At night Momma or Dad would make a pretty decent supper of meat and potatoes of some kind and we always had plenty of milk to drink. However, I think my limited diet and the stress of dealing with my mother, when she was off, must have affected me physically. I was always quite small and skinny for my age. At the age of sixteen, when I received my driver's license, I weighed eighty-five pounds and stood four feet eleven inches tall as it stated on my driver's license. I did not hit puberty until I was eighteen. At school I stayed in trouble most of the time, as I felt I constantly had to prove myself by not allowing anyone to bully me around because of my size. I was a pretty tough kid, or at least I thought I was. My grades were usually passing, although not always. I made a habit of cramming at the last minute and it eventually caught up with me as I came up short credits and spent two years in the eleventh grade. In 1964, after finally, becoming a senior I was still one of the smallest kids, boys or girls, in our four year high school of about 1200 students. I'm sure plenty of people were convinced I had a chip on my shoulder. I was involved in about one or more fights every couple of weeks, trying to prove how tough I was, and because of the fighting I was kicked out of school numerous times my last four years. After I turned eighteen in July, I had to register for the draft and started thinking about the military. In October of 64, I was just short at of 5 foot seven and skinny as a rail. I was fed up with school and school was fed up with me. Soooo, I decided to quit school and join the Navy! It seemed like an easy way to get away from my dead end life. The Navy uniform looked cool, and girls seemed to like it more than the other uniforms at the time. I knew that as a sailor, I would I would get to see the world and more important, just get away from home. However, at the recruiting station I just failed to make the minimum weight at the weigh in. The recruiter took me over to a scuttlebutt and told me to start drinking. I drank water until I thought I would pop, after which he weighed me again and I topped out at one hundred and seventeen pounds. This was apparently enough as not long thereafter I was on my way to Boot Camp.

BOOT CAMP! OH MY GOD WHAT HAVE I DONE!!! Shortly after arriving at the United States Naval Training Center in San Diego I was issued a full sea bag, sized to meet my 5 foot almost seven inch - less than 117 pound frame. Not being accustomed to discipline it did not take me long to get into trouble. At my very first inspection I was written up for having peach fuzz on my face. I mean come on you've got to be kidding me! At every turn I was doing something wrong. I was constantly in trouble. In addition to all the added calisthenics, and extra chores, it seemed that daily I was getting kicked in the rear by my drill instructor while I was trying to march, and it really hurt sometimes. To this day I don't think my legs were long enough for me to keep in step, but eventually the kicking stopped. I also remember another form of punishment where I had to stand in a corner with my knees bent and successfully hold both arms and hands straight out while keeping a pencil horizontally between my index fingers for several consecutive minutes with muscles burning in pure agony. Another thoroughly disgusting punishment was the day I had to crawl around outside the

barracks on my hands and knees and pick cigarette butts up off the ground with my lips and spit them into a wash bucket. And by far the most embarrassing punishment I ever received was when I had to stand nude on a picnic table with my M-1 rifle, and recite over and over "This is my rifle and this is my gun, this is for shooting and this is for fun" while demonstrating which was what. It did not take me long to realize that I needed to straighten up to make life in the Navy easier; or boot camp at least. Eventually I decided to apply myself, and began taking the PT and classroom training seriously. Like every recruit I was tested and surprise, surprise I did very well. Apparently I scored well enough on the exams that the Company Commander assigned me as the educational recruit Petty Officer to help recruits that were having difficulties with studies and testing. The irony of this amazed me… but I responded positively! I had to attend a religious service every Sunday and I needed that spiritually. Along with the grueling physical exercise, I was also eating three square meals every day and GROWING. Soon my clothes did not fit any longer because I had gained thirty four pounds of muscle and bone and getting taller. Before my graduation ceremony my Company Commander had to have my sea bag re-issued because I could no longer fit into my uniform. I don't know how much taller I grew in boot camp, but before I left the Navy I was a little taller than five feet eleven and weighed one hundred and eighty pounds (I'll never see that again). I remember that prior to boot camp the recruiter asked me what type of job I wanted and I told him I would like to be a "welder." Well fortunately for me, that did not happen. I was assigned to Fire Control Training (FT) School in Bainbridge, Maryland. Little did I know that becoming an FT would be the start of my career in the Electronics field. After FT school I was assigned to the USS Johnston and while assigned to the ship I received my General Equivalency Diploma (GED). In addition I was sent to various electronics equipment schools. With the help of the additional training I eventually became the ship's Gun Fire Control Radar operator/ technician. The Gun Fire Control Radar Dish was located on top of the Director and the Director was located above the Captains Bridge at the top of the ship.

The Radar transmitter and radar indicator was located

inside the Director and this was my assigned Battle Station. The Radar was used to "lock-on" to targets that were discernible on the sea or air but was basically ineffective when looking at a land mass other than determining the range to the beach. In the Director I had an optical Range Finder that could be used to determine the range to an object that was inland during the day, but it was useless at night. In Vietnam as a Gun Fire Control Technician, on the night of the TET Offensive, I could not use the Radar or the Range Finder so I sat on the top of the Gun Fire Control Director and witnessed an awesome combat experience with the enemy. As I watched and listened with my headphones, most if not all of targets were called in by spotters who were under attack in the middle of the firefight. From my position I experienced a spectacular assault on my senses. Our ships pounded the enemy relentlessly all night long. Our five inch thirty-eights were smoking. I remember the ship shaking constantly as we fired those guns. The huge donut rings of smoke, combined with the brilliant flashes of light and sonic booms, feeling the intense heat from the ignited gun powder as those projectiles left the barrels. Star shells were exploding everywhere that night. They floated to earth with brilliant light as we relentlessly pounded the enemy and turned night into day. Explosion after explosion, with back and forth red machine gun tracers and what appeared to be yellow and red flames from what I thought were side winder missiles flying through the air with subsequent explosions as they hit their targets. I remember thinking about the men who were out there on the beach fighting for their very lives. Knowing they were feeling the terror that besieged them because they knew that death was everywhere as wounded men had to be yelling screaming in agony around them. That night I also remember thanking God that I had volunteered and not waited to be drafted into the Army or Marines. If I had waited, I very well could have been one of those unfortunate souls crawling around in that cauldron of Hell on earth that was created during that battle and possibly not made it out of there alive. I left Vietnam a changed man. I had experienced firsthand what real sacrifice for freedom meant. I had learned to honor and respect all of the men and women that had lived and sorrowfully died to protect all the rights and freedoms, over the two hundred plus years, only we as Americans have under our unique Constitution and Bill Of Rights. From then on whenever I see our flag and hear the Star Spangled Banner played, chills run up and down my spine. I am indelibly changed by those experiences. I was proudly, and most notably, honorably discharged after four tumultuous years and a few earned disciplinary lessons along the way. Fortunately, right out of the Navy I was hired by Texas Instruments Inc. (TI) as an Electronics Technician at a whopping $2.39/ hour. In my job at TI, I was working alongside electrical and mechanical engineers and felt that a few of them thought they were superior to me. This fueled my ambition and I started taking courses at the local junior college where TI and the VA picked up the tab and also gave me a little extra to boot (pun intended) which was an incentive because I needed the money. TI noticed that my grades for the junior college courses I was taking were very good and in turn, TI gave me a full scholarship to Southern Methodist University where I would earn a Bachelor of Science degree in Electrical Engineering and work there for almost forty years where I became a project engineer or Program Manager for several Radar and Infrared systems that were used on Navy Aircraft such as Navy P3s and S3s. I look back now after retirement and I know that I owe my successful beginnings to the Navy's metamorphosis of me. I went in as a small troubled underdeveloped kid and that absolutely without the intervention of the Navy, I would probably have been headed for much bigger trouble or if drafted into the Army or Marines possibly much worse. The Navy shaped me into a responsible human being. They instilled much of the moral and ethical character I developed along with skills necessary to perform my job and serve my country. There I learned what it really meant to be an American. The sacrifice men and women have made for freedom. And for my service, the VA and my country aided me by giving me an opportunity to help myself as long as I worked to improve my standing in society by providing me and my family a way to a better life that honest, hard work and perseverance deserves. I am not alone in this regard because the military has helped thousands of troubled kids like me find their way to a better life if you try. In most cases, especially mine, discipline that the military provides is necessary and paves the way for success. Go Navy!

RETURNING FROM VIET NAM

By: John "Mick" Potter, Fire Control Technician (FTG-1)

Years on board the Johnston: 1967 to 1971

The summer of 68 found us crossing the peaceful Pacific Ocean. We had completed a very successful mission in Viet Nam and were returning home. Our call sign, "Tampico" was well known to our military spotters for our accuracy. It was a perfect day. Warm, not hot, a gentle breeze, and the Pacific was like glass.

The Johnston had an "unauthorized" outside urinal on the port bridge wing for use by the bridge watch and signal gang. It was probably installed during a shipyard overhaul using a 20 lb. can of coffee for cash. The signal gang had a coffee mess and instead of going all the way down to the forward head to dump the grounds, they would pour them in this urinal.

Not always, of course but eventually the urinal became plugged up. The bridge watch notified the DC shop to unplug it. Not knowing how the salt-water supply was connected to this urinal, the DC man hooked-up a 1-1/2 inch hose to the fire main.

While this was going on, the CO was enjoying himself, sitting on his crapper in his sea cabin.

You can see the handwriting on the wall on this one, right?

Well, the "duty DC man" charged the hose with 150 pounds of pressure from the fire main. As it turns out the outside urinal was connected to the CO's crapper. It blew the CO completely off the crapper. He came storming onto the bridge covered in coffee grounds, toilet paper, etc. He was not happy!!! The "duty DCman" realizing what had happened, quickly disappeared, forgetting to shut off the valve. The valve was secured, the CO's cabin was cleaned up, and so was the CO.

They never found out which DCman answered the trouble call as no one would own up to it, so no one was held accountable. It was the only time in my naval career that I ever saw a CO looking like that.

I'm glad I was there, the image will last a lifetime.

The Lost Crepe Paper
By: John "Mick" Potter, Fire Control Technician (FTG-1)

While I was a 2nd class & master-at-arms, one of my duties included holding the keys to the Welfare & Rec locker. During one particular deployment we were at sea through Christmas so we bought Christmas items to decorate the mess decks. At various times the duty MAA was asked for the keys to this locker. We thought nothing of loaning the keys out and the keys were always returned as required. Christmas time came and we decided to decorate. After looking for a while we couldn't find any of the crepe paper we purchased. When we asked around, the younger guys said "Crepe paper is just the right size for rolling your own weed." Johnston sailors can be ingenious.

The Fighting Brothers
By: John "Mick" Potter, Fire Control Technician (FTG-1)

At one time the Johnston had two brothers who were both gunners mates and on board at the same time. They were fighters. When they hit the beach, they would look for someone to fight with. If they couldn't find anyone, they would fight each other. At the time, I slept on the bottom bunk, one slept in the middle, and the other slept on top.

One particular night, they returned from the beach and drunk as usual. They both climbed into their bumps for some shut-eye. However, the one in the top bunk kept rolling off his bunk and hit the metal deck with a "splat". We would pick him up; put him back in his bunk and a few minutes later the same thing would happen. After about four times of falling, we decided to let him sleep it off on the deck. The next morning, when he woke, he had no idea who he had fought the night before, but he said he hurt from head-to-toe. We never told him the real reason for his hurts.

Another "Jolly J" Story

By: John "Mick" Potter, Fire Control Technician (FTG-1)

I served aboard the "Jolly J" from 67 to 71. During that time many sailors reported aboard. This story is about a non-designated striker that came aboard during that time. Shortly after his arrival, he told us a story about how he had served aboard a nuclear submarine that had a 5" gun mount on its bow. He immediately earned the nickname, "Nukey."

No matter what Nukey tried, somehow it got screwed up. Because of this he was transferred from division-to-division hoping to find his nitch. His was finally transferred to 2nd division. On his first assignment, the gunnersmate in charge of mount 52 showed Nukey how to wash down the mount. They hosed the mount down with fresh water, applied soap, scrubbed it down, then rinsed it off.

The gunner's mate, figuring nothing could go wrong, left Nukey alone while he went to get a cup of coffee. His parting words were, "Nukey, do the same thing to the inside."

Nukey carried out the task to the letter. He opened the door to the mount, sprayed the inside with the hose, applied the soap, scrubbed everything down and then hosed down the whole inside of the mount.

The gunner's mate returned to find water pouring out the bottom of the mount. Needless to say, Nukey got transferred to another division.

You might ask, "Is there anything that Nukey could do and not screw it up?" The answer is YES. Somewhere along the line, Nukey came into possession of a camera. It turned out he was a natural photographer.

He took a picture of an ASROC missile as the missile left the launcher and showed the end of the flames touching the launcher.

He took a picture of a sunset through the bullnose just as the sun touched the horizon.

He took many other very good pictures; however, those two stick out in my mind.

I was transferred shortly after, so I don't know whatever became of Nukey.

Best Fire Control Gang Ever!
By: John "Mick" Potter, Fire Control Technician (FTG-1)

In my 22 year Navy career, the closest and best fire control gang I was ever privileged to be a part of was the one that went to Viet Nam. Jim Jay was our LPO and the rest of us were: John Argonti, Billy Cook, Sam Hall, Mike Lawson, Dave Nabor and myself.

A lot of training went into preparing us for combat and it showed when we experienced our real first counter-battery. Enemy shore batteries had bracketed us with heavy fire and we knew the next round would hit us. The training kicked in and without thinking, we returned fire and destroyed the enemy. When we finally pulled away to a safe distance, that's when the nervous shakes kicked in.

We enjoyed each other's company on and off the ship. You could often see us on the beach searching the closest watering hole. Once found, we'd gather around the table to quench our thirst. Hard as we tried, we never found a beer we didn't like.

Upon returning to the States, the Johnston's wartime complement was reduced to 100 men. I'm not sure what happened to most of the gang, however, thanks to the "Jolly J" reunions I'm back in contact with Billy and John.

A STORY FROM THE USS JOHNSTON DD-821 (continued)

By: Daun "Harry" H. Harris, Radarman (RD-3)

Years on board the Johnston: 1968 to 1970

Although I had planned to start this biography where I left off in "The Real Story of the USS Johnston DD-821", I decided a short introduction of my pre-Navy years would be in order. I was born and raised in South Dakota which is typical small town USA. I grew up living in a house with a big yard which enabled me to raise pigeons and ferrets in the back yard. Aside from attending school I spent my free time playing baseball, school sports, etc., fishing and swimming at the lake, hunting, trapping, delivering newspapers, working at a grocery store, and later working for a plumber through whom I later earned my journeyman plumber's license. My father was a school superintendent so after graduating from high school I attended a nearby college that specialized mostly in teacher education, where I earned my B.A. & teaching certificate. I joined the Naval Reserve while in school and was given deferments through the years to attend college, and upon graduation from college I started my two year tour of active duty. My first experience with culture shock (my second will come later) was when I reported aboard ship and was taken to the OI division living quarters. I saw that the compartment where I would be living for the next two years would be approximately the same size as my room back in SD, only there were no windows, no carpet on the floor, no pennants and deer horns on the walls, no baseball bat and glove leaning in the cornier, and I would be sharing this "room" with 21 other radarmen. As most of us did, I also survived and now look back at all the good times I experienced with my fellow shipmates while serving about the Jolly-J, the greatest ship in the Navy.

Anyway now back to where I left off in the first book. I had just been separated from the USS Johnston and the Navy and was heading north on my 100 CC Yamaha motorcycle. I still had my atrocious beard and long hair that we were allowed to grow on the Johnston, and my expired S.D. driver's license. Just as I crossed over the Ohio River from Kentucky into Ohio I was stopped at a road-block put up by Ohio State Troopers looking for traffic violators. After looking me over, these State Troopers couldn't quite believe that I had just been released from the Navy. It took a while to explain my beard, hair, and driver's license, but since my paperwork all checked out, I was finally able to continue my trip home. I stopped off to see my brother & his family who lived in a suburb of Detroit on my way home. Since I planned to continue with my education they convinced me to start my graduate work during the summer session at the nearby Eastern Michigan University (EMU). I still had my beard from the Navy, but before seeing my graduate school advisor for the first time I decided to "clean up a bit" and shave off the beard. When I walked in to see my advisor I found that he had a full beard, HA! I decided to take the fall semester off so I could go back to S.D. to see my parents, and also do a bit of pheasant hunting. Although I really liked EMU, it was a bit too urban for an old country boy like me, so rather than go back to Michigan I continued by education at the University of South Dakota. I stayed at USD for several years and earned what could be the equivalent of three masters degrees as I ended up with endorsements in history, school administration, and counseling. At that time the job market was getting tight, and I decided that if I didn't want to be a professional student forever, I had better find a job. I wrote something like 75 letters applying for various jobs and finally was hired as the secondary principal at a school in western S.D. As I had no actual teaching experience before this, it took some time to get me temporarily certified for this job, but after taking my education and navy experience into consideration the state department of education finally granted me the certification.

    I stayed on this job from 1972 through 1976, and it was here that I met my wife Joan (the math & science teacher) who has put up with me now for 36 years. Although the community, kids, people, hunting, fishing, etc. were great, after four years I decided (after talking Joan into it) that it was time to pursue another dream I always had, and that was to go to Alaska. We wrote some letters applying for jobs up there and we were finally hired in a bush school district (as a principal & teacher) which was north and west of Fairbanks. Our school district office was located in the town of Nenana and since we had been hired over the phone, sight unseen, shortly after arriving in Alaska we decided that we should meet the superintendent of our new school district. Since our job applications included pictures (mine without a beard), before meeting the Supt. I decided to "clean up a bit again" so the night before I shaved off my beard, and before going into his office building I spit my chewing tobacco into a nearby flower bed. Well when we went into the superintendent's office what did I find? (You guessed it) The superintendent had a full beard and a mouth full of chewing tobacco. I knew right then and there we would be getting along, HA!

  The school in which we were assigned was fly-in only, and located along a river approximately half way between Nome and Fairbanks. Upon arrival we found that there was only one telephone in town (that sometimes even worked), the mail plane arrived on Mondays, Wednesdays & Fridays (weather permitting), and that aside from the other teachers we were virtually the only white people in a village that was populated by Athabascan Indians. This turned out to be a real culture shock too, especially since both of us were raised in the virtually all-white Midwest. We soon found out that making friends here was really no different than anywhere else, and being a principal of a school over 300 miles from the district office did have some benefits. One time the school in our district just up river burned to the ground. I worried that the Supt. And district board may want to send all of the students down to our school, I would have to find boarding homes, etc., so for close to two months I never called or contacted the district office, and only sent in the necessary & required time sheets, attendance & grade reports, etc.

    After spending four years in this remote village, we decided it was time for a change so we ended up taking jobs at the school district office which was in Nenana and on the highway system about 55 miles from Fairbanks. Here we could return to a more normal life where we could go shopping on weekends, go out to eat in restaurants, go to movies, etc. On the job Joan was hired as a correspondence study teacher, and I was a district guidance counselor. Joan's job involved flying into sites that were so remote that there were no schools and the pupils had to be home schooled. Most of her pupils were the children of gold miners, trappers, homesteaders, etc. With my job I had to fly to our district's 10 schools and work with the students. Since we both traveled, we sometimes only saw each other on weekends, but still, in some ways our jobs were pretty neat. We would often think of other people in large cities commuting or riding busses to and from work, while we commuted in small airplanes flying over the Yukon, Koyukuk, and Tanana Rivers. We stayed with these jobs until we retired in 1989. As we were still quite young and didn't know how well we would adapt to retirement we first took a leave-of-absence from our jobs. Flying in small planes is lots of fun, but it is also quite dangerous. All of you probably heard about former Alaska Senator Ted Stevens dying in a plane crash during the second week in August 2010, but he was certainly not the first. We had a really good friend who taught out in one of our district's schools. He was married and had 5 children. He and his family were flying back to their school, the plane crashed along the Yukon River, and our friend along with three of his children were killed. As we figured we had pushed our luck far enough we decided to officially retire.

We spent the next 10 years living up in Alaska spending our time camping, hunting, fishing, etc., and although we both really loved Alaska, the long winters finally started to get to us. We decided to spend a winter down south and ended up in the Florida Panhandle. We enjoyed ourselves so much that after we returned home in May (there was still snow on the ground) we put our home up for sale, and drove down the Al-Can highway for the last time. We didn't have any idea where we would end up, but knew it would be somewhere in the South as I always loved the rural areas around Charleston when aboard the Johnston. We always tell people that before leaving Alaska we tied our snow shovel to the front of our pickup/camper and headed south. When we arrived in Timpson, Texas and stopped for gasoline, the attendant looked at our snow shovel, scratched his head, and asked, "What's that thing?" Upon hearing this I turned to Joan and said, "Honey I think we found our new home".

Anyway we are now busier than ever, retired on a small hobby ranch in the Piney Woods of Deep East Texas, about 20 miles from the Louisiana line. If any of you old Johnston sailors ever decide to take a trip to Alaska in your motorhome, and plan to spend the summer, be sure to get in contact with us as we can tell you how to find some really great fishing spots.

MED CRUISE SEPTEMBER '66 TO FEBRUARY '68

By: Gary "Benje" Benjestorf, Radarman (RD-2)

Years on board the Johnston: 1966 to 1969

The Med Cruise of Sept '66 to Feb of '68 was like most cruises with good times you won't forget, but some that you would like to.

The Seaman Makes the Coffee. Crossing the Atlantic on mid watch PO2 Brown decided that a fresh pot of coffee was in order. Here we were in CIC with heavy seas making us hang on just to watch the radar and Brown wanted coffee. I was deemed the man for the job. I unplugged the 1/2 full huge pot of hot coffee and protested. Naturally, the effort was in vein. As I went out the door I took a last shot. "I don't think I can make it!" I was right. I didn't get more than three steps down the ladder when the pot lid popped up and coffee spilled on a couple of steps. I stepped on the coffee. The pot, coffee and Benje fell down to the bottom of the ladder. My back was up against the bulkhead, one leg one way the other between steps. Out from the Captain's Cabin came Captain Mingo. The crash brought Brown out to the top of the ladder. His eyes were wide as he heard the Captain ask if I was OK. If I had to guess some words come to mind as to what Brown was thinking! "I just slipped on the ladder sir", was my response to the Captain. Browns face shifted to relief. I continued my mission. After probably an hour of pot watching, Brown saw the first perks. He waited impatiently with cup in hand. Finally drew some and took a sip, which he promptly spewed out of his mouth. It seems I got the wrong faucet in the after head. Somehow Brown forgave me and was actually pretty understanding - a newbie, first cruise and all.

It ended up that Brown was a good guy when you got past his gruff exterior. We ended up going on liberty together in Charleston several times after the Med cruise.

American Meat and Potatoes! While in Naples we were granted liberty for a trip to Rome. We had booked a hotel that was in our price range and it was clean and adequate but will never challenge a destination hotel anytime soon. From there our day excursions were the typical tourist attraction stuff...St Peters Cathedral, the Vatican, catacombs, coliseum, and so on. One remarkable thing that we enjoyed was the fact that the Italian girls in Rome don't see many American Sailors. Night life was good.

One dinner at our hotel was especially memorable. The menu said "American Meat and Potatoes". It was the thinnest slice of meat I had ever seen but the color was strangely familiar. It was a bit spicy and pink in color. I tried hard to place where I had seen this before. It was when they brought out the Ice Cream that I remembered. In high school advanced biology we had dissected a cat......

Casino Royale: One great port of call was Beirut. Five miles out approaching port, with the afternoon sun was at our backs, the city looked like it was made of gold. It's probably the most beautiful city I've ever seen. There were broad tree lined boulevards and almost pristine in cleanliness (just months later fighting there destroyed much of it). One late afternoon two shipmates of mine and I went to a casino a few miles up the coast. Located along a rocky shore the top floors offered a commanding view of the Med.

When we arrived, we found our way to the lounge. There was an older and obviously rich man there sitting at a table with drop dead beautiful young women. At the prompting of my buddies, I approached this couple and asked the gentleman if I might have a dance with the lady. He just ever so slightly shook his head no. She was clearly disappointed, but not as nearly disappointed as I was. It provided a good laugh for my buddies.

Later, we were approached by the Casino manager who was from Southern California! He offered to take us on a tour of the place. The higher you went in the building, the more exclusive it got until we arrived on the top floor. A big set of double doors guarded by two well-dressed and obviously competent security guys greeted us. Behind those doors was what looked like a scene from a James Bond movie. There was quiet conversation and sounds of the gaming machines. Absent were slots or T Shirts! There were stacks of chips with a number five or ten and so on there in front of each of the players sitting at the Baccarat tables. Our host explained that the numbers on the chips corresponded to thousands of Lebanese pounds. In US dollars the manager said bets were in the tens of thousands of American dollars. As I was catching my breath, a security guy approached the manager with some kind of problem. It wasn't long before we learned that two Jolly J sailors had found a way to climb into a false ceiling over the women's restroom. They fell through! I wonder what they thought they were doing? Having had enough entertainment for the night we made our way back to the ship.

Merry Christmas! We found ourselves in Jidah, Saudi Arabia, just a few days before Christmas. We were just 30 miles from Mecca, so we didn't see a sign of Christmas anywhere. It was near 100 outside on a couple of days, but in the 80's most of the time. Capt. Mingo and Cdr. Jonasz received an invitation from the American Embassy to an Embassy dinner. The invitation included 2 enlisted to attend as well. I was one of the enlisted to go, which blew me away. When the dinner was served I was lost. I was raised in the Sierras in Northern California so I didn't know which of the forks or spoons to use for what, so I watched the guy across from me. He caught me watching and just smiled. He was the Operations Chief for Trans World Airlines for the Middle East. At the reception prior to the dinner he had approached me and asked what I'd heard from home. I told him that our mail was stuck in Naples, so we haven't heard in 3 or 4 weeks. He excused himself to go speak to Capt Mingo. I saw him ask an attendant for a phone. The next day, we got our mail. We celebrated Christmas Eve reading our mail from home.

NATO OPS: As to the part I'd like to forget? The Johnston didn't wear all the E's with hash marks at no cost. We were over there in the Persian Gulf to do NATO Ops with other nations. Grueling. In CIC we were working around the clock. If Ops were not going on there were watches to stand. It got to a point where you had a decision to make. You had to ask yourself, "Am I too hungry and smelly to get sleep, or sleep for a couple of hours?" We would often nap behind the status boards. In the first 6 days I got about 15 hours of sleep. Finally, Sunday holiday routine was scheduled. I happened to be on the bridge when the Exec reminded the Captain that our last ASROC Casualty drill could have been better. The Capt. ordered ASROC drills. It was very tough, but it brought the guy's in our division together. When you got so little sleep and was awakened far sooner than you'd like, you jumped up because you knew the guy you were relieving was just as tired as you were.

Blow'en Off Steam: Liberty was scheduled in Bander Abbas, Iran. We needed a break. But I think the Captain didn't want us to tear up the town, so he ordered liberty on Kharg Island, Iran. It was barren except for a concrete block communications building. The Captain's launch was loaded up with beer and sailors. Many trips back and forth and the results were predictable. We didn't tear up the town when Liberty Call came 2 days later.

Liberty Call: The most amazing thing about Bander Abbas was the shopping place. Tiny shops side by side down narrow streets. The amazing part was that when a shop was closed. The rollup chicken wire door was rolled down and a piece of twine was wrapped around the corner post and the chicken wire. The orientation officer had told us on our arrival that if we ever thought of theft, don't! The embassy couldn't respond in time to save your right hand have being severed in the town square. Shia Law was at work in Iran. I didn't see any people in that busy shopping area with a hand missing. It seemed to be very effective crime prevention.

The International Incident: The village or town of Assab, Ethiopia is a prototypical 3rd world town. There were few glass windows. The few stores in town had very little inventory. Poverty and dust was at home here. It's was very dry. Water was scarce. We were there on a good will mission and we gave those folks cases of bubble bath and advanced medical books written in English. However, there was a British guy there that asked if we could help a local Catholic mission. There were plaster walls desperately in need of paint, the DC electrical system was a mess, and the well pump had died. Our volunteers went over for about a four days. The electricians managed to fix the well pump and the other electrical needs. Fifteen sailors started the project and, at completion, there were still nine guys left. As a token of his appreciation the British guy said he could take five guys on a safari of sorts in the Ethiopian bush. He had already met with the Captain who had given permission for them to go and use weapons from the armory. When The Brit asked who would like to go nine hands shot up. I was number six. When they returned from the hunt they had a story to tell. It seems that one of the sailors saw what he thought was some kind of Antelope. One shot and the thing was dead. Then Bushmen appeared and surrounded the group. They were fighting mad. The sailor had shot a tribesman's Goat! The Brit negotiated a settlement with the goat owner. All the sailors had to pool their money to pay the ransom, and the tribesman kept the goat. Thus, an international incident was avoided.

West Pac November 1967-June of 1968
By: Gary "Benje" Benjestorf, Radarman (RD-2)

Butt Pucker Time: The Westpac cruise literally started with a bang. A tug skipper misjudged something and hit us a pretty good wallop getting us away from the pier. An inspection revealed no apparent harm, but it didn't take long before we knew something was amiss. We ended up with a pit stop in a Jacksonville shipyard to replace a bearing on one of the main shafts. It's only a story because by the time we got to Yokosuka major problem forced us to dry dock, where a worker cleaning barnacles off the bottom put his hammer through the hull. The hole got bigger as workers tried to get enough thickness in steal to weld to with the new bottom. Consequently, a very large section of the bottom sheeting was replaced. A shaft was taken out up through a hole cut in the main deck and I believe rudder bushing repairs were done was well.

While there, I was assigned to do maintenance on the air and surface radar antennas. I was up on the mast with the ship on blocks and an earthquake hit! You would have thought we were underway with a pretty good swell! It took a bit of time to stop the shaking. The same could be said about me. But, on the bright side, we had been assigned to go with the carrier to cover the Pueblo incident when the dry dock call was made. Our sister ship took our place and a friend of mine told me later that it was 58 days of boredom and ice. He said that making figure eights for fifty some days wasn't his idea of a good time. I enjoyed the liberty in Yokosuka, thank you!

Stormy Weather: Anyone who has spent any time at all at sea has gone through storms. I was in one I thought to be pretty severe with 110 knot winds in the Caribbean. I was sent out on deck with 4 other guys to secure a line on the corner of a tarp covering the ASROC launcher. Bow into the wind, we got the line. I made the bad decision to wrap the line around my wrist a turn. Yes, just like they tell you in boot camp as the thing NOT to do! A burst of wind came with the ships roll the tarp responded. 4 guys let go and I hung on. The tarp flipped me over and up against the life line. I was glad I was just banged up...overboard in that weather would have been by my deadly mistake.

But that storm was minor league compared to the one we went through running solo just off Midway Island. The swell was severe and we stood off Midway for several days trying to get in and refuel. No dice. We'd been pumping sea water into the fuel tanks to maintain ballast. While on the bridge, I saw the gauge that indicated roll would cross the danger line with unnerving regularity. We had enough power rung up to do 18-20 knots but were simply keeping ships head. While in the trough you could see the top of the next swell ONLY IF you leaned across the metal counter at the forward bulkhead and looked up through the window. The swells had to be 60-70 feet high. We'd crest the swell, nosedive down and hear the sounds and vibration of the screws coming out of the water and make like a submarine until some violent shaking and struggling took place until the bow would raise sending water smashing across our deck.

Finally, time had run out for the Johnston to stay put. I'm told we were at less than 50% of our fuel capacity. An oiler was passing some 300 miles to the north and we were on a heading south. It was a very serious moment and everybody knew it. If we roll over it's not going to be like the movie of the ship that rolls over and people make way to the bottom of the ship and get rescued. I looked at the Captain (Commander Curran) and I saw leadership. I saw confidence. I saw courage. And seeing his example gave every man on that bridge a sense of confidence that we would get through this thing. If we knew then what we would come to learn in Yokosuka when that shipyard worker put his chipping hammer through our hull...wow!

The Aftermath: When seas laid down enough we went out on deck. All the life lines were gone. The hydrant just aft of the after compartment door was 4" pipe, maybe

6" long with hydrant on top and welded to the deck and then strapped to the bulkhead. It was bent flat to the deck. The sheet steel that covered the underside of the flight deck was caved in. Inside the length of the inside passageway needed cleaning and paint. Scuff marks on the lower 25% or so on both bulkheads indicated the roll in the storm. One foot on the deck, the other on the bulkhead, alternating the length of the passageway was required for walking. Oh well, it's not like we were strangers to the paint locker!

10 Minutes of Drama! While on station in the South China Sea, I had the opportunity to do a duty swap with another RD2 from the carrier. I took the chopper ride over for what I thought would be a good opportunity to see how things work on a carrier and a change of scenery. The first day I tried to get my bearings on that floating city. I found the 3 important places, the chow hall (which to my surprise was open 24/7), my rack, and CIC. It was to be a 3 or 4 day stay. My first watch came up and I was assigned to the air search radar. It needs to be noted that in a carrier CIC RD2's are not watch supervisors, as they are on a can. I settled in. Ho Hum. There were Phantoms on station doing their thing guarding the 4 corners of the carrier and one 2 engine recon plane to the north. He was snooping just off Hanan Island. Not that long into the watch, to my amazement, a contact came off Hanan Island. The contact wasn't "squawking IFF" (friend/foe identification), so I made the call, "Bogey

Alpha bearing.....range...." The place burst into activity and there are at least 30 people in CIC. A Phantom was immediately given a flight vector to intersect the contact. The recon plane was ordered back to the carrier. With each sweep of the radar the scene was painted. The Recon was peddling his bicycle toward home as fast as he could, the MIG was closing fast and the crotch rocket Phantom was on afterburner operation to intercept. The audio of the communications between the Carrier, prop job recon, and Phantom was overhead in a speaker near me. Each sweep brought more anticipation. The Phantom asks the carrier for permission to shoot. No response. He asks again warning he would overshoot his target soon....permission granted. Phantom says, "Bird away" (or something like that!) There's a pause, then the Phantom pilot says, "I have visual contact"! (the explosion of the MIG). I watched it all with each sweep of the radar. I saw the Phantom approaching the target from the west, the Recon heading from north to south toward the carrier, the MIG, which was WELL WITHIN range to fire on the recon, just getting closer and closer. A few sweeps later and the radar painted the Phantom and Recon, but No MIG. Through overhead speaker came the voice of a relieved recon pilot to the Phantom, "thank you!" and Cool Dude in the Phantom said, "You are welcome, anytime!" I didn't go back to that 'Ho Hum' mindset for the remainder of my stay.

A Call for Fire came in. We were accustomed, by this time in the cruise to have many nights of Harassment and Interdiction Fire, or H&I fire, on too many nights to count. I often wondered who we were harassing. Below our decks you would hear the shots fired with no rhythm as to the timing intervals. Meanwhile, the gentle roll of the ship would roll shell casings back and forth across the deck. Sleep was out of the question. But, occasionally a daytime gig would come up. We shot at some walls surrounding Hue, but they were too thick for us to penetrate. Supposedly Charlie was within inner passageways, etc. Command brought in the heavyweight in. We watched the Missouri arrive. She was quite a sight. We were about 6 miles away when she positioned to fire and then opened up. What a sight it was to see those big guns flash and hear the roar. It was like we were watching what we'd only seen in movies or old "Victory at Sea" films. I don't know how successful she was, but the sight of her in action is something I won't forget. It was like seeing history in action.

Several hundred rounds of fire and we made the news. Most of our duty was spent with I corps Marines up around the DMZ. One day we got a call to fire on a battalion strength force of NVA coming south. It was going to be long range fire on the back side of a ridge. We had to snuggle in against the beach very close to the shore. The chart had circles on it - Danger, extreme danger, and imminent danger. Yes, that's where we went, imminent danger. The Captain pointed our bow south and had all the boilers going in case we had to bug out. Our first rounds hit smack center of the column. No adjustment necessary. The spotter went nuts, and they never do that. He nearly yelled, "You are dead on. Repeat, repeat, 4 guns 10 rounds fire for effect", so we did. A bunch gathered under a bridge and it was up against the side of the hill so he adjusted our fire. It took a bit but we got most of it. Then five artillery pieces started firing on us from the cape. They actually bracketed us but nothing hit closer than 30 yards according to a lookout. The column was very scattered by then and the Captain advised that we were under fire and leaving. Our F/T guys visually sighted on the mounts and knocked out 4 of the 5 guns that shot at us.

A few weeks later one of the guys got a letter from his home in Ohio. Enclosed in the letter was a short article about us. It made it look like the battle raged through the night. We were all heroes.

Excuse Me: We were refueling on from the carrier one stormy night. I was the bridge talker for the Captain. When we got connection to the carrier the Captain got on the line and gave a warm greeting, "Pleasure to be alongside". The carrier skipper said, "Ah bull...." The captain turned to me with a smile and said, "Musta been something he ate!"

Blistered Gun Barrels Mark DesDiv 42's Long Vietnam Voyage

Editor's note: This story appeared in the "Cruiser-Destroyerman" Magazine, August 1968.

The 1,230 officers and men of Destroyer Division 42 and the guided missile destroyer Dewey were reunited with their families and friends on June 22. The Charleston-based DesDiv 42 ships, *Cone*, *James C. Owens* and *Johnston*, and the Norfolk-based *Dewey* returned to their homeports following a seven month Western Pacific deployment.

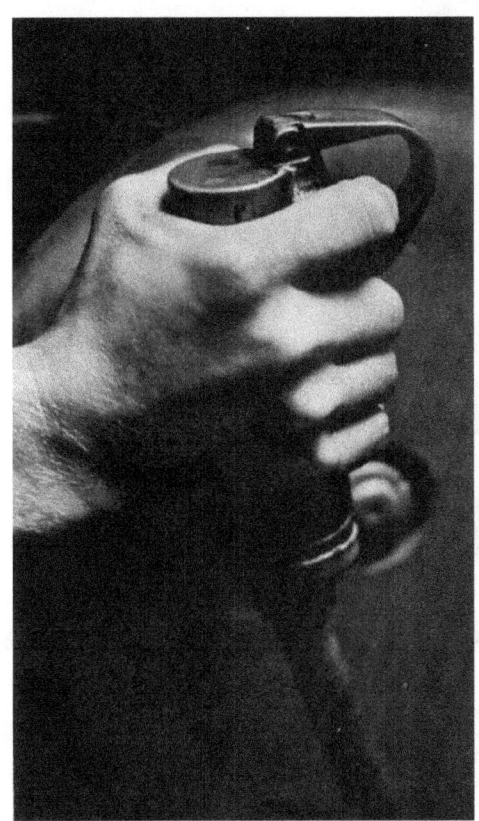

Photo on left - A steady hand waits for the order to fire aboard a Destroyer Division 42 ship while on gunline duty off the Vietnam coast.

Since departure from the U.S. last November, the ships have transited the South Atlantic Ocean, Caribbean Sea and Pacific Ocean; and operated in the East China Sea, South China Sea, Philippine Sea, Gulf of Tonkin and Sea of Japan. Each ship steamed 55,000 miles - the equivalent of nine round trips to Europe from New York. Included in the ship's port calls were Rodman, Panama Canal Zone; Manzanillo, Mexico; San Diego, Calif.; Pearl Harbor, Hawaii; Midway Island; Yokosuka, Sasebo, Beppu and Shimoda, Japan; Buckner Bay, Okinawa; Subic Bay, Republic of the Philippines; Kaohsiung, Taiwan; DaNang, Nha Trang and Cam Ranh Bay, Republic of Vietnam and Hong Kong, British Crown Colony.

While in Vietnamese waters DesDiv 42 ships daily harassed Viet Cong junks carrying supplies to the enemy.

For the men of DesDiv 42, the times were good – hours spent in exotic liberty ports from the South Atlantic to the South China Sea. But the times were tough too – days and weeks on the gunline, where there is little time for sleep, and at-sea ammunition replenishments must be conducted at night, cutting even deeper into resting hours.

A destroyer struggles through the turbulent wake of an aircraft carrier while "Puppy Dogging" on Yankee Station.

Guns slammed away for nearly 24 hours a day, and there was no liberty call in the Gulf of Tonkin - especially when shore batteries bracketed a ship. For the men of DesDiv 42 the war is now reality. Whether they were stationed aboard a battle-scarred veteran, or cruising with their ship into her first battle, they wrote another chapter in Naval History.

While in Vietnamese waters the four men-of-war fired 31,000 rounds of ammunition in naval gunfire support missions against the Viet Cong and North Vietnamese troops and installations. Nearly one-third of these missions were observed and controlled visually by airborne spotters or ground spotters in forward observation posts. The official gun damage assessment by the spotters totaled 59 enemy killed; 135 bunkers and fortifications destroyed, more than 468 structures were destroyed or damaged, five sampans sunk; three bridges damaged and miles of supply and escape routes interdicted. In addition, many other unobserved missions were fired.

In addition to their fire power, DesDiv 42 ships made other vital contributions to the war effort without firing a gun. *Dewey* and *Cone*, for example, spent 11 days as a Search and Rescue (SAR) team in the Gulf of Tonkin. The SAR station was within range of enemy jet aircraft and PT Boats. The two men-of-war participated in three separate SAR operations and rescued a total of six American airmen.

Dewey's primary mission was to provide an advanced SAR command and control center for Navy and Air Force Search and Rescue. In addition, she provided a mobile helicopter landing platform for SAR copters on station in the Tonkin Gulf. As an added part of her duties, *Dewey* also provided anti-air protection for Yankee Station carriers and controlled several hundred aircraft during the deployment.

Photo on left – Cleaning empty brass while on gunline duty is an all hands job, with little time to relax while a destroyer's 5-inchers roar in battle.

While *Dewey* and *Cone* were providing SAR and naval gunfire coverage around the Tonkin Gulf area, *Owens* and *Johnston* joined the attack aircraft carrier *Ranger* for a brief gunline tour. *Owens* then shifted operations to the Sea of Japan.

While in Vietnamese waters *Owens* completed a tour of duty as a Naval Gunfire Support ship for allied ground forces ashore. No newcomer to combat, *Owens* performed similar gunline duties during World War II and the Korean Conflict.

While on the gunline off the Demilitarized Zone (DMZ), she immediately responded to calls from Marines ashore to attack enemy troop concentrations north of Hue. Using her five-inch batteries, *Owens* blasted enemy emplacements for more than 15 hours before being diverted to other gunfire assignments.

In contrast to the combat veteran *Owens*, war was a new experience for *Cone* and her crew. Despite her 23 years of service the Charleston-based destroyer had never fired a shot in anger. This situation changed quickly after she steamed to her station off the DMZ in February. Arriving there shortly after the start of the Tet offensive, the Third Marine Division wanted all the help that *Cone's* 5-inchers could give. For 11 days, 293 officers and men worked around the clock, pouring in 7,500 rounds on the enemy.

Gun barrels became so hot the paint blistered. Men who were not on watch voluntarily backed up the crews in the magazines and handling rooms so that high rates of fire could be sustained. On occasion found *Cone* being called upon to saturate an area infiltrated by more than 800 Viet Cong troops. After bombarding the area and driving the enemy out, Marine Corps units mopping up afterward credited the ship with 22 enemy killed.

During a Destroyer Division 42 gunline mission, bluejackets cool gun barrels with cold sea water and an old fire hose.

Johnston had the distinction of being the only one of the four ships to come under enemy fire. The incident occurred when the U.S destroyer was completing two hours of suppression fire against enemy troops. She was taken under fire simultaneously by three artillery emplacements just north of the DMZ. At least five enemy rounds were observed to fall close aboard. Immediately, the destroyer's guns returned the fire, knocking out one of the Viet Cong's shore batteries.

The Charleston-Based destroyer Johnston's guns blast the Viet Cong, lighting of the night sky with the flash of war.

Not long after that incident, *Johnston* was again called in to bombard an estimated battalion-sized force of Viet Cong regulars discovered near Gio Linh. Following the directions of shore-based spotters, *Johnston* guns pounded relentlessly againbst the enemy. U.S. troops moving through the area backed by the destroyer's guns reported that *Johnston* had destroyed many structures and killed 22 enemy troops.

In all, *Johnston* spent 32 uninterrupted days on the gunline, delivering more than 7,500 rounds of 5-inch projectiles onto enemy targets. An additional 3,100 rounds were fired during subsequent gunline assignments.

As the four ships left the Vietnam area for their return to the U.S., the DesDiv 42 ships received the following message from Vice Admiral W.F. Bringle, "As you depart, I congratulate the officers and men of each ship in your division on the fine job you have done while deployed to the Seventh Fleet. Your ships performed well in all assignments, including SAR, escort, radar pickett and Naval Gunfire Support duty. Their long days at sea are greatly appreciated. You have made a significant contribution to the United States mission in Southeast Asia. Best wishes on your long trip home, and for a pleasant reunion with your families and loved ones."

World Traveled
By: George A. Sites, Radarman (RD-2)

Years on board the Johnston: 1968 to 1971

As a young kid I loved to travel however our family didn't have lots of money so the travel was usually limited to one short, week-long vacation during the summer months. These vacations usually meant going to a local amusement park or to a state park and usually during the same vacation. However in 1960 our family headed south to Florida. On the way, we visited my uncle who lived in Georgia. We spent the night and left in the morning headed for Pensacola, Florida. I couldn't wait to see the beach and the Gulf of Mexico.

I had never seen a body of water any larger than Lake Erie. We arrived, changed into our bathing suits and hit the water. After a little while, my Mom decided to get us a snack, went to the car for her purse, only to find it missing. She carried most of the cash and there were no credit cards in those days. The family decided it wasn't stolen so we called my uncle and he said it was there sitting by the chair my mom had occupied the night before. As a result, we headed back to Georgia and then home. Our Florida vacation cut short because of a silly mistake.

Once having seen the beach and the water, I knew that someday I would visit it again and hopefully live by it.

Move forward about seven years, I graduate from High School and join the Navy to see the world and the water. I couldn't wait. I signed up for an East Coast ship after Radarman "A" School and was assigned to the USS William C. Lawe in Mayport Florida. I was only on the Lawe for a matter of months before being transferred to the USS Johnston DD-821 homeported in Charleston, South

Carolina. The ship was going through a yard period which turned out to be my second time through the yards. Charleston didn't seem like it would be as great as Mayport but I knew it was close to the ocean and had lots of beaches.

The first time at sea on the Johnston was a short trip to GITMO (my second time, first was on the Lawe). After that we headed for the first of my two Med cruises. We left on September 8, 1969 and returned on March 28, 1970. I loved the cities and countries we visited and to me, the cruise was far too short. I couldn't wait until the next one.

The next Med cruise came in mid-summer of 1971. Although we visited many of the same cities and countries, it was still wonderful to see how others in the world lived compared to us in the good ol' USA. My travels in the Navy made me appreciate the United States even more than before. In fact I believe if all young men and women were required to join the military, many of them would appreciate what we have here more than they do. Most young people take our freedom and liberties for granted. My enlisted ended during the Med cruise so the Navy flew me back to the states for discharge in October. Like many of you, I ordered a "Cruise Book" for the '71 Med cruise. Did you ever what happened to it? I found out recently from Admiral Mike McCaffrey the books were lost a sea. All these years I thought I had lost it.

It was hard for me to imagine having parties at sea back then, but do you remember the parties on the fantail during the Med cruise?

Again more forward more than forty years later, I still love to travel. At the time of this writing, I have visited 45 of the United States and many countries. I loved sailing the seas during my four-year enlistment in the Navy and continue that tradition by taking Ocean Cruises as often as possible. The cruises have allowed Alida and me to visit nearly all of the Caribbean Islands, some northern parts of South American, the Panama Canal, Costa Rica, Hawaii and the West Coast of Mexico. We currently have both an Alaskan and an Eastern Caribbean cruise scheduled for summer and fall of 2013. We hope to do a Baltic cruise in 2014 and a return (for me) to the Mediterranean Sea in 2015 nearly 35 years after my first trip to the Mediterranean Sea. I can't wait.

Alida and I hope to continue our travels both here in the United States and overseas! The USS Johnston DD-821 Association Reunions have given us reason to visit many places we probably would not have visited on our own. You should consider Johnston reunions in the future.

Traveling is kind of a Sites family tradition. If you consider all the travels of my Dad in the US Navy during WWII, my youngest son Brent in the Navy during the War on Iraq and my Navy travels, the three of us have covered nearly the entire world with the exception of the North and South Pole areas! I credit the Navy for actually introducing me to world traveling.

And by the way, where did you do all of your growing up? If like me, it was during your Navy enlistment.

Bio – RD2 George A Sites

After WWII, my Dad returned home from the US Navy. Shortly thereafter, he was hired by General Motors as a production worker while my Mother worked at the local five & dime store. I was born in

1948 to George and Frances Sites in Columbus, Ohio. They both worked hard at their respective jobs in life and instilled in me the work ethic I possess today. There is nothing else they could have taught me that would be more important in my adult life.

I led a pretty normal life growing up in the Midwest, sheltered, going to high school, working, etc. I played guitar in several local garage bands, built a model railroad and studied electronics in high school. Having listened to my Dad's sea stories for years, I knew that someday I would also join the Navy. Not long after turning 18, I received my 'Draft Notice' for the US Army and immediately headed for the Navy recruiter and 'signed my life away'. My 'coming of age' story is mostly based upon those four years in the Navy.

I left for Boot Camp at Great Lakes on October 25, 1967, graduated about 12 weeks later and moved across the street to attend 13 weeks of Basic Electric and Electronics (BE&E) school and 26 weeks of Radarman 'A' school. Upon graduation I was assigned to the USS William C. Lawe DD-763 stationed in Jacksonville, Florida which was going through a yard period in Charleston, South Carolina. Upon arrival, I was assigned to 'Mess Cooking' and we headed for GITMO. Upon return from GITMO, I got my orders to report aboard the USS Johnston DD-821. Off I went to the 'Jolly J' and upon arrival I was once again assigned to 'Mess Cooking' and then off to GITMO again. Wow, 6 months of 'Mess Cooking'. I was stuck in a rut – however Chief Jackson and RD1 Dawson came to my rescue and allowed me in CIC (Combat Information Center) to learn even though I was assigned to the galley. I achieved 3rd class and then 2nd class quickly and had passed 1st class exams but did not have enough time left to be advanced. I was the lead guitar player in "SMOKE", the Johnston's Rock & Roll band. Hindsight tells me I should have shipped over for the two months that I was short and enjoyed 1st class status and of course the extra money. I loved the Navy life!

At the end of my four years I headed home and joined a Rock & Roll band. We played all over the country but I decided I probably wasn't going to make the big time so I quit the band and got a job at Halmar Electronics as a stock clerk. While employed there, I got married, had two sons, went to college and got my bachelors degree in Electronics, advanced to Engineering Manager, received two United States Patents and helped double the product offering at Halmar. I spent 19 years at Halmar before moving on to HDR Power Systems as Vice President of Engineering and starting up the 'Power Products Group'. I spent 20 years at HDR, wrote and published two technical books and while developing the 'Power Products' product line. A third technical book is currently in the works. HDR is now the leader in their industry. My connection to the Navy did not end at discharge, as I developed industrial power supplies for use in "Waste to

Energy" being used by the US Navy, the US Air Force and multiple companies around the word.

I retired from HDR on March 4, 2011 and thought I was on a fun filled journey I had been working my whole life for. Unfortunately on the day I retired, my 85 year old Dad had a stroke (resulting from Hernia surgery) and six weeks later my 28 year old son, Brent took his own life suffering from PTSD from three tours in the war zone. He had served five years honorably while stationed most of the time on the USS Enterprise CVN-65 as a MM3. He was only five weeks from graduating from college. He loved his country and was proud of his Navy service. Years later I'm still mourning our loss of Brent as I always will. They say 'time heals all wounds', I'm not so sure about that. To say my retirement got off to a rocky start would be an under-statement!

As a retiree, I find myself splitting my time between my home town of Columbus, Ohio and my new home in Venice, Florida. I've always wanted to spend time in Florida every since my Navy days in Jacksonville, Florida. I finally made it! People always say, "What are you going to do with all your time?" I seem busier now than I ever was. I've always had an interest in writing as evidenced by my two technical books and the "USS Johnston" book which I am very proud of. I am currently working on a third technical book, a book about my son Brent, a horror story and my life story. Not sure any of them will be a 'Best Seller'. I also have G.A.

Sites Engineering, LLC in which I am a consultant to the industries I worked in during my near 40 year career. In addition to all of this, Alida and I take long walks nearly every day, while in Florida. We walk the beach every opportunity we get and generally try to have some down time that neither of us had during our working career. I guess the moral of this story is work hard but find time to enjoy life. Life is far too short……enjoy it while you can!

Chapter 6

YEARS 1970 THROUGH 1983

Tail Ends on Fire

By: William P. "Bill" Watson III, Midshipman Third Class

Year on board the Johnston: 1970

During the summer of 1970, I was a NROTC midshipman third class from Tulane University on board the USS Johnston based in Charleston, South Carolina. Midshipmen were rotated through the divisions on the ship and we all had books that contained various assignments that had to be signed off. Of course, sailors on board the ship enjoyed harassing unsuspecting midshipman at every opportunity. On one hot, steamy South Carolina day, after being told to paint an area below an actively leaking water valve, another midshipman and I were assigned to dust the gun barrels of the forward gun mount. We were told that the fire control system was so sensitive that dust on the barrels affected the accuracy of the guns. That did not make any sense at all, but we dutifully found some rags and clambered up on the gun mount, straddled each barrel, and shimmied our way out as we dusted off the barrels. Perhaps 1/4 of the way out on the barrels and to the delight of the sailors who were watching and knew what was coming, the heat from the guns which had been baking in the sun began to burn through our dungaree trousers and put our tail ends on fire. At about the same time, we both yelled and jumped down from the barrels as we sheepishly endured the laughs of those on the forward deck.

Not the Fastest Learners
By: William P. Watson III, Midshipman Third Class

Not being fast learners and for some reason continuing to trust the sailors of the Johnston, sometime later another midshipman and I were assigned to frap the bow lines. Of course we had no idea what frap the lines even meant, but dutifully reported forward where we were each given lengths of white rope and were told that a VIP was coming on board and the lines had to be dressed up. We were told to carefully wrap each line with each wrap evenly spaced from the top of the line down to the bollard. Of course, the only way to accomplish this vital mission was to straddle the lines and shimmy our way down. We were told to be careful not to fall as the white rope would get wet and we would have to start over with dry rope. It appeared to be a long way down to the water and neither of us was interested in falling. We quickly found that balancing ourselves on the line was quite difficult and it did not seem to be a safe endeavor. Like dusting gun barrels, frapping lines was also not listed in our midshipman assignment books, but were anxious to learn all of this real Navy stuff. As we were about halfway down the lines, sailors on the pier grabbed the lines and began to sway them back and forth. Again to the delight of the sailors, one midshipman quickly fell into the water. I managed to hang on inverted and make my way to the pier, though my blue ringed Dixie cup followed the other midshipman into the drink. A CPO then came up and after laughing at the sight, told the sailors to fish the other midshipman out of the water and get back to work.

There are many other stories, but the two above may be remembered by those who participated in the time honored practice of making life on board a ship interesting for midshipmen. It permitted the sailors to get in a few good natured digs at future officers and taught the midshipmen more about a ship than they could ever learn from following a checklist in an assignment book.

I ended up serving 28 years in the a Marine Corps as an aviator, but my time served on board the USS Johnston provided experiences that remained with me throughout my career and reminded me to always look at situations from the deck level. Serving as a midshipman and later deploying on board ships as an aviator provided a background that served me well as an Assistant U.S. Naval Attaché in China and as a Defense and Naval Attaché in West Africa.

Thanks to the sailors of the USS Johnston who harried, harassed, pulled wool over the eyes, and played jokes on midshipman while at the same time teaching valuable lessons from the bilges to the O levels that made all of us better Navy and Marine Corps officers.   William P. Watson III LtCol, USMC (Ret.)

The NTPI

By: Burnham C. "Mike" McCaffree, Commander (Rear Admiral, USN Retired)

Years on board the Johnston: 1970 to 1972

The NTPI. I wonder how many of our shipmates remember the dreaded **N**avy **T**echnical **P**roficiency **I**nspections the ship had to undergo periodically to certify that JOHNSTON was safe to carry nuclear weapons – in our case, nuclear-tipped ASROCs. These inspections were exhaustive (and exhausting): they included ASROC loading/unloading drills, and simulated launching of one of the nuclear ASROCs; they tested our fire-fighting capabilities; they examined the ship's Personnel Reliability Program (PRP); they looked at torque wrenches and other tools and weapons handling equipment; and they looked at and tested the various alarm systems associated with our ASROC weapons system. The NTPI involved every department in some way.

We had prepared and gone through advance inspections and we were ready. Then the Defense Nuclear Agency inspection team arrived and the NTPI began. All was going apparently well until I heard an alarm sound. Shortly thereafter LT Bruce Cannon, our Weapons Officer, and LTJG Mo Gauthier, our ASW Officer, came into my cabin to tell me the bad news: the inspector had tried to gain access to the FZ alarm panel in Main Battery Control, and had triggered the access alarm. This would automatically result in an UNSATISFACTORY grade on the NTPI. However, Mr. Gauthier told me that it wasn't a fair test, in his opinion. He went on to recount that the inspector, a 250-pound Air Force Captain build like an NFL lineman, had grabbed hold of the cage surrounding the FZ alarm controls and jerked the cover so vigorously that

Mo was afraid he would rip it from the bulkhead. The alarm contacts between cage door and the rest of the cage were interrupted; hence the access alarm went off.

The senior inspector did not agree with our assessment that his inspector had been unrealistically vigorous in his test of the access alarm. It looked like we were sunk on the inspection, but we let our Commodore, CAPT Larry Fay, know of our objections and he took the matter to our CRUDES Flotilla Commander. The Admiral listened to our story, talked to the senior inspector, and called the Type Commander on the ship's behalf. A long day of waiting later we were told that the FZ alarm cage was not to be ruled as a serious deficiency. We had done very well on all other aspects of the NTPI, and we were given a SATISFACTORY. [After the DNA inspectors left, our shipfitters welded additional supports to the

FZ alarm cage so that not even King Kong could get into it without the key!]

A Brindisi Highlight

By: Burnham C. "Mike" McCaffree, Commander (Rear Admiral, USN Retired)

<u>Brindisi, Italy</u>. One of the highlights of our 1971 Mediterranean deployment was going to be a Restricted Availability in Valleta, Malta. However, the Prime Minister of Malta became angry at Great Britain, and more generally at NATO, so our port visit there was cancelled. Instead, we went to Brindisi. It didn't have the attractions of Valleta, but there was an Air Force Security Station there that made us feel really welcome. We played a lot of softball (officers vs. chiefs, departments against departments, etc.) during the visit. My wife and daughters were there; the four of us went to most of the games and we all got sunburn! Our teams seemed never to run out of beer between innings. And the games made up in physicality what they lacked in talent - a couple of our CPOs broke legs or arms and wound up in the Station's Sick Bay.

One Friday afternoon SMOKE was performing on the ASROC deck. My family and I were sitting at the hotel's outdoor café across the street where JOHNSTON was moored right down town. Cars driving by were slowing down and their passengers gawking, and it looked like there would soon be a traffic jam. We saw two Italian policemen walk to the Quarterdeck, and LT Cannon, the ship's Command

Duty Officer, came down to meet them. I figured that we were about to get a ticket or something worse for causing a civic annoyance and maybe I better go over to the ship. But I waited. The two policemen climbed the ladder to the ASROC deck where there were a number of crewmembers, and even a couple of guests, enjoying SMOKE. But instead of disrupting the scene, the two rested their elbows on the lifelines and became enthusiastic spectators! And there they stayed for the next half hour. So I stayed put at the café and watched the show of the Italians on the quay and our crewmembers on the ship enjoying SMOKE's performance.

Bio – Rear Admiral Burnham C. McCaffree Jr.

Captain of USS Johnston: 1970 to 1972

BURNHAM C. McCAFFREE JR. (Mike) Rear Admiral U. S. Navy (Retired) was a surface warfare officer. He was born in San Diego, CA, as the son of a career naval officer. During his childhood, he moved frequently with his family and graduated from high school in Bethesda, MD.

He enlisted in the Naval Reserve in 1948, attended the Naval Academy and was commissioned an officer in 1954. He then served in the aircraft carrier USS *Midway*, the heavy cruiser USS *Newport News*, and the destroyer USS *Gearing*. He next served as Executive Officer of the landing ship USS *Traverse County*, the landing ship dock USS *Rushmore*, and the destroyer USS *Rich*. In 1970-1972 he commanded the destroyer USS *Johnston*, and later the amphibious transport dock USS *Shreveport* and Amphibious Squadron TWO, conducting operations in the Atlantic Ocean and deploying to the Caribbean, Mediterranean, and

Norwegian Seas and the Indian Ocean. As a junior officer, he spent three years ashore in Norfolk as an ASW project officer on the Operational Test and Evaluation Force staff; and later in his career was the Torpedo Officer for the Atlantic Cruiser and Destroyer Force commander in Newport. He was the Assistant Chief of Staff (Plans) for the Commander Naval Support Activity (Danang) for one year in South Vietnam, and served in the Strategic Plans and Policy Division on the Chief of Naval Operations' staff in Washington. As a flag officer, he was Director of two divisions on the CNO's staff (OPNAV), he commanded Amphibious Group ONE in the Western Pacific and Indian Ocean, and he served as the Assistant Deputy Chief of Naval Operations (Logistics).

Since retiring from the Navy in 1988, Admiral McCaffree has been a consultant for several defense-related research companies and for the federal government. He is now a research scientist for CNA, a federally funded research and development center in northern Virginia. He and his wife Lynn have two daughters and five grandchildren.

Mike has served in various capacities in church and community organizations associated with retirement living and seniors services, both in northern Virginia and in the Episcopal Diocese of Virginia. He is very active at Goodwin House Alexandria, a retirement community where he and Lynn have lived since 2001.

VISIT TO TUNIS, TUNISIA

By: Bruce Sauerwine, Quartermaster (QM-2)

Years on board the Johnston: 1971 to 1975

During the 1971 Mediterranean cruise the Johnston was detached on a solo mission to visit Tunis, Tunisia for a weekend to "show the flag". The lone mission itself was unusual in that even when detached from the fleet, ships usually traveled in a group of 2 or 3.

I had duty on our arrival on Friday but was determined to see what I could of an Arab city, perhaps the only chance I would ever get. Therefore, on Saturday my buddy YN3 Jim Thomsen and I set off down the pier to go into the city. We had heard there was a commuter train line not far from the pier and planned to use that to get into the city.

As we started down the pier we met an American civilian and his young daughter who had come to the ship to pick up some supplies. He and his wife were both teachers at the American embassy, he originally from New York, she from Philadelphia. As we talked he offered us a ride into the city in his van. We accepted and he was glad to give us a short "guided tour" of the center of the city and point out and explain some things we no doubt would not have gotten from an official tour.

Jim Thomsen at a Coffee House, Tunis Tunisia

He seemed happy to speak with fellow countrymen who were not part of the embassy. Next he offered us a tour of the Medina, the old city, explorable only on foot. He dropped us off in a central square to look around on our own while he went home to drop off his daughter and explain to his wife what he was going to do (no cell phones back then).

On his return we walked in the Medina with him. He explained that in the shops the owners loved to bargain. If you see something interesting, he said, don't act interested, just tell me and I'll do the talking. Tunisia had been a French colony so all signs are in French and Arabic. Many Tunisians of course spoke only Arabic.

Keeping in mind, as we all knew, that anything purchased had to be small (the rugs, for instance were wonderful but not a practical buy for sailors with nowhere to store them) I selected a brass item (another Tunisian specialty). The shopkeeper wanted $5-, our "guide" offered $2- and they settled on $3-. I still have the item today.

The Medina, Tunis Tunisia 1971

Our teacher friend then left us but not without a recommendation for dinner if we decided to eat ashore. We took his advice and went to a Greek restaurant where of course the menu had no English and the waiters spoke no English. We finally determined that one item was, of all things, spaghetti which we figured was a safe choice.

Brass souk (shop) at The Medina

We certainly appreciated our luck at having met the teacher. We got to see and learn a lot more than we would have on our own. Sometimes in life it's those chance meetings that work out really well.

The next day, Jim and I went took the commuter train to the ancient city of Carthage, only a few miles in the opposite direction. The train line had been built by the French in the 1880's and the Tunisians were still using the original equipment 90 years later. It was an interesting train ride because basically the cars were boxcars where the riders could only stand as there were no seats.

A few footnotes to this story:

1. In 1976 my wife and I went to Iowa where I served as best man when Jim got married.

2. In 1999, 28 years after the USS Johnston's visit, my wife and I had the chance to visit Tunis on a Mediterranean cruise but this time on an actual cruise ship without gun turrets or having to stand watch. It was great to see the city again and to have my wife enjoy it as I had. One of the highlights of that visit was to see the North Africa American Cemetery outside of Tunis where 2,841 Americans are buried who fought in the North Africa campaign in WWII. This cemetery lies over part of what was the ancient city of Carthage which was destroyed by the Romans in 146 BC. Those interested in the cemetery can view it at:

www.abmc.gov/cemeteries/cemeteries/na.php

Time Erodes Everything
By: Stephen Zenes, Radioman (RM-1)

Years on board the Johnston: 1975 to 1977

When I arrived at the USS Johnston it was home ported in Philadelphia, Pennsylvania as a Reserve ship. I spent 3 years on her - 1975 to 1977.

I was in charge of training the Reserves in the Radio room and had to put up with Reserve Officers. We took weekend cruises out into the Atlantic and down to the Caribbean. We also visited GTMO. I think we made one visit to the Med. on a 2 week cruise.

Since our ship was dockside so much, all of our communication sitreps and other messages were at the Communication Center on the base. We had to walk to the Comm. Center and back to the ship.

While I was stationed on the Johnston, I was able to see all of the numerous greyhounds of the sea at the ship graveyard there. There were Destroyers, LST's, Cruisers, PT Boats Refrigerator ships, and other ships that were part of the mothball fleet. I loved seeing them but felt so very sad at seeing them decaying and no one wanting to restore them.

I now know that our ship is no longer, the naval base is no longer, the Mothball fleet is no longer and the Naval Hospital is no longer. It seems that time erodes everything.

Memories: Good and Sad
By: Carl Williams, Machinist Mate (MM-1)

Years on board the Johnston: 1976 to 1980

I served on USS Johnston from April 1976 to September 8, 1980. While on USS Johnston, we were involved in several activities: the Bicentennial celebration in tow trips to Guantanamo Cuba for refresher training; a test ship for the SQS-56 Sonar system; and a small part in the Israel/Egypt peace accord. These were just a few things that USS Johnston was involved in during the four and a half years I was part of her crew.

In June 1976 DESRON 30 had its two week training cruise for its reserves. The ships of DESRON 30 that took part in the reserve training cruise were USS Johnston, USS Rich, USS Corry and USS Ellison; all four of these ships were home ported in Philadelphia, Pennsylvania.

One morning during the first week of the reserve training cruise the Commodore of DESRON 30 had the Johnston, Rich, Corry and Ellison form up in a line abreast of one another. I was up on the main deck of the Johnston amidships while this took place. It was quite a sight to see: four Gearing Class Destroyers in a line abreast of each other. The Commodore of DESRON 30 had all four ships increase speed to twenty four knots and hold at that speed.

Normal operation for a Gearing Class Destroyer at sea is to run two boilers with a maximum speed of twenty four knots.

All four ships came up to twenty four knots and maintained that speed for about 30 minutes. Then one by one the Rich, Corry, and Ellison started to slow down and fall behind, unable to maintain the twenty four knot speed. At approximately 50 minutes the Johnston was the only ship that was able to maintain the twenty four knot speed. At one hour the Commodore of DESRON 30 had the Johnston slow down while the other three ships caught up. Then he had all ships proceed at twenty knots, which all ships were able to do.

I was very proud to be part of the USS Johnston's crew that day and that the ship was able to do what was asked of her. It was a mild sunny morning with relatively calm seas somewhere off the northern coast of the United States in the Atlantic Ocean.

The sadist time I can remember while on the Johnston happened in February of 1980. We were in Mayport, Florida, for a couple of weeks alongside a tender/repair ship for minor repairs and up-keep.

While the Johnston was in Mayport, Florida, the ship received its schedule for the next six months. The schedule was a very busy and aggressive one; it was more like a fleet ship's schedule than a reserve ship's schedule. This schedule had the Johnston going down into the southern parts of the Caribbean and making several port calls there. This schedule even had us making port calls in the Dutch Antilles and crossing the equator. This schedule for would have been a challenge for a fleet ship but we knew that we were up to the challenge. The crew of Johnston was excited about the new schedule and was all that we talked about for the next week.

On Tuesday during the second week of the tender availability in Mayport, Florida, our Captain, Commander Kronz called an all hands meeting on the flight deck. As we assembled on the flight deck for the meeting, everyone was wondering what this was for -- maybe more and better information about our new schedule. When our Captain and Executive Officer came out on deck we all knew that something was wrong just from their expressions. We all got quiet without anything being said. Then our Captain told us that USS Johnston was going to be decommissioned. The results from a hull survey of the Johnston showed that eighty percent of the hull below the water line was one eighth of an inch or less. With the hull survey information plus USS Johnston's age (33+ years old) and the cost to replace the ship's hull the Navy deemed that the ship was no longer fit for service and would be decommissioned. As our Captain told this news to us, we could see that he was on the brink of tears.

While our Captain was telling this information to us, you could feel the upbeat mood of the crew go down. Our Captain must have seen this change of mood in the crew as he told about what our near future would be. Our Captain had a change in his tone and mood as he tells us that we the crew of USS Johnston should be proud of all that we had done while on the ship and that the ship's thin hull was just the result of many years at sea, and to remember that these "Old Tin Cans" were made to be expendable and that USS Johnston had proud history and a long life.

Our Captain said that we would finish our repair time alongside the tender and then go back to our home port of Philadelphia, Pennsylvania, and start preparing the Johnston to be decommissioned. Our Captain told us that we had a lot of work to do to get the Johnston ready and that we would have many challenges to deal with and that some of us would be transferred off the ship to other ships before the decommissioning.

I stayed on the Johnston as the ship was made ready to be decommissioned. I was discharged from the Navy on September 8, 1980, and on that day I left USS Johnston DD 821 for my last time.

USS Johnston DD 821 was decommissioned on October 1, 1980.

These are just a few of my many memories of USS Johnston DD 821 and the men with whom I served.

FROM THE HOME FRONT
By: Donna Williams, Wife of Carl Williams

Editor's Note: I met Carl and his wife at one of the Johnston reunions and she asked if it would be appropriate to tell her side of the story. I think it's great and I'm sure you will too. It never hurts to have another perspective. This is Carl's story as his wife Donna remembers it.

My dad, a USS New Mexico veteran: "A sailor's wife is a lonely life…"

My husband (then my fiancé): "Oh, baby, this isn't a typical destroyer. She's too old. We don't go on Mediterranean deployments, those six- to nine-month things. We go out one weekend a month and two weeks during the summer with the reservists, and that's about it. Sometimes we even stay in port with the reservists."

I was torn about which one to believe, and, as it turns out, they were both right - and both wrong. This is the story of the days before and the first months of our marriage.

Carl arrived home (Houston, Texas) on 3 January 1977 for our wedding on 7 January. I had just graduated from a secondary teacher education program at a university about an hour from Houston and had just completed student teaching at a high school in Houston. We are high school sweethearts, but we knew the wisdom of waiting a few years; however, I completed my degree requirements early so that we could get married sooner.

The night Carl arrived home, his wallet went missing. Not only was a considerable amount of money, especially by 1977 standards, gone, but so were his health records for the marriage license and his military ID. Fortunately, his leave papers were not among the missing items.

In spite of the missing money and records, the wedding did go on as planned -- early in the morning of 7 January. I chose a morning wedding for two reasons: The sanctuary of the church we officially belonged to is pretty that time of morning, with the sun coming through the stained glass, and we weren't sure how much travel time we'd have - or need - to get to Philadelphia.

We left Houston for Philadelphia on Monday, 10 January, after a stop at the bank to trade our money - almost all the money we had, including wedding gift money - into traveler's checks so that the funds could be recovered if they went missing. That could be considered a smart move, but, since I had no ID in my married name, they were all on Carl's signatures. So it turned out to be a not-so-good move later. We also rented a small U-Haul trailer to move all our belongings. Yes, we were two twenty-year-old newlyweds with little more than dreams, starting a new life.

So on to Philadelphia we went. That winter was an unusually cold one, even in Texas; we started seeing snow when we went through Dallas, and I did not see ground again for a month. After a few days visiting with Carl's aunt and uncle in northern Missouri (where, by the way, I saw my first live pigs), we stopped in Columbia, Missouri, one night and ended up staying an extra night. The car battery was too cold to start the car - and with good reason. The actual temperatures were about -30 F, with the wind chills -50 F. The canned food I had from the house in Houston literally turned into frozen food; and any time we had to leave the room, Carl would rummage through all my clothes (intended more for relatively mild Houston winters than weather like that) to find enough of something to protect me.

We did arrive in the Philadelphia area on 19 January, and, of course, our first stops there were to obtain new military IDs and to see the housing officer. He referred us to an apartment complex in Bellmawr, New Jersey, about ten miles from the shipyard. It wasn't much, but it had what we needed; an A and P grocery store is within walking distance, and a strip mall was easily accessible by bus. When the managers found out we had no place to go, they allowed us to spend the night in one of the model apartments.

We took occupancy of the apartment the next morning, a third- floor one-bedroom walkup. That included having the electricity turned on and the delivery of rented furniture. We also went to a local mall to buy some warmer clothes for me. We also phoned my parents from a pay phone with our address. But it was the following Monday when everything seemed to start going wrong again.

Carl returned to the Johnston that Monday morning, 24 January. I expected him home that evening; no Carl. *Okay,* I thought, *He's written many times about overnight duty. That's probably what's going on. But I'll sleep on the couch so that I can hear the bell if he's just very late...*

So that Tuesday I continued settling in; that night – still no Carl. I was becoming worried, but I remembered that he had said someone from the ship had told him that loss of the military ID could lead to restriction to the ship. *Is he just very late, did he get restriction – what's going on here? I'll sleep on the couch again, and if he doesn't show up by morning, I'll go find a public phone...*

That Wednesday morning, I was quite worried and had indeed decided I'd waited long enough without any news. When I left the apartment complex, I saw a group of youngsters – about junior high age—walking to school. *Kids,* I think, *but any port in a storm...At least they appear to be old enough to be of help....* "Hello," I call out to them, "Can you tell me where I could find a public phone?"

"Um..." one of the youngsters answers, "maybe if it's important, the principal at school will let you use the office phone...."

Married not even three weeks, and I don't know where my husband is--I think that's important...but these kids don't need to know the whole story, and it may be nothing after all …. "That's your school, over there?" I ask, pointing to a nearby building.

"Yes."

"Okay, but I don't know how to walk in this snow. You'll have to help me, if I'm going to keep up with you at all."

The bewildered looks on the youngsters' faces was absolutely priceless.

"I just moved here, from a part of Texas where it doesn't snow."

That explanation definitely seemed to satisfy the young people, because they then formed a line and "handed" me from one to another. We reached the school, and I asked for the use of the phone to call the shipyard.

"Naval shipyard, Philadelphia."

"Yes. Can you put me through to the Johnston?"

"Ma'am, the Johnston got under way Monday morning for GITMO and won't be back until early March…"

Is this guy telling the truth? I wonder. *I don't know whom to trust, and who not to trust…Carl said something about the Johnston going to Guantanamo shortly after the wedding, but I thought it was in February. And almost every cent we have is in traveler's checks on his signature …. What will I do for money for six weeks?*

That evening, I decide that the man on the base switchboard must have been telling the truth, and I go to a neighbor's apartment to ask to use their phone to call my parents.

"Now, you two didn't have a quarrel or something like that, did you?" she asks.

"No, nothing like that."

"I know someone else whose husband is on that ship. Let me call her." She does so. "I have a young neighbor girl here whose husband is also on the Johnston. She's a long way from home, doesn't know anyone, and doesn't know what's going on….. OK…. So the first Friday in March, they should be back…. OK… Thanks… I'll tell her."

After she ended the call, she said, "Yes, that man told you the truth. They're gone until early March."

"OK, then I have to call my parents, please."

"Daddy?"

"Yes, honey, what's up?"

I explain, in tears, that I had just found out that Carl will be gone for six weeks. "And, Daddy, it's cold."

"Nothing I can do about that, baby. Just be careful on the ice and snow."

"I'm scared… and lonely…"

"Nothing I can do about that, either."

"And… I don't have any money. We put all but about five dollars into traveler's checks in Carl's name."

"Now, that I can do something about! Do you have any idea how much you'll need to manage until he gets home?"

"Yes." And I told him the amount I thought would hold me.

"OK. I'll have it wired to you in the morning. You don't have a bank yet?"

"No, but there's one right on the corner. We were going to go to them and didn't have time before he left." I told him the name and location of the bank.

"OK. Expect to hear from them tomorrow."

"OK, Daddy, thanks. I'll repay you as I can."

The next day, there was a note on the door from the apartment manager to come to the office. The bank had called them, and the money from my parents was there; the bank needed me to come open an account with it. In the regular mail that same day was a telegram from Carl that was supposed to have been hand-delivered to me that previous Monday explaining that Johnston was under way until March, as well as a letter with money orders in it.

I managed the best I could for the remainder of Carl's absence. I stayed busy doing handcrafts; I actually finished knitting a very large throw within about a month, and even knitted a pair of booties for some neighbors who were expectant parents. I had been – and still am – accustomed to attending church, so I walked to a nearby church for the first time on 6 February. It was still very cold outside – about ten degrees – but I was determined. I had many layers of underclothing on, including one of Carl's t-shirts and two pair of pantyhose, as well as church clothes and outerwear. I find the people of that church to be friendly, helpful people; one of them was another Johnston wife who reminded me the Sunday before the men were due home that they should be home that Friday.

I also worked for the apartment managers a few hours a day while Carl was gone, taking care of their then-toddler-age son. That was an experience for me, because they were Jewish and kept a kosher kitchen. I had to learn and take careful notes about what dishes were to be used for what foods, and what to give the baby and when and how to give it.

One big memory of that time was that Valentine's Day. That was the day that I saw ground for the first time in about five weeks! The ice and snow melted. It was a false spring; there was more cold weather to come. But seeing the ice and snow melt did help me feel more hopeful.

Another strong memory of that time had to do with the heating in the apartment - steam from the baseboard area. Because warm air rises and because of solar gain from the windows, our apartment was much warmer than was actually permitted by township ordinance because of a fuel shortage. I remember seeing on television that police were actually checking people's thermostats to be sure they didn't exceed a certain temperature. The thermostat to the apartment was set at a "legal" temperature, but I was concerned that if the police did come and check, they wouldn't believe me. I reported the situation to maintenance on numerous occasions, but nothing they did, short of completely turning off the heat to the apartment, seemed to help.

On the day that the men were due home, I made up my mind not to look for Carl until the next day - in case he had duty or some other situation came up. There was still a lot of, "I'll believe he's home when I see him!" in my attitude. However, about 1100 on the day they were due home, something told me to look out the window. There was Carl's car, pulling into the parking lot! I was down those stairs in personal-best time!

Our marriage, obviously, did not get off to an easy start, but I have to admit that I did need to learn the self-sufficiency I learned from this first deployment. We both learned to be better-prepared for times when Carl would be away, as well. Two young dreamers grew up very quickly.

Bitter Sweet
By: Jeffrey Phillps, Machinist Mate (MM-3)

Years on board the Johnston: 1980

It was 1980 and I was a "Baby Nuke" third class right out of Machinist Mate A-School and sent to the USS Johnston DD-821 for 6 months while I waited for my class to start in Orlando. She was in the Philadelphia reserve basin, and she had sailed her last voyage before I ever had the privilege of reporting aboard. As an A-gang member, I got to see a lot of her, and even helped put one of her Emergency Diesel Generators back together and start it back up.

My stay was bitter sweet though I must confess. I was sad for her, a ship past her prime and her days were numbered. Some dog stole her Bell and brass fire station strainers no doubt for brass salvage, and it seemed to me that her crew was slowly eating her up. I look at pictures of her in her day and wonder what it would have been like.

As a Navy Nuke I went to the Enterprise CVN-65, then the Orion AS-18 in Italy to tend subs. I was supposed to go to the Truxtun for my last tour but my orders got dropped for budget cuts and I stayed in Italy. I always wanted to be a Tin Can sailor but never got the chance.

Chapter 7

JOLLY "J" PORTS OF CALL

Editor's Note: All information pertaining to each port is courtesy of Wikipedia and is just a small portion of the information available. For more information simply enter the name of the port into your search engine and then select the one with Wikipedia at the end of the description.

The names of all "Ports of Call" have been provided by the following shipmates and are assumed to be accurate: Admiral Mike McCaffree, Bob "Frosty" Frost, Captain John Mingo, Dick Schultz, Gary "Benje" Benjestorf, Gauthier

"MO" Maurice, George Nugent, George A. Sites, Herman Sudholz, Johnny "Jonesy" Jones, Stephen Zenes, Toby Mack. All photos for the ports with a "Johnston" theme were provided by various shipmates.

Annapolis, MD is the capital of the U.S. state of Maryland, as well as the county seat of Anne Arundel County. It had a population of 38,394 at the 2010 census and is situated on the Chesapeake Bay at the mouth of the Severn River, 26 miles (42 km) south of Baltimore and about 29 miles (47 km) east of Washington, D.C. Annapolis is part of the Baltimore-Washington Metropolitan Area. The city was the temporary capital of the United States in 1783-1784 and the site of the Annapolis Peace Conference, held in November 2007, at the United States Naval Academy. Annapolis is the home of St. John's College.

The United States Naval Academy was founded in 1845 on the site of Fort Severn, and now occupies an area of land reclaimed from the Severn River next to the Chesapeake Bay.

Amsterdam, Holland is the largest city and the capital of the Netherlands. Its principal language is Dutch. The city's status as the capital of the nation is governed by the constitution. Amsterdam has a population of 820,256 within city limits, an urban population of 1,209,419 and a metropolitan population of 2,289,762. The city is located in the province of North Holland in the west of the country. It comprises the northern part of the Randstad, one of the larger conurbations in Europe, with a population of approximately 7 million.

Amsterdam 28 Jan. - 5 Febr. 1953

Amsterdam's name is derived from *Amstelredamme*, indicative of the city's origin: a dam in the river Amstel. Settled as a small fishing village in the late 12th century, Amsterdam became one of the most important ports in the world during the Dutch Golden Age, a result of its innovative developments in trade. During that time, the city was the leading center for finance and diamonds. In the 19th and 20th centuries, the city expanded, and many new neighborhoods and suburbs were formed. The 17th-century canals of Amsterdam (in Dutch: 'Grachtengordel'), located in the heart of Amsterdam, were added to the UNESCO World Heritage List in July 2010.

As the commercial capital of the Netherlands and one of the top financial centers in Europe, Amsterdam is considered an alpha world city by the Globalization and World Cities (GaWC) study group. The city is also the cultural capital of the Netherlands. Many large Dutch institutions have their headquarters there, and 7 of the world's top 500 companies, including Philips and ING, are based in the city. In 2010, Amsterdam was ranked 13th globally on quality of living by Mercer, and previously ranked 3rd in innovation by 2thinknow in the Innovation Cities Index 2009.

The Amsterdam Stock Exchange, the oldest stock exchange in the world, is located in the city center. Amsterdam's main attractions, including its historic canals, the Rijksmuseum, the Van Gogh Museum, Stedelijk Museum, Hermitage Amsterdam, Anne Frank House, Amsterdam Museum, its red-light district, and its many cannabis coffee shops draw more than 3.66 million international visitors annually.

Argentia, Newfoundland is a community on the island of Newfoundland in the Canadian province of Newfoundland and Labrador. It is situated on a flat headland located along the southwest coast of the Avalon Peninsula on Placentia Bay. It is within the municipal boundaries of the Town of Placentia.

It was originally settled by the French in the 1630s that fishing settlement was called Petit Plaisance, meaning "Pleasant Little Place". The name was retained in English (Little Placentia) when the French lost control of the area following the Treaty of Utrecht in 1713. The census of 1706 records 149 individuals in 14 habitations. The community adopted its present name (unofficially in 1895 and officially in 1901) for the presence of silver ore in the Broad Cove region of the community. The name "Argentia" is Latin, meaning "Land of Silver" and was chosen Father John St. John, the parish priest at Holy Rosary Parish from September 18, 1895 to February 11, 1911. The Silver Cliff Mine operated until the early 1920s but was never profitable. Through most of the 19th century, the fishery was the lifeblood of the community; the Commission of government built a herring factory at Argentia in 1936.

The first church and school were established by Father Pelagius Nowlan in 1835. He was from Ireland and moved to Newfoundland as a missionary priest. In 1836, population was made up 484 people in 76 houses.

Argostoli, Greece is a town and a former municipality on the island of Kefalonia, Ionian Islands, Greece. Since the 2011 local government reform it is part of the municipality Kefalonia, of which it is a municipal unit. It has been the capital and administrative center of Kefalonia since 1757, following a population shift down from the old capital of Agios Georgios (also known as Kastro) to take advantage of the trading opportunities provided by the sheltered bay upon which Argostoli sits. Argostoli developed in to one of the busiest ports in Greece, leading to prosperity and growth. The 2001 census recorded a population of 12,589 in the Argostoli municipal unit. Its largest towns are Argostóli (pop. 9,037), Dilináta (739), Farakláta (411), and Kardakáta (362).

Augusta Bay, Sicily is located on the east coast of Sicily, Italy, about 270 nm south-southeast of Naples.

It is the location of the **Auguate Bay Port Facility** which supports the Sixth Fleet of the US Navy. The facility is distributed among Porto Megarese, Porto Xifonio and Seno del Priolo.

Assab, Ethiopia (now part of Eritrea) is a port city in the Southern Red Sea Region of Eritrea. It is situated on the west coast of the Red Sea.

Assab is known for its large market, beaches and nightlife. It is served by the Assab International Airport.

The city is very hot during summer months; temperatures can touch a scorching high of 54°C (129°F) in July and August.

In 1989, Assab had a population of 39,600 inhabitants. It possesses an oil refinery, which was shut down in 1997 for economic reasons. Nearby is the site of the ancient city of Arsinoe.

The port facilities were greatly expanded in the early 1990s, with the construction of the new terminal, but the port has declined since trade with Ethiopia was terminated in 1998 as a consequence of the Eritrean-Ethiopian War.

Athens, Greece is the capital and largest city of Greece. Athens dominates the Attica region and is one of the world's oldest cities, with its recorded history spanning around 3,400 years. Classical Athens was a powerful city-state. A center for the arts, learning and philosophy, home of Plato's Academy and Aristotle's Lyceum, it is widely referred to as the cradle of Western civilization and the birthplace of democracy,[5][6] largely due to the impact of its cultural and political achievements during the 5th and 4th centuries BC in later centuries on the rest of the then known European continent. Today a cosmopolitan metropolis, modern Athens is central to economic, financial, industrial, political and cultural life in Greece. In 2008, Athens was ranked the world's 32nd richest city by purchasing power and the 25th most expensive in a UBS study.

The city of Athens has a population of 664,046 (796,442 in 2004) within its administrative limits and a land area of 39 km^2 (15 sq mi). The urban area of Athens (*Greater Athens* and *Greater Piraeus*) extends beyond the administrative municipal city limits, with a population of 3,074,160 (in 2011), over an area of 412 km^2 (159 sq mi). According to Eurostat, the Athens Larger Urban Zone (LUZ) is the 7th most populous LUZ in the European Union (the 4th most populous capital city of the EU), with a population of 4,013,368 (in 2004). Athens is also the southernmost capital on the European mainland.

The heritage of the classical era is still evident in the city, represented by ancient monuments and works of art, the most famous of all being the Parthenon, considered a key landmark of early Western civilization. The city also retains Roman and Byzantine monuments, as well as a smaller number of Ottoman monuments.

　　Athens is home to two UNESCO World Heritage Sites, the Acropolis of Athens and the medieval Daphni Monastery. Landmarks of the modern era, dating back to the establishment of Athens as the capital of the independent Greek state in 1834, include the Hellenic Parliament (19th century) and the Athens Trilogy, consisting of the National Library of Greece, the Athens University and the Academy of Athens. Athens was the host city of the first modern-day Olympic Games in 1896, and 108 years later it welcomed home the 2004 Summer Olympics. Athens is home to the National Archeological Museum, featuring the world's largest collection of ancient Greek antiquities, as well as the new Acropolis Museum.

Aden (Now Yemen) is a seaport city in Yemen, located by the eastern approach to the Red Sea (the Gulf of Aden), some 110 miles (170 kilometers) east of Bab-el-Mandeb. Its population is approximately a million people. Aden's ancient, natural harbor lies in the crater of a dormant volcano which now forms a peninsula, joined to the mainland by a low isthmus. This harbor, *Front Bay*, was first used by the ancient Kingdom of Awsan between the 5th and 7th centuries BCE. The modern harbor is on the other side of the peninsula.

Aden consists of a number of distinct sub-centers: Crater, the original port city; Ma'alla, the modern port; Tawahi, known as "Steamer Point" in the colonial period; and the resorts of Gold Mohur. Khormaksar, located on the isthmus that connects Aden proper with the mainland, includes the city's diplomatic missions, the main offices of Aden University, and Aden International Airport (the former British Royal Air Force station RAF Khormaksar), Yemen's second biggest airport. On the mainland are the sub-centers of Sheikh Othman, a former oasis area; Al-Mansura, a town planned by the British; and Madinat ash-Sha'b (formerly Madinat al-Itihad), the site designated as the capital of the South Arabian Federation and now home to a large power/desalinization facility and additional faculties of Aden University.

Aden encloses the eastern side of a vast, natural harbor that comprises the modern port. The volcanic peninsula of Little Aden forms a near-mirror image, enclosing the harbor and port on the western side. Little Aden became the site of the oil refinery and tanker port. Both were established and operated by British Petroleum until they were turned over to Yemeni government ownership and control in 1977.

Aden was the capital of the People's Democratic Republic of Yemen until that country's unification with the Yemen Arab Republic. On that occasion, the city was declared a free trade zone. Aden gives its name to the Gulf of Aden.

Bahrain is a small island country situated near the western shores of the Persian Gulf. It is an archipelago of 33 islands, the largest being Bahrain Island, at 55 km (34 mi) long by 18 km (11 mi) wide. Saudi Arabia lies to the west and is connected to Bahrain by the King Fahd Causeway. Iran lies 200 km (120 mi) to the north of Bahrain, across the Gulf. The peninsula of Qatar is to the southeast across the Gulf of Bahrain. The planned Qatar Bahrain Causeway will link Bahrain and Qatar and become the world's longest marine causeway. The population in 2010 stood at 1,234,571, including 666,172 non-nationals.

Bahrain is believed to be the site of the ancient land of the Dilmun civilization. Bahrain came under the rule of successive Persian empires, the Parthians and Sassanid's empires respectively. Bahrain was one of the earliest areas to convert to Islam in 628 AD. Following a successive period of Arab rule, the country was occupied by the Portuguese in 1521. The Portuguese were later expelled, in 1602, by Shah Abbas I of the Safavid Empire. In 1783, the Bani Utbah tribe captured Bahrain from the Persians and was ruled by the Al Khalifa royal family since, with Ahmed al Fateh being the first hakim of Bahrain. In the late 1800s, following successive treaties with the British, Bahrain became a protectorate of the United Kingdom. Following the withdrawal of the British from the region in the late 1960s, Bahrain declared independence in 1971. Formerly a state, Bahrain was declared a kingdom in 2002. Since early 2011, the country has experienced sustained protests and unrest inspired by the regional Arab Spring.

Bahrain today has a high Human Development Index (48nd highest in the world) and the World Bank identified it as a high income economy. Bahrain is a member of the United Nations, World Trade Organization, the Arab League, the Non-Aligned Movement, the Organization of the Islamic Conference as well as being a founding member of the Cooperation Council for the Arab States of the Gulf.[6] Bahrain was also designated as a major non-NATO ally by the George W. Bush administration in 2001.

Oil was discovered in Bahrain in 1932 (the first in the Arabian side of the Gulf). In recent decades, Bahrain has sought to diversify its economy and be less dependent on oil by investing in the banking sector and tourism.

The country's capital, Manama, is home to many large financial structures, including the Bahrain World Trade Center and the Bahrain Financial Harbor. The *Qal'at al-Bahrain* (the harbor and capital of the ancient land of Dilmun) and the Bahrain pearling trail were declared UNESCO World Heritage Sites in 2005 and 2012, respectively. The Bahrain Formula One Grand Prix takes place at the Bahrain International Circuit.

Bandar Abbas, Iran is a port city and capital of Hormozgān Province on the southern coast of Iran, on the Persian Gulf. The city occupies a strategic position on the narrow Straits of Hormuz, and it is the location of the main base of the Iranian Navy. Bandar Abbas is the capital and also largest city of the province Hormozgān. At the 2006 census, its population was 367,508, in 89,404 families.

Bandar Abbas has always been a port, and as such its various names have all addressed this function. The most common name over time (Gameroon) has traditionally been said to derive from Persian *gümrük*, customhouse (from Late Greek *kommerkion*, from Latin *commercium*, "commerce"), but is now speculated to be from Persian *kamrūn*, shrimp (which in Portuguese is *camarão*, similar to the former Portuguese name).

Barcelona, Spain is the capital of Catalonia and the second largest city in Spain, after Madrid, with a population of 1,620,943 within its administrative limits on a land area of 101.4 km² (39 sq mi). The urban area of Barcelona extends beyond the administrative city limits with a population of between 4.2 and 4.5 million within an area of 803 km² (310 sq mi), being the sixth-most populous urban area in the European Union after Paris, London, the Ruhr, Madrid and Milan. About five million people live in the Barcelona metropolitan area. It is also the largest metropolis on the Mediterranean Sea. It is located on the Mediterranean coast between the mouths of the rivers Llobregat and Besòs and is bounded to the west by the Serra de Collserola ridge (512 m/1,680 ft).

Founded as a Roman city, Barcelona became the capital of the County of Barcelona. After merging with the Kingdom of Aragon, Barcelona became the most important city of the Crown of Aragon. Besieged several times during its history, Barcelona has a rich cultural heritage and is today an important cultural center and a major tourist destination. Particularly renowned are the architectural works of Antoni Gaudí and Lluís Domènech i Montaner, which have been designated UNESCO World Heritage Sites. The headquarters of the Union for the Mediterranean is located in Barcelona. The city is known for hosting the 1992 Summer Olympics as well as world-class conferences and expositions and also many international sport tournaments.

Barcelona is today one of the world's leading tourist, economic, trade fair/exhibitions and cultural-sports centers, and its influence in commerce, education, entertainment, media, fashion, science, and the arts all contribute to its status as one of the world's major global cities. Indeed, it is a major cultural and economic center in southwestern Europe (Iberian Peninsula), 26th in the world (after Moscow, before Dubai) and a growing financial center (Diagonal Mar and Gran Via). It is the fourth economically powerful city by GDP in the European Union and 35th in the world with an output amounting to €177 billion. As of 2009 the city was ranked Europe's third and one of the world's most successful as a city brand. At the same time, the city was ranked Europe's fourth best city for business and fastest improving European city, with growth improved by 17% per year. Barcelona is the transport hub with one of Europe's principal ports, Barcelona international airport, which handles above 35 million passengers per year, extensive motorway network and also is a hub of high-speed rail, particularly that which is intended to link Spain with France and the rest of Europe as the second longest in the world.

Beirut, Lebanon is the capital and largest city of Lebanon. As there has been no recent population census, the exact population is unknown; estimates in 2007 ranged from slightly more than 1 million to slightly less than 2 million. Located on a peninsula at the midpoint of Lebanon's Mediterranean coast, it serves as the country's largest and main seaport. The Beirut metropolitan area consists of the city and its suburbs. The first mention of this metropolis is found in the ancient Egyptian Tell el Amarna letters, dating from the 15th century BC. The city has been inhabited continuously since then.

Beirut is Lebanon's seat of government and plays a central role in the Lebanese economy, with many banks and corporations based in its Central District, Hamra Street, Rue Verdun and Ashrafieh. The city is the focal point of the region's cultural life, renowned for its press, theatres, cultural activities and nightlife. After the destructive Lebanese Civil War, Beirut underwent major reconstruction, and the redesigned historic city center, marina, pubs and nightlife districts have once again made it a tourist attraction.

Identified and graded for accountancy, advertising, banking/finance and law, Beirut is ranked as a Beta World City by the Globalization and World Cities Research Network coming ahead of cities like Rio de Janeiro, Geneva, and Abu Dhabi.

Beirut was named the top place to visit by *The New York Times* in 2009, and as one of the ten liveliest cities in the world by Lonely Planet in the same year. According to a 2010 study by the American global consulting firm Mercer comparing high-end items such as upscale residential areas and entertainment venues, Beirut was ranked as the 4th most expensive city in the Middle East and 15th among the Upper Middle Income Countries included in the survey. Beirut came in first place regionally and 10th place internationally in a 2010 study by "EuroCost International" about the rental markets for high quality housing. 2011 MasterCard Index revealed that Beirut had the second-highest visitor spending levels in the Middle East and Africa, totaling $6.5 billion. Beirut was chosen in 2012 by Condé Nast Traveler as the best city in the Middle East, beating Tel Aviv and Dubai.

The Lebanese capital hosted the Mediterranean Games in 1959, FIBA Asia Champions Cup in 1999, 2000, 2012, the AFC Asian Cup in 2000, and the FIBA Asia Cup in 2010. Beirut was the host city for the 6th Annual Games of the Jeux de la Francophonie in 2009. Beirut also hosted the Pan Arab Games in 1957, 1997, and will do again in 2015.

Booth Bay, ME is a town in Lincoln County, Maine, United States. The population was 3,120 at the 2010 census. It includes the villages of East Boothbay and Trevett. The Boothbay region is a center of summer tourist activity, and a significant part of its population does not live there year round.

The first European presence was a British fishing station on Cape Newagen in 1623. By the 1630s, there were a few families. Henry Curtis purchased from the sachem Mowhotiwormet (commonly known as Chief Robinhood) the right to settle here in 1666. The inhabitants fled in 1676 during King Philip's War and returned in 1677. In 1689 during King William's War, they were driven out again, and the village remained a desolate waste for 40 years.

Colonel David Dunbar, governor of the Territory of Sagadahock, laid out a town in 1730 known as Townsend, and convinced about 40 families of Scots-Irish Presbyterians, largely from the north of Ireland, to settle here. Some were veterans of the Revolution of 1688. Named for Lord Charles Townshend, this settlement survived and was incorporated November 3, 1764. It was renamed Boothbay in 1842 after the hamlet of Boothby, which is located about a mile east of Welton le Marsh in Lincolnshire, England. Southport was set off in 1842 and incorporated as a town, followed in 1889 by Boothbay Harbor.

Boston, MA is the capital and largest city of the U.S. state of Massachusetts, officially the Commonwealth of Massachusetts; Boston also serves as county seat of the state's Suffolk County. The largest city in New England, the city proper, covering 48 square miles (125 square km), had an estimated population of 626,000 in 2011, making it the 21st largest city in the United

States. The city is the anchor of a substantially larger metropolitan area called Greater Boston, home to 4.5 million people and the tenth-largest metropolitan area in the country.[6] Greater Boston as a commuting region is home to 7.6 million people, making it the fifth-largest Combined Statistical Area in the United States.

One of the oldest cities in the United States, Boston was founded on the Shawmut Peninsula in 1630 by Puritan colonists from England. It was the scene of several key events of the American Revolution, such as the Boston Massacre, the Boston Tea Party, the Battle of Bunker Hill and the Siege of Boston. Through land reclamation and municipal annexation, Boston has expanded beyond the original peninsula. After the coming of American independence the city became an important port and manufacturing center, and a center of education and culture as well.[13] Its rich history helps attract many tourists, with Faneuil Hall alone attracting over 20 million visitors. Boston's many "firsts" include the United States' first public school (1635), and first subway system (1897).

The area's many colleges and universities make Boston an international center of higher education and medicine, leading many to dub the city "The Athens of America", and the city is considered to be a world leader in innovation for a variety of reasons. Boston's economic base also includes finance, professional and business services, and government activities. The city has one of the highest costs of living in the United States, though it remains high on world livability rankings.

Bremerhaven, Germany is a city at the seaport of the Free Hanseatic City of Bremen, a state of the Federal Republic of Germany. It forms an enclave in the state of Lower Saxony and is located at the mouth of the River Weser on its eastern bank, opposite the town of Nordenham. Though a relatively new city, it has a long history as a trade port and today is one of the most important German ports, playing a crucial role in Germany's trade.

The port of Bremerhaven is the sixteenth-largest container port in the world and the fourth-largest in Europe with 4.9 million twenty-foot equivalent units (TEU) of cargo handled in 2007. In addition, more than 1,350,000 cars are imported or exported every year via Bremerhaven. Bremerhaven imports and exports more cars than any other city in Europe except for Rotterdam, and this traffic is also growing. In 2011 a new panamax-sized lock has been opened, replacing the 1897 *Kaiserschleuse*, then the largest lock worldwide.

Brindisi, Italy is a city in the Apulia region of Italy, the capital of the province of Brindisi, off the coast of the Adriatic Sea. Historically, the city has played an important role in commerce and culture, due to its position on the Italian Peninsula and its natural port on the Adriatic Sea. The city is a major port for trade with Greece and the Middle East. Brindisi has an active industry in agriculture, chemical and energy production.

Brindisi is situated on a natural harbor that penetrates deeply into the Adriatic coast of Apulia. Within the arms of the outer harbor islands are Pedagne, a tiny archipelago, currently not open and in use for military purposes (United Nations Group Schools used during the intervention in Bosnia). The entire municipality is part of the Brindisi Plain, characterized by high agricultural uses of its land. It is located in the northeastern part of the Salento plains, about 40 km (24.85 mi) from the Itria Valley, and the low Murge. Not far from the city is the Natural Marine Reserve of the World Wide Fund for Nature of Torre Guaceto. The Ionian Sea is located about 45 km (27.96 mi) away.

Cannes, France is a city located in the French Riviera. It is a busy tourist destination and host of the annual Cannes Film Festival. It is a commune of France located in the Alpes-Maritimes department.

The city is also famous for its luxury shops, restaurants, and hotels. On 3 November 2011 it played host to the G20 organization of industrialized nations.

By the 2nd century BC the Ligurian Oxybii established a settlement here known as Aegitna. Historians are unsure what the name means. The area was a fishing village used as a port of call between the Lérins Islands.

In 69 AD it became the scene of violent conflict between the troops of Othos and Vitellius.

Shipmates - Cannes 1957

In the 10th century the town was known as Canua. The name may derive from "canna", a reed. Canua was probably the site of a small Ligurian port, and later a Roman outpost on Le Suquet hill, suggested by Roman tombs discovered here. Le Suquet housed an 11th-century tower which overlooked swamps where the city now stands. Most of the ancient activity, especially protection, was on the Lérins islands and the history of Cannes is the history of the islands.

An attack by the Saracens in 891, who remained until the end of the 10th century, devastated the country around Canua. The insecurity of the Lérins islands forced the monks to settle on the mainland, at the Suquet. Construction of a castle in 1035 fortified the city by then known as Cannes, and at the end of the 11th century construction was started on two towers on the Lérins islands. One took a century to build; the other, three.

Around 1530, Cannes detached from the monks who had controlled the city for hundreds of years and became independent.

During the 18th century, the Spanish and British both tried to gain control of the Lérins Islands, but were chased away by the French. The islands were later controlled by many, such as Jean-Honoré Alziary, and the Bishop of Fréjus. The islands had many different purposes; at the end of the 19th century, one was a hospital for soldiers in the Crimean War.

Henry Brougham, 1st Baron Brougham and Vaux bought land at the Croix des Gardes and constructed the villa Eleonore-Louise. His work to improve living conditions attracted the English aristocracy, who also built winter residences.

At the end of the 19th century, several railways were completed. This prompted the arrival of streetcars.

In Cannes, projects such as the Boulevard Carnot, the rue d'Antibes and the Carlton Hotel on the Promenade de la Croisette were carried out. After the closure of the Casino des Fleurs (hôtel Gallia), a luxury establishment was built for the rich winter clientele, the Casino Municipal next to the pier Albert-Edouard. This casino was demolished and replaced by the new Palace in 1979.

With the 20th century came new luxury hotels such as the Miramar and the Martinez. The city was modernized with a sports centre, street cars, a post office, and schools. There were fewer British and German tourists after the First World War but more Americans. Winter tourism gave way to summer tourism and the summer casino at the Palm Beach was constructed.

The city council had the idea of starting an international film festival shortly before World War II. The first opened on 20 September 1946, held in the Casino Municipal.

Cape Canaveral, Florida from the Spanish *Cabo Cañaveral*, is a headland in Brevard County, Florida, United States, near the center of the state's Atlantic coast. Known as Cape Kennedy from 1963 to 1973, it lies east of Merritt Island, separated from it by the Banana River.

It is part of a region known as the Space Coast, and is the site of the Cape Canaveral Air Force Station.

Since many U.S. spacecraft are launched from both the station and the Kennedy Space Center on Merritt Island, the terms "Cape Canaveral," "Canaveral", or "the Cape" have become metonyms that refer to both as the launch site of spacecraft. In homage to its spacefaring heritage, the Florida Public Service Commission allocated area code 321 to the Cape Canaveral area.

Other features of the cape include the Cape Canaveral lighthouse and Port Canaveral. The city of Cape Canaveral is a few miles south of the cape. Mosquito Lagoon, the Indian River, Merritt Island National Wildlife Refuge and Canaveral National Seashore are also features of this area.

During the middle archaic period, from 5000 BCE to 2000 BCE, the Mount Taylor period culture region covered northeast Florida, including the area around Cape Canaveral. Late in the archaic period, from 2000 BCE to 500 BCE, the Mount Taylor culture was succeeded by the Orange culture, which was among the earliest cultures in North America to produce pottery. The Orange culture was followed by the St. Johns culture, from 500 BCE until after European contact. The area around the Indian River was in the Indian River variant of the St. Johns culture, with influences from the Belle Glade culture to the south.

During the first Spanish colonial period the area around the Indian River, to the south of Cape Canaveral, was occupied by the Ais people, while the area around the

Mosquito Lagoon, to the north of the Cape, was occupied by the Surruque people. The Surruque were allied with the Ais, but it is not clear whether the Surruque spoke a Timucua language, or a language related to the Ais language.

In the early 16th century Cape Canaveral was noted on maps, although without being named. It was named by Spanish explorers in the first half of the 16th century as *Cabo Cañareal*. The name "Canaveral" (*Cañaveral* in Spanish, meaning "reed bed" or "sugarcane plantation") is the third oldest surviving European place name in the US. The first application of the name, according to the Smithsonian Institution, was from the 1521-1525 explorations of Spanish explorer Francisco Gordillo. A point of land jutting out into an area of the Atlantic Ocean with swift currents, it became a landing spot for many shipwrecked sailors. An early alternate name was "Cape of Currents." By at least 1564, the name appeared on maps.

English privateer John Hawkins and his journalist John Sparke gave an account of their landing at Cape Canaveral in the 16th century. A Presbyterian missionary was wrecked here and lived among the Indians. Other histories tell of French survivors from Jean Ribault's colony at Fort Caroline, whose ship the *Trinite* wrecked on the shores of Cape Canaveral in 1565, and who built a fort from its timbers.

The last naval battle of the American Revolutionary War was fought off the shores of Cape Canaveral in 1783, between the USS *Alliance* and the HMS *Sybill*, the American frigate being captained by Captain John Barry.

Because of the hazards of the cape from coral shoals to shipping, the first Cape Canaveral Lighthouse was built and completed in January 1848.

The 1890 graduating class of Harvard University started a gun club called the "Canaveral Club" at the Cape. This was founded by C.B. Horton of Boston and George H. Reed. A number of distinguished visitors including presidents Grover Cleveland and Benjamin Harrison were reported to have stayed here. In the 1920s the grand building fell in disrepair and later burned to the ground.

In the 20th century several communities sprang up in Cape Canaveral with names like Canaveral, Canaveral Harbor, and Artesia.

While the area was predominantly a farming and fishing community, some visionaries saw its potential as a resort for vacationers.

In the 1930s a group of wealthy journalists started a community called "Journalista" which is now called Avon by the Sea. The Brossier brothers built houses in this area and started a publication entitled the *Evening Star Reporter* that was the forerunner of the *Orlando Sentinel*.

The first rocket launch from the Cape was Bumper 8 from Launch Complex 3 on July 24, 1950. On February 6,

1959 the first successful test firing of a Titan intercontinental ballistic missile was accomplished. NASA's Project Mercury and Gemini space flights were launched from Cape Canaveral, as were all of the Apollo flights and Space Shuttles.

Cape Canaveral was chosen for rocket launches to take advantage of the Earth's rotation. The linear velocity of the Earth's surface is greatest towards the equator; the relatively southerly location of the cape allows rockets to take advantage of this by launching eastward, in the same direction as the Earth's rotation. It is also highly desirable to have the downrange area sparsely populated, in case of accidents; an ocean is ideal for this. The east coast of Florida has logistical advantages over potential competing sites. The Spaceport Florida Launch Complex 46 of the Cape Canaveral Air Force Station is at the tip of the cape.

Cardiff, Wales is the capital and largest city in Wales and the tenth largest city in the United Kingdom. The city is the country's chief commercial centre, the base for most national cultural and sporting institutions, the Welsh national media, and the seat of the National Assembly for Wales. The unitary authority area's mid 2011 population was estimated to be 346,100, while the population of the Larger Urban Zone was estimated at 861,400 in 2009. Cardiff is a significant tourist centre and the most popular visitor destination in Wales with 18.3 million visitors in 2010. In 2011, Cardiff was ranked sixth in the world in National Geographic's alternative tourist destinations.

The city of Cardiff is the county town of the historic county of Glamorgan (and later South Glamorgan). Cardiff is part of the Eurocities network of the largest European cities. The Cardiff Urban Area covers a slightly larger area outside of the county boundary, and includes the towns of Dinas Powys and Penarth. It was a small town until the early 19th century, its prominence as a major port for the transport of coal following the arrival of

industry in the region contributed to its rise as a major city.

Cardiff was made a city in 1905, and proclaimed the capital of Wales in 1955. Since the 1990s, Cardiff has seen significant development. A new waterfront area at Cardiff Bay contains the Senedd building, home to the Welsh Assembly and the Wales Millennium Centre arts complex. Current developments include the continuation of the redevelopment of the Cardiff Bay and city centre areas with projects such as the Cardiff International Sports Village, a BBC drama village, and a new business district in the city centre. Cardiff is the largest media centre in the UK outside of London.

Sporting venues in the city include the Millennium Stadium (the national stadium for the Wales national rugby union team and the Wales national football team), SWALEC Stadium (the home of Glamorgan County Cricket Club), Cardiff City Stadium (the home of Cardiff City football team), Cardiff International Sports Stadium (the home of Cardiff Amateur Athletic Club) and Cardiff Arms Park (the home of Cardiff Blues and Cardiff RFC rugby union teams). The city is also HQ of the Wales Rally GB and was awarded with the European City of Sport in 2009 due to its role in hosting major international sporting events. It has been announced that Cardiff will again be the European City of Sport in 2014. The Millennium Stadium hosted 11 football matches as part of the 2012

Summer Olympics, including the games' opening event and the men's bronze medal match.

Cartagena, Spain is a Spanish city and a major naval station located in the Region of Murcia, by the Mediterranean coast, south-eastern Spain. As of January 2011, it has a population of 218,210 inhabitants being the Region's second largest municipality and the country's 6th non-Province capital city.

Cartagena has been inhabited for over two millennia, being founded around 227 BC during the Phoenician conquest as **Qart Hadasht.** The city lived its heyday during the Roman Empire, when it was known as **Carthago Nova** (the New Carthage) and **Carthago Spartaria**, capital of the province of Carthaginensis. It was one of the important cities during the Umayyad invasion of Hispania, under its Arabic name of Qartayannat al-Halfa.

Much of the historical weight of Cartagena in the past goes to its coveted defensive port, one of the most important in the western Mediterranean. Cartagena has been the capital of the Spanish Navy's Maritime Department of the Mediterranean since the arrival of the Spanish Bourbons in the 18th century. As far back as the 16th century it was one of the most important naval ports in Spain, together with Ferrol in the North. It is still an important naval seaport, the main military haven of Spain, and is home to a large naval shipyard.

The confluence of civilizations as well as its strategic harbor, together the rise of the local mining industry is manifested by a unique artistic heritage, with a number of landmarks such as the Roman Theatre, the second largest of the Iberian Peninsula after the one from Mérida, an abundance of Phoenician, Roman, Byzantine and Moorish remains, and a plethora of Art Nouveau buildings, a result of the bourgeoisie from the early 20th century. Cartagena is now established as a major cruiser destination in the Mediterranean and an emerging cultural focus.

It is the first of a number of cities which eventually have been named Cartagena, most notably Cartagena de Indias (*Cartagena of the Indies*) in Colombia.

Catania, Sicily is an Italian city on the east coast of Sicily facing the Ionian Sea, between Messina and Syracuse. It is the capital of the homonymous province, and is the second-largest city in Sicily and the tenth in Italy.

Catania is known for its seismic history, having been destroyed by a catastrophic earthquake in 1169, another in 1693, and several volcanic eruptions from the neighboring Mount Etna volcano, the most violent of which was in 1669.

Catania has had a long and eventful history, having been founded in the 8th century BC. In the 14th century and the Renaissance, Catania was one of Italy's most important and flourishing cultural, artistic, and political centers, having witnessed the opening in 1434 of the first university in Sicily. Today, Catania is one of the main economic, touristic, and educational centers in the island, being an important hub of industry, thus gaining the nickname, "European Silicon Valley".

Catania is located on the east coast of the island, at the foot of the Mount Etna.

The position of Catania at the foot of Mount Etna was the source, as Strabo remarks, both of benefits and evils to the city. On the one hand, the violent outbursts of the volcano from time to time desolated great parts of its territory; on the other, the volcanic ashes produced fertile soil, adapted especially for the growth of vines.

Under the city runs the river, Amenano, visible in just one point, south of Piazza Duomo, and the river, Longane or Lognina.

Charleston, SC is the oldest and second-largest city in the southeastern U.S. state of South Carolina, the county seat of Charleston County, and principal city in the Charleston-North Charleston-Summerville Metropolitan

Statistical Area. The city lies just south of the geographical midpoint of South Carolina's coastline and is located on Charleston Harbor, an inlet of the Atlantic Ocean formed by the confluence of the Ashley and Cooper rivers.

Founded in 1670 as **Charles Towne** in honor of King Charles II of England, Charleston adopted its present name in 1783. It moved to its present location on Oyster Point in 1680 from a location on the west bank of the Ashley River known as Albemarle Point. By 1690, Charles Towne was the fifth largest city in North America and it remained among the ten largest cities in the United States through the 1840 census. With a 2010 census population of 120,080 (and a 2012 estimate of 124,632), current trends put Charleston as the fastest-growing municipality in South Carolina. The city's metropolitan area population was counted by the 2010 census at 664,607 – the second largest in the state – and the 75th-largest metropolitan statistical area in the United States.

Known for its rich history, well-preserved architecture, restaurant community and mannerly people, Charleston has received a large number of accolades; they include "America's Most Friendly [City]" by *Travel + Leisure* in 2011 and subsequently *Southern Living* magazine naming Charleston "the most polite and hospitable city in America".

Charleston's unique dialect has long been noted in the South and elsewhere for its singular attributes.

Alone among the various regional Southern accents, the Charleston accent traditionally has ingliding or monophthongal long mid-vowels, raises *ay* and *aw* in certain environments, and is non-rhotic (although non-rhoticity was definitely not unique to Charleston and some or all of the above features may not have been either). Some attribute these unique features of Charleston's speech to its early settlement by the French Huguenots and Sephardic Jews, both of which played influential parts in Charleston's development and history. However, given Charleston's high concentration of African-Americans that spoke the Gullah language, the speech patterns probably were more influenced by the dialect of the Gullah African-American community.

The "Charleston accent" can be particularly noted in the local pronunciation of the city's name itself. A Charleston native will typically ignore the *r*, elongate the middle vowel, and shorten the ending vowel, pronouncing the name as "Ch-\aw\lst-un."

Today, the Geechee language and dialect is still spoken among African-American locals. However, rapid development, especially on the surrounding sea islands, is slowly diminishing its prominence.

Two important works shed light on Charleston's early dialect: *Charleston Provincialisms* and *The Huguenot Element in Charleston's Provincialisms,* both by Sylvester Primer. Further scholarship is needed on possible influence of Sephardic Jews on Charleston speech patterns.

Charlotte Amalie, St. Thomas USVI is the capital and largest city of the U.S. Virgin Islands, founded in 1666 as **Taphus** (meaning "beer houses" or "beer halls). In 1691, the town was renamed to Amalienborg (in English *Charlotte Amalie*) after Charlotte Amalie of Hesse-Kassel

(1650-1714), queen consort to King Christian V of Denmark. It contains a deep-water harbor that was once a haven for pirates and is now one of the busiest ports of call for cruise ships in the Caribbean, with about 1.5 million cruise ship passengers landing there in 2004. Protected by Hassel Island, the harbor has docking and fueling facilities, machine shops, and shipyards and is also a U.S. submarine base. The town has been inhabited for centuries. When Christopher Columbus came here in 1493, the area was inhabited by both Carib- and Arawak Indians. It is located on the southern shore at the head of Saint Thomas Harbor. In 2010 the city had a population of 18,481, which makes it the largest city in the Virgin Islands Archipelago. Hundreds of ferries and yachts pass through town each week, and at times the population more than doubles.

The city is known for its Danish colonial architecture, building structure and history, and a dozen streets and places throughout the city have Danish names. Charlotte Amalie has buildings of historical importance including St. Thomas Synagogue, the second-oldest synagogue in the Western Hemisphere, and the oldest Lutheran church in the Western Hemisphere, the Frederick Lutheran Church. The town has a long history of pirates, especially stories of Bluebeard and Blackbeard (Edward Teach). In the 17th-century, the Danes built both Blackbeard's Castle and Bluebeard's Castle attributed to the pirates. Blackbeard's Castle is a U.S. National Historic Landmark and one of the most visited attractions in town. Another tourist attraction is Fort Christian, the oldest standing structure in the Virgin Islands Archipelago. A copy of the Liberty Bell is located in Emancipation Park, which is a tourist attraction.

Christiansted, US Virgin Islands is a town on Saint Croix, one of the main islands comprising the United States Virgin Islands, an unincorporated territory of the United States. It is a former capital of the Danish West Indies and home to the Christiansted National Historic Site. Christiansted as of 2004, has a population of about 3,000, the 2000 census population of the town was 2,637; that of the larger sub-district was 2,865. Christiansted has preserved the 18th-century Danish-style buildings constructed by African slaves. Solid stone buildings in pastel colors with bright red tile roofs line the cobblestone sidewalks, adding a touch of 18th century European architectural style. Because the town was constructed by African slaves, there are many African influences in Christiansted's design as well, making it one of the few "African-Danish" towns in the world. The town's symmetry, with streets running at right angles to the waterfront, makes it popular for walking tours. The commercial area centers on King and Company streets, adjacent to the Christiansted National Historic Site. The residential area, including portions that were originally settlements for free blacks, extends inland and uphill from the commercial area.

The town has several small hotels and many restaurants. Several scuba shops operate in the town, as the wharf has easy access to many diving attractions on the north side of the island.

The botanist Julius von Röhr started a botanic garden in Christiansted in the 18th century and produced a number of landscapes of the island.

Corfu, Greece is a Greek island in the Ionian Sea. It is the second largest of the Ionian Islands, and including its small satellite islands, forms the edge of the northwestern frontier of Greece. The island is part of the Corfu regional unit, and is administered as a single municipality. The municipality includes the island Corfu and the smaller islands Ereikoussa, Mathraki and Othonoi. The principal city of the island and seat of the municipality (pop. 32,095) is also named Corfu. Corfu is home to the Ionian University.

The island is bound with the history of Greece from the beginning of Greek mythology. Its Greek name, *Kerkyra* or *Korkyra*, is related to two powerful water symbols: Poseidon, god of the sea, and Asopos, an important Greek mainland river.[5] According to myth, Poseidon fell in love with the beautiful nymph Korkyra, daughter of Asopus and river nymph Metope, and abducted her. Poseidon brought Korkyra to the hitherto unnamed island and, in marital bliss, offered her name to the place: *Korkyra*, which gradually evolved to *Kerkyra* (Doric). Together, they had a child they called *Phaiax*, after whom the inhabitants of the island were named: *Phaiakes*. This term was transliterated via Latin to Phaeacians.

The island's history is laden with battles and conquests. The legacy of these struggles is visible in the form of castles punctuating strategic locations across the island. Two of these castles enclose its capital, which is the only city in Greece to be surrounded in such a way. As a result, Corfu's capital has been officially declared a *Kastropolis* ("castle city") by the Greek government. Corfu was long controlled by Venice, which repulsed several Turkish sieges, before falling under British rule following the Napoleonic Wars. Corfu was eventually ceded by the British Empire along with the remaining islands of the United States of the Ionian Islands, and unification with modern Greece was concluded in 1864 under the Treaty of London.

In 2007, the city's old city was designated for the UNESCO World Heritage List, following a recommendation by ICOMOS.

Corfu is a very popular tourist destination. Up until the early 20th century, it was mainly visited by the European royals and elites, including Emperor Wilhelm II of Germany and Empress Elisabeth of Austria; today it is also widely visited by middle class families (primarily from the UK, Scandinavia and Germany), leading to mass tourism. It is still popular with the global elite however, and in the island's northeast the homeowners include members of the Rothschild family and Russian oligarchs.

Da Nang, RVN is one of the major port cities in Vietnam (in addition to Ho Chi Minh city and Hai Phong) and the biggest city on the South Central Coast of Vietnam; the city is situated on the coast of the South China Sea, at the mouth of the Hàn River. Đà Nẵng is the commercial and educational center of Central Vietnam, with a well-sheltered, easily accessible port; its location on the path of National Route 1A and the North-South Railway makes it a hub for transportation. It is located within 100 km of several UNESCO World Heritage Sites, including the Imperial City of Huế, the Old Town of Hội An, and the Mỹ Sơn ruins. The city was previously known as **Cửa Hàn** during early Đại Việt settlement, and as **Tourane** (or **Turon**) during French colonial rule. It is the fourth biggest economic center in Vietnam (after Ho Chi Minh City, Ha Noi, and Hai Phong).

Before 1997, the city was part of Quảng Nam-Đà Nẵng Province. On 1 January 1997, Đà Nẵng was separated from Quảng Nam province to become one of five independent (centrally controlled) municipalities in Vietnam. Đà Nẵng is listed as a first class city, and has a higher urbanization ratio than any of Vietnam's other provinces or centrally governed cities. In terms of urban population, Đà Nẵng is the 4th largest city in Vietnam.

Djibouti officially the **Republic of Djibouti**, is a country located in the Horn of Africa. It is bordered by

Eritrea in the north, Ethiopia in the west and south, and Somalia in the southeast. The remainder of the border is formed by the Red Sea and the Gulf of Aden at the east. Djibouti occupies a total area of just 23,200 km^2 (8,958 sq mi).

In antiquity, the territory was part of the Land of Punt. The Djibouti area, along with other localities in the Horn region, was later the seat of the medieval Adal and Ifat Sultanates. In the late 19th century, the colony of French Somaliland was established following treaties signed by the ruling Somali and Afar Sultans with the French. It was subsequently renamed to the French Territory of the Afars and the Issas in 1967. A decade later, the Djiboutian people voted for independence. This officially marked the establishment of the *Republic of Djibouti*, named after its capital city. Djibouti joined the United Nations the same year, on September 20, 1977. In the early 1990s, tensions over government representation led to armed conflict, which ended in a power sharing agreement in 2000 between the ruling party and the opposition.

Djibouti is a multi-ethnic nation, with a population of over 790,000 inhabitants. The Somali and Afar make up the two largest ethnic groups. Both speak Afro-Asiatic languages, which serve as recognized national languages. Arabic and French constitute the country's two official languages. About 94% of residents adhere to Islam, a religion with a long-standing presence in the region.

Djibouti is strategically located near the world's busiest shipping lanes, controlling access to the Red Sea and Indian Ocean. It serves as a key refueling and transshipment center, and is the principal maritime port for imports to and exports from neighboring Ethiopia. A burgeoning commercial hub, the nation is the site of various foreign military bases, including Camp Lemonnier. The Intergovernmental Authority on Development regional body also has its headquarters in Djibouti City.

Together with northern Somalia, Eritrea and the Red Sea coast of Sudan, Djibouti is considered the most likely location of the land known to the ancient Egyptians as *Punt* (or "Ta Netjeru", meaning "God's Land"), whose first mention dates to the 25th century BC. The Puntites were a nation of people that had close relations with Ancient Egypt during the times of Pharaoh Sahure and Queen Hatshepsut. According to the temple reliefs at Deir el-Bahari, the Land of Punt was ruled at that time by King Parahu and Queen Ati.

Through close contacts with the adjacent Arabian Peninsula for more than 1,000 years, the Somali and Afar ethnic groups in the region became among the first populations on the continent to embrace Islam.

Dundee, Scotland officially the **City of Dundee** is the fourth-largest city in Scotland and the 38th most populous settlement in the United Kingdom. It lies within the eastern central Lowlands on the north bank of the Firth of Tay, which feeds into the North Sea. Under the name of *Dundee City*, it forms one of the 32 council areas used for local government in Scotland.

The town developed into a burgh in medieval times, and expanded rapidly in the 19th century largely due to the jute industry. This, along with its other major industries gave Dundee its epithet as the city of "jute, jam and journalism".

In mid-2012, the population of the City of Dundee was estimated to be 156,561. Dundee's recorded population reached a peak of 182,204 at the time of the 1971 census, but has since declined.

Today, Dundee is promoted as 'One City, Many Discoveries' in honor of Dundee's history of scientific activities and of the RRS *Discovery*, Robert Falcon Scott's Antarctic exploration vessel, which was built in Dundee and is now berthed in the city harbor. Biomedical and technological industries have arrived since the 1980s, and the city now accounts for 10% of the United Kingdom's digital-entertainment industry. Dundee has two universities—the University of Dundee and the University of Abertay Dundee. A £1,000,000,000 master plan to regenerate and to reconnect the Waterfront to the city centre which started in 2001 is expected to be completed within a 30 year period, with the Dundee Victoria & Albert Museum opening by 2015, at a cost of £45 million.

Dundee is also known for the Dandy, the Beano, Desperate Dan, Oor Wullie, and was said to be built on the 'three Js': jam, jute, and journalism. There is a new Victoria and Albert Museum to be built on waterfront near the Tay Bridge on a plot vacated by the soon-to-be-replaced public swimming baths. Visitors wishing to orient themselves should consider taking a walk (or drive) up the Law, Dundee which offers a 360 degree uninterrupted view of Dundee, the Tay estuary and the two Tay Bridges.

Earle, New Jersey Naval Weapons Station is a United States Navy base in New Jersey. Its distinguishing feature is a 2.9-mile pier in Sandy Hook Bay where ammunition can be loaded and unloaded from warships at a safe distance from heavily-populated areas.

The Station is divided into two sections: Mainside, located in parts of Colts Neck Township, Howell Township, Wall Township, and Tinton Falls at 40°15'00"N 74°09'00"W40.25000°N 74.15000°W; and the Waterfront Area (which includes the pier complex), on Sandy Hook Bay, located in the Leonardo section of Middletown Township, at 40°24'30"N 74°04'30"W40.40833°N 74.07500°W. The areas are connected by **Normandy Road**, a 15-mile (24 km) military road and rail line.

World War II operations demanded an ammunition depot near the greater New York metropolitan area but away from high-population sectors. Planning was hastened in early 1943 after the ammunition ship *SS El Estero* caught fire while moored in Bayonne, New Jersey. If the stowed and dockside explosives had detonated at once, in the manner of the great Halifax Explosion, the blast could have damaged parts of Bayonne and even Lower Manhattan. A board was established to locate a suitable site, and chose Sandy Hook Bay, which featured a safe, sheltered, and nearby port where ships could take on ammunition. Rail lines could bring in the ammunition from the west, where the majority of ammunition shipments originated. The rural area meant few local residents would be affected.

On August 2, 1943, construction began on Naval Ammunition Depot Earle, named after Rear Admiral Ralph Earle, the Chief of the Bureau of Ordnance during World War I. The depot was commissioned on December 13, 1943, though work continued on the military road and railway connecting the mainside complex, the waterfront complex and the pier, which stretches 2.9 miles (4.7 km) into the Sandy Hook Bay and comprises 2.9 miles (4.7 km) of pier / trestle surface area.

Earle continued to develop after World War II, keeping pace with the changing needs of the Navy. In 1974, the depot's name was changed to Naval Weapons Station Earle.

School-aged children of active military personnel at Naval Weapons Station Earle in grades K through 8 attend the schools of the Tinton Falls School District. Students in grades 9 through 12 attend Monmouth Regional High School in Tinton Falls, part of the Monmouth Regional High School District.

Genoa, Italy is the capital of Liguria and the sixth largest city in Italy, with a population of 608,676 within its administrative limits on a land area of 243.6 km^2 (94 sq mi). The urban zone of Genoa extends beyond the administrative city limits with a population of 718,896. The urban area of Genoa has a population of 800,709. In the metropolitan area live over 1.5 million people. Genoa is one of Europe's largest cities on the Mediterranean Sea and the largest seaport in Italy.

Genoa has been nicknamed *la Superba* ("the Superb one") due to its glorious past and impressive landmarks. Part of the old town of Genoa was inscribed on the World Heritage List (UNESCO) in 2006 (see below). The city's rich art, music, gastronomy, architecture and history, allowed it to become the 2004 European Capital of Culture. It is the birthplace of Christopher Columbus.

Genoa, which forms the southern corner of the Milan-Turin-Genoa industrial triangle of north-west Italy, is one of the country's major economic centers. The city has hosted massive shipyards and steelworks since the 19th century, and its solid financial sector dates back to the Middle Ages. The Bank of Saint George, founded in 1407, is among the oldest in the world and plays an important role in the city's prosperity since the middle of the 15th century. Today a number of leading Italian companies are based in the city, including Fincantieri, Ansaldo Energia, Ansaldo STS and Edoardo Raffinerie Garrone.

Gaeta, Italy is a city and *commune* in the province of Latina, in Lazio, central Italy. Set on a promontory stretching towards the Gulf of Gaeta, it is 120 km from Rome and 80 km from Naples.

The town has played a conspicuous part in military history: its fortifications date back to Roman times, and it has several traces of the period, including the 1st-century mausoleum of the Roman general Lucius Munatius Plancus at the top of the Monte Orlando.

Gaeta's fortifications were extended and strengthened in the 15th century, especially throughout the history of the Kingdom of Naples (later the Two Sicilies). Present day Gaeta is a fishing and oil seaport, and a renowned tourist resort. NATO maintains a Naval base of operations at Gaeta.

It is the ancient **Caieta**, situated on the slopes of the Torre di Orlando, a promontory overlooking the Mediterranean Sea. Gaeta was an ancient Ionian colony of the Samians according to Strabo, who believed the name stemmed from the Greek *kaiétas*, which means "cave", probably referring to the several harbors. According to

Virgil's *Aeneid* (vii.1-9), *Caieta* was Aeneas' (another legend says Ascanius') wet-nurse, whom he buried here.

In the classical age *Caieta*, famous for its lovely and temperate climate, like the neighboring Formia and Sperlonga, was a tourist resort and site of the seaside villas of many important and rich characters of Rome. Like the other Roman resorts, Caieta was linked to the capital of the Empire by Via Appia and its end trunk Via Flacca (or Valeria), through an opposite *diverticulum* or bye-road. Its port was of great importance in trade and in war, and was restored under Emperor Antoninus Pius. Among its antiquities is the mausoleum of Lucius Munatius Plancus.

Gibraltar is a British Overseas Territory located on the southern end of the Iberian Peninsula at the entrance of the Mediterranean. It has an area of 6.8 square kilometres (2.6 sq mi) and a northern border with Andalusia, Spain. The Rock of Gibraltar is the only landmark of the region. At its foot is the densely populated city area, home to almost 30,000 Gibraltarians and other nationalities.

An Anglo-Dutch force captured Gibraltar from the Kingdom of Castile in 1704 during the War of the Spanish Succession on behalf of the Habsburg pretender to the Spanish throne. The territory was subsequently ceded to Britain "in perpetuity" under the Treaty of Utrecht in 1713. It was an important base for the Royal Navy; today its economy is based largely on tourism, online gaming, financial services, and shipping.

The sovereignty of Gibraltar is a major point of contention in Anglo-Spanish relations as Spain asserts a claim to the territory.

Gibraltarians rejected proposals for Spanish sovereignty in a 1967 referendum and again in 2002. Under the Gibraltar constitution of 2006, Gibraltar governs its own affairs, though some powers, such as defense and foreign relations, remain the responsibility of the UK Government.

The name *Gibraltar* is the Spanish derivation of the Arabic name *Jabal-ı Tārıq*, meaning "mountain of Tariq." It refers to the geological formation, the Rock of Gibraltar, which in turn was named after the Umayyad general Tariq ibn-Ziyad who led the initial incursion into Iberia in advance of the main Umayyad force in 711 under the command of Umayyad Caliph Al-Walid I. Earlier, it was known as *Mons Calpe*, one of the Pillars of Hercules.

Golfe Juan, France is a seaside resort on France's Côte d'Azur. The distinct local character of Golfe-Juan is indicated by the existence of a demonym, "Golfe-Juanais," which is applied to its inhabitants.

Golfe-Juan belongs to the commune of Vallauris in the Grasse arrondissement of the Alpes-Maritimes department, which belongs in turn to the Provence-Alpes-

Côte d'Azur region of France. The area is served by the *Golfe Juan-Vallauris* railway station.

On March 1, 1815, Napoléon Bonaparte landed at Golfe-Juan with 600 men, having escaped exile on the island of Elba. His return to Paris, commemorated by the Route Napoléon, and the campaign that led to his ultimate defeat at the Battle of Waterloo are known as the "Hundred Days".

"Golfe Juan" is also the name of a pointillist painting done by Paul Signac, a French neo-impressionist, in 1896.

Guam is an organized, unincorporated territory of the United States in the western Pacific Ocean. It is one of five U.S. territories with an established civilian government. Guam is listed as one of sixteen Non-Self-Governing Territories by the Special Committee on Decolonization of the United Nations. The island's capital is Hagåtña (formerly Agaña). Guam is the largest and southernmost of the Mariana Islands.

The Chamorros, Guam's indigenous people, first populated the island approximately 4,000 years ago. The island has a long history of European colonialism, beginning with its discovery by Ferdinand Magellan during a Spanish expedition on March 6, 1521. The first colony was established in 1668 by Spain with the arrival of settlers including Padre San Vitores, a Catholic missionary. For more than two centuries Guam was an important stopover for the Spanish Manila Galleons that crossed the Pacific annually. The island was controlled by Spain until 1898, when it was surrendered to the United States during the Spanish-American War and later formally ceded as part of the Treaty of Paris.

As the largest island in Micronesia and the only U.S.-held island in the region before World War II, Guam was captured by the Japanese on December 8, 1941, just hours after the bombing of Pearl Harbor, and was occupied for two and a half years.

During the occupation, the people of Guam were subjected to acts that included torture, beheadings and rape, and were forced to adopt the Japanese culture. Guam was subject to fierce fighting when U.S. troops recaptured the island on July 21, 1944, a date commemorated every year as Liberation Day.

Today, Guam's economy is supported by its principal industry, tourism, which is composed primarily of visitors from Japan. Guam's second largest source of income is the United States military.

Guam was first discovered by people from southeastern Indonesia around 2000 BC. Most of what is known about pre-contact ("Ancient") Chamorros comes from legends and myths, archaeological evidence, Jesuit missionary accounts, and observations from visiting scientists like Otto von Kotzebue and Louis de Freycinet.

Guantanamo Bay, Cuba is a bay located in Guantánamo Province at the southeastern end of Cuba. It is the largest harbor on the south side of the island and it is surrounded by steep hills which create an enclave that is cut off from its immediate hinterland.

The United States assumed territorial control over the southern portion of Guantánamo Bay under the 1903 Cuban-American Treaty. The United States has complete jurisdiction and control over this territory, while Cuba retains ultimate sovereignty. The current government of Cuba regards the U.S. presence in Guantánamo Bay as illegal and insists the Cuban-American Treaty was obtained by threat of force in violation of international law. Some legal scholars judge that the lease may be voidable. It is the home of the Guantanamo Bay detention camp, which is governed by the United States.

The bay was called Guantánamo by its original inhabitants, the Taínos. Christopher Columbus landed in 1494, naming it *Puerto Grande*. On landing, Columbus' crew found Taíno fishermen preparing a feast for the local chieftain. When Spanish settlers took control of Cuba, the bay became a vital harbor on the south side of the island.

The bay was briefly known as Cumberland Bay when the British seized it in 1741, during the War of Jenkins' Ear. British Admiral Edward Vernon arrived with a force of eight warships and 4,000 soldiers with plans to march on Santiago de Cuba. However, he was defeated by local guerrilla forces of Creole and Spaniards and forced to withdraw or face becoming a prisoner. In late 1760, boats from HMS *Trent* and HMS *Boreas* cut-out the French privateers *Vainquer* and *Mackau*, which were hiding in the bay. The French were also forced to burn the *Guespe*, another privateer, to prevent her capture.

During the Spanish-American War, the U.S. Navy fleet attacking Santiago needed shelter from the summer hurricane season. They chose Guantánamo because of its excellent harbor. U.S. Marines landed with naval support in the 1898 invasion of Guantánamo Bay. As they moved inland, however, Spanish resistance increased and the Marines required support from Cuban scouts.

The Guantanamo Bay Naval Base surrounds the southern portion of the bay. Since 2002, the base has included the detainment camp for people of risk to US national security. In 2009, U.S. President Barack Obama gave orders for the detention camp to be closed by January 22, 2010. As of present day, the detention camp remains open.

The naval base, nicknamed "GTMO" or "Gitmo", covers 116 km² (about 45 square miles) on the western and eastern banks of the bay. It was established in 1898, when the United States took control of Cuba from Spain following the Spanish-American War. A perpetual lease for the area around Guantánamo Bay was offered February 23, 1903, from Tomás Estrada Palma, the first President of Cuba. The newly formed American protectorate incorporated the Platt Amendment in the Cuban Constitution. The Cuban-American Treaty held, among other things, that the United States, for the purposes of operating coaling and naval stations, has "complete jurisdiction and control" of the Guantánamo Bay, while the Republic of Cuba is recognized to retain ultimate sovereignty.

Halifax, Nova Scotia is the capital of the province of Nova Scotia, Canada. The Regional Municipality had a population of 390,096 in 2011 Canadian Census and the urban area had a population of 297,943. Halifax is the largest population centre in Atlantic Canada and largest in Canada east of Quebec City. Halifax was ranked by *MoneySense* magazine as the fourth best place to live in Canada for 2012, placed first on a list of "large cities by quality of life" and placed second in a list of "large cities of the future", both conducted by *fDi Magazine* for North and South American cities.

Halifax is a major economic centre in eastern Canada with a large concentration of government services and private sector companies. Major employers and economic generators include the Department of National Defense, various levels of government, and the Port of Halifax. Agriculture, fishing, mining, forestry and natural gas extraction are major resource industries found in the rural areas of HRM.

The area comprising present day Halifax County was settled for thousands of years by the Mi'kmaq. Those who settled on Halifax Harbor called it Jipugtug (anglicised as "Chebucto"), meaning Great Harbor. The first permanent European settlement in the HRM was on the Halifax Peninsula. The establishment of the *Town of Halifax* named after the British Earl of Halifax, in 1749 led to the colonial capital being transferred from Annapolis Royal.

The establishment of Halifax marked the beginning of Father Le Loutre's War. The war began when Edward Cornwallis arrived to establish **Halifax** with 13 transports and a sloop of war on June 21, 1749. By unilaterally establishing Halifax the British were violating earlier treaties with the Mi'kmaq (1726), which was signed after Father Rale's War. Cornwallis brought along 1,176 settlers and their families. To guard against Mi'kmaq, Acadian, and French attacks on the new Protestant settlements, British fortifications were erected in Halifax (Citadel Hill)(1749), Bedford (Fort Sackville) (1749), Dartmouth (1750), and Lawrencetown (1754), all areas within the HRM. St. Margaret's Bay first got settled by French-speaking Foreign Protestants at French Village, Nova Scotia who migrated from Lunenburg, Nova Scotia during the American Revolution.

HMS (His Majesty's Station) Juffair, Manama, Bahrain is a suburban neighborhood of Manama, Bahrain. It was originally a separate village inhabited by Bahrani Shia Muslims but it has been absorbed by the suburban expansion of Manama, and also includes large parts of land reclaimed from the sea.

It is now home to many hotels, restaurants, flats, and villas.[2] In fact, Juffair is built on a massive land reclamation scheme which has extended Bahrain's coastline by two kilometers to the east.

The area is the site of frenetic building activity, with new apartment buildings and hotels constructed each year. Most of those who live in the area are established foreigners or upwardly mobile young Bahrainis. It is also the site of Bahrain's largest mosque, the huge domed Al Fateh Mosque, which houses the new National Library. All Bahraini road calculations are made from the Grand Mosque — Zero Point.

A British naval installation known as HMS Juffair was established near old Juffair village on April 13, 1935 in the area where ASU-SWA is located today. In 1950, the United States Navy leased office space aboard HMS JUFFAIR from the British. In 1971, after their treaty expired, the British left Bahrain, granting the island total independence. The United States, through agreement with the Bahraini government, took over part of HMS JUFFAIR, renaming it Administrative Support Unit Bahrain, subsequently Naval Support Activity Bahrain.

The offices of the *Ministry of Islamic Affairs*, *Central Informatics Organization*, *Bahrain Society of Engineers*, and the *Bahrain Tribune* newspaper are all located in Juffair. The Bahrain School and Modern Knowledge School are both also located in Juffair.

There is a new commercial road in Juffair (Al Shabab Road) that houses many restaurants and retail outlets, such as McDonalds, Chilli's, Nando's, Asian Zyng, Dairy Queen, Hardee's, Starbucks, Abraj Grills, and Burger King etc. The road also has Juffair's only pharmacy, "Juffair Pharmacy". Near the entrance of Juffair, there is a building called Murjan Shopping Center that has a large supermarket, a restaurant, Post Office, and Coffee Bean and Tea Leaf coffee shop.

The American Naval Support Center is located in the Corner of Juffair.

Hong Kong is a Special Administrative Region of the People's Republic of China. It is situated on China's south coast and, enclosed by the Pearl River Delta and South China Sea; it is known for its expansive skyline and deep natural harbor. With a land mass of 1,104 km^2 (426 sq mi) and a population of seven million people, Hong Kong is one of the most densely populated areas in the world. Hong Kong's population is 95 percent ethnic Chinese and 5 percent from other groups. Hong Kong's Han Chinese majority originate mainly from the cities of Guangzhou and Taishan in the neighboring Guangdong province.

Hong Kong became a colony of the British Empire after the First Opium War (1839-42). Originally confined to Hong Kong Island, the colony's boundaries were extended in stages to the Kowloon Peninsula in 1860 and then the New Territories in 1898. It was occupied by Japan during the Pacific War, after which the British resumed control until 1997, when China resumed sovereignty. The region espoused minimum government intervention under the ethos of positive non-interventionism during the colonial era. The time period greatly influenced the current culture of Hong Kong, often described as "East meets West", and the educational system, which used to loosely follow the system in England until reforms implemented in 2009.

Under the principle of "one country, two systems", Hong Kong has a different political system from mainland China. Hong Kong's independent judiciary functions under the common law framework. Hong Kong Basic Law, its constitutional document, which stipulates that Hong Kong shall have a "high degree of autonomy" in all matters except foreign relations and military defense, governs its political system. Although it has a burgeoning multi-party system, a small-circle electorate controls half of its legislature. That is, the Chief Executive of Hong Kong, the head of government, is chosen by an Election Committee of 400 to 1,200 members, a situation that will be in effect during the first 20 years of Chinese rule.

As one of the world's leading international financial centers, Hong Kong has a major capitalist service economy characterized by low taxation and free trade, and the currency, Hong Kong dollar, is the eighth most traded currency in the world. The lack of space caused demand for denser constructions, which developed the city to a centre for modern architecture and the world's most vertical city. Hong Kong has one of the highest per capita incomes in the world. The dense space also led to a highly developed transportation network with public transport travelling rate exceeding 90 percent, the highest in the world. Hong Kong has numerous high international rankings in various aspects. For instance, its economic freedom, financial and economic competitiveness, quality of life, corruption perception, Human Development Index, etc., are all ranked highly. According to estimates from both UN and WHO, Hong Kong has the longest life expectancy of any country/special administrative region in the world in 2012, surpassing Japan.

Izmir, Turkey is a large metropolis in the western extremity of Anatolia and the third most populous city in Turkey. Izmir's metropolitan area extends along the outlying waters of the Gulf of İzmir and inland to the north across Gediz River's delta, to the east along an alluvial plain created by several small streams and to a slightly more rugged terrain in the south. The ancient city was known as Smyrna, and the city was generally referred to as **Smyrna** in English, until the Turkish

Postal Services Law of 1930 made "Izmir" the internationally recognized name.

The city of Izmir is composed of several metropolitan districts. Of these, Konak district corresponds to historical Izmir, this district's area having constituted the "Izmir Municipality" (Turkish: *İzmir Belediyesi*) area until 1984, Konak until then having been a name for a central neighborhood around Konak Square, still the core of the city. With the constitution of the "Greater Izmir Metropolitan Municipality" (Turkish: *İzmir Büyükşehir Belediyesi*), the city of Izmir became a compound bringing together initially nine, and more recently eleven metropolitan districts, namely Balçova, Bayraklı, Bornova, Buca, Çiğli, Gaziemir, Güzelbahçe, Karabağlar, Karşıyaka, Konak and Narlıdere. Almost all of these settlements are former district centers or neighborhoods which stood on their own, with their own distinct features and temperament. In an ongoing processes, the Mayor of Izmir was also vested with authority over the areas of additional districts reaching from Aliağa in the north to Selçuk in the south, bringing the number of districts to be considered as being part of Izmir to twenty-one under the new arrangements, two of these having been administratively included in Izmir only partially.

According to the Turkish Statistical Institute, as of 2011 the city of Izmir had a population of 2,783,866 and its metropolitan municipality 3,366,947.

İzmir has almost 3,500 years of recorded urban history (see Timeline of İzmir) and possibly even longer as an advanced human settlement. Lying on an advantageous location at the head of a gulf running down in a deep indentation midway on the western Anatolian coast, the city has been one of the principal mercantile cities of the Mediterranean Sea for much of its history. Its port is Turkey's primary port for exports in terms of the freight handled and its free zone, a Turkish-U.S. joint-venture established in 1990, is the leader among the twenty in Turkey. Its workforce, and particularly its rising class of young professionals, concentrated either in the city or in its immediate vicinity (such as in Manisa and Turgutlu), and under either larger companies or SMEs, affirm their name in an increasingly wider global scale and intensity. İzmir is widely regarded as one of the most progressive Turkish cities in terms of its values, lifestyle, dynamism and gender roles. Politically, it is considered a stronghold of the Republican People's Party.

Iraklion, Crete (also known as Heraklion or Heraclion) is the largest city and the administrative capital of the island of Crete, Greece. It is the 4th largest city in Greece.

Iraklion is the capital of Heraklion regional unit. The ruins of Knossos, which were excavated and restored by Arthur Evans, are nearby. The Heraklion is named after Nikos Kazantzakis.

The Arab raiders from Andalusia who founded the Emirate of Crete moved the island's capital from Gortyna to a new castle they called *rabḍ al-ḫandaq* 'Castle of the Moat' in the 820s. This was hellenized as Χάνδαξ (*Handax*) or Χάνδακας and Latinized as **Candia**, which was taken into other European languages: in Italian as Candia (used under the Venetian rule), in French as *Candie*, in English as *Candy*, all of which could refer to all of Crete as well as to the city itself; the Ottoman name was *Kandiye*.

After the Byzantine reconquest, the city was locally known as Megalo Kastro or Castro (the Big Castle in Greek) and its inhabitants were called Kastrinoi or Castrini (Castle-dwellers in Greek).

The ancient name Ηράκλειον was revived in the 19th century and comes from the nearby Roman port of Heracleum ("Heracles' city"), whose exact location is unknown. English usage formerly preferred the classicizing transliterations "Heraklion" or "Heraclion", but the form "Iraklion" is becoming more common.

Iran officially the **Islamic Republic of Iran**, is a country in Western Asia. The name "Iran", which in Persian means "Land of the Aryans", has been in native use since the Sassanian era, in antiquity. It came into use internationally in 1935, before which the country was known to the Western world as **Persia**. Both "Persia" and

"Iran" are used interchangeably in cultural contexts; however, "Iran" is the name used officially in political contexts.

The 18th-largest country in the world in terms of area at 1,648,195 km^2 (636,372 sq mi), Iran has a population of around 75 million. It is a country of particular geopolitical significance owing to its location in three spheres of Asia (West, Central, and South). Iran is bordered on the north by Armenia, Azerbaijan and Turkmenistan. As Iran is a littoral state of the Caspian Sea, which is an inland sea, Kazakhstan and Russia are also Iran's direct neighbors to the north. Iran is bordered on the east by Afghanistan and Pakistan, on the south by the Persian Gulf and the Gulf of Oman, on the west by Iraq and on the northwest by Turkey. Tehran is the capital, the country's largest city and the political, cultural, commercial and industrial center of the nation. Iran is a regional power, and holds an important position in international energy security and world economy as a result of its large reserves of petroleum and natural gas. Iran has the second largest proven natural gas reserves in the world and the fourth largest proven petroleum reserves.

Iran is home to one of the world's oldest civilizations. The first dynasty in Iran formed during the Elamite kingdom in 2800 BC. The Iranian Medes unified Iran into an empire in 625 BC. They were succeeded by the Iranian Achaemenid Empire, the Hellenic Seleucid Empire and two subsequent Iranian empires, the Parthians and the Sassanids, before the Muslim conquest in 651 AD. Iranian post-Islamic dynasties and empires expanded the Persian language and culture throughout the Iranian plateau. Early Iranian dynasties which re-asserted Iranian independence included the Tahirids, Saffarids, Samanids and Buyids.

The blossoming of Persian literature, philosophy, medicine, astronomy, mathematics and art became major elements of Muslim civilization. Iranian identity continued despite foreign rule in the ensuing centuries and Persian culture was adopted also by the Ghaznavid, Seljuk, Ilkhanid and Timurid rulers. The emergence in 1501 of the Safavid dynasty, which promoted Twelver Shia Islam as the official religion of their empire, marked one of the most important turning points in Iranian and Muslim history. The Persian Constitutional Revolution established the nation's first parliament in 1906, within a constitutional monarchy. Following a coup d'état instigated by the UK and US in 1953, Iran gradually became a more autocratic country. Growing dissent with foreign influence culminated during the Iranian Revolution which led to establishment of an Islamic republic on 1 April 1979.

Iran is a founding member of the UN, NAM, OIC and OPEC. The political system of Iran, based on the 1979 constitution, comprises several intricately connected governing bodies. The highest state authority is the

Supreme Leader. Shia Islam is the official religion and Persian is the official language.

Istanbul, Turkey is the largest city in Turkey, constituting the country's economic, cultural, and historical heart. With a population of 13.9 million, the city forms one of the largest urban agglomerations in Europe and is among the largest cities in the world by population within city limits. Istanbul's vast area of 5,343 square kilometers (2,063 sq mi) is coterminous with Istanbul Province, of which the city is the administrative capital. Istanbul is a transcontinental city, straddling the Bosphorus—one of the world's busiest waterways—in northwestern Turkey, between the Sea of Marmara and the Black Sea. Its commercial and historical center lies in Europe, while a third of its population lives in Asia.

Founded on the Sarayburnu promontory around 660 BC as Byzantium, the city now known as Istanbul developed to become one of the most significant cities in history. For nearly sixteen centuries following its reestablishment as Constantinople in 330 AD, it served as the capital of four empires: the Roman Empire (330-395), the Byzantine Empire (395-1204 and 1261-1453), the Latin Empire (1204-1261), and the Ottoman Empire (1453-1922). It was instrumental in the advancement of Christianity during Roman and Byzantine times, before the Ottomans conquered the city in 1453 and transformed it into an Islamic stronghold and the seat of the last caliphate. Although the Republic of Turkey established its capital in Ankara, palaces and imperial mosques still line Istanbul's hills as visible reminders of the city's previous central role.

Istanbul's strategic position along the historic Silk Road, rail networks to Europe and the Middle East, and the only sea route between the Black Sea and the Mediterranean have helped foster an eclectic populace, although less so since the establishment of the Republic in 1923. Overlooked for the new capital during the interwar period, the city has since regained much of its prominence. The population of the city has increased tenfold since the 1950s, as migrants from across Anatolia have flocked to the metropolis and city limits have expanded to accommodate them. Arts festivals were established at the end of the 20th century, while infrastructure improvements have produced a complex transportation network.

Seven million foreign visitors arrived in Istanbul in 2010, when it was named a European Capital of Culture, making the city the world's tenth-most-popular tourist destination. The city's biggest draw remains its historic center, partially listed as a UNESCO World Heritage Site, but it's cultural and entertainment hub can be found across the city's natural harbor, the Golden Horn, in the Beyoğlu district. Considered a global city, Istanbul hosts the headquarters of many Turkish companies and media outlets and accounts for more than a quarter of the country's gross domestic product. Hoping to capitalize on its revitalization and rapid expansion, Istanbul is currently bidding for the 2020 Summer Olympics.

Jeddah, Saudi Arabia is a city in the Tihamah region on the coast of the Red Sea and is the major urban center of western Saudi Arabia. It is the largest city in Makkah Province, the largest sea port on the Red Sea, and the second largest city in Saudi Arabia after the capital city, Riyadh. With a population currently at 3.2 million, Jeddah is an important commercial hub in Saudi Arabia.

Jeddah is the principal gateway to Mecca, Islam's holiest city, which able-bodied Muslims are required to visit at least once in their lifetime. It is also a gateway to Medina, the second holiest place in Islam.

Economically, Jeddah is focusing on further developing capital investment in scientific and engineering leadership within Saudi Arabia, and the Middle East. Jeddah was independently ranked 4th in the Africa / Mid-East region in terms of innovation in 2009 in the Innovation Cities Index.

Jeddah is one of Saudi Arabia's primary resort cities and was named a Gamma world city by the *Globalization and World Cities Study Group and Network* (GaWC).

Historically, Jeddah has been well known for its legendary money changers. The largest of said money changers at the time (the late Sheikh Salem Bin Mahfouz) eventually founded Saudi Arabia's first bank, the National Commercial Bank (NCB). Other notable trading families that have greatly impacted Saudi Arabia include the Ba-eshen, Bajubair, Bajammal, Bakhashab, Bakhashwain, Ali-Reda, Bin Zagr, Bin Mahfouz, Abdulfatah, Balubaid, and Kamel families, respectively.

Kaohsiung, Taiwan officially **Kaohsiung City**, is one of the five special municipalities in Taiwan. Located in southern-western Taiwan and facing the Taiwan Strait, Kaohsiung is the largest municipality in Taiwan at 2,947.62 km^2 (1,138.08 sq mi), and second most populous with a population of approximately 2.77 million. Since its start at 17th century, Kaohsiung has grown from a small trading village, into the political, economic, transportation, manufacturing, refining, shipbuilding, and industries centers of southern Taiwan. It is a global city with sufficiency which categorized by GaWC in 2010.

The Kaohsiung International Airport serving the city is the second largest airport in Taiwan. The Port of Kaohsiung is the largest harbor in the Taiwan, but not officially part of Kaohsiung City. The southern terminal of the Sun Yat-sen Freeway is in Kaohsiung. For north-south travel on railway, the city is served by the Taiwan Railway Administration stations of Western Line and Pingtung Line. The Taiwan High Speed Rail also provides fast and frequent railway connection to Taipei City. The Kaohsiung Mass Rapid Transit, the city's subway system, launched in early 2008. Kaohsiung was the host city of the 2009 World Games, a multi-sport event primarily composed of sports not featured in the Olympic Games. The city is also home to the Republic of China Navy fleet headquarter and academy.

Key West, FL is an island in the Straits of Florida on the North American continent at the southernmost tip of the Florida Keys. The island is about 90 miles (140 km) from Cuba.

Key West is politically within the limits of the city of Key West, Monroe County, Florida, United States. The city also occupies portions of nearby islands.

The island is about 4 miles (6.4 km) long and 2 miles (3.2 km) wide. In the late 1950s many of the large salt ponds on the eastern side were filled in, nearly doubling the original land mass of the island. The island is 3,370 acres (13.6 km^2) in area.

In Pre-Columbian times Key West was inhabited by the Calusa people. The first European to visit was Juan Ponce de León in 1521. As Florida became a Spanish colony, a fishing and salvage village with a small garrison was established here.

Cayo Hueso is the original Spanish name for the island of Key West. Spanish-speaking people today also use the term **Cayo Hueso** when referring to Key West. It literally means "Bone Island" or "Bone Cay" (a low-lying island). It is said that the island was littered with the remains (bones) from a Native American battlefield or burial ground. The most widely accepted theory of how the name changed to Key West is that it is a false-friend anglicization of the word, on the ground that the word *hueso* ['weso]) sounds like "west" in English. Other theories of how the island was named are that the name indicated that it was the westernmost Key, or that the island was the westernmost Key with a reliable supply of water.

Many businesses on the island use the name, such as *Casa Cayo Hueso*, *Cayo Hueso Resorts*, *Cayo Hueso Consultants*, *Cayo Hueso y Habana Historeum*, etc.

In 1763, when the Kingdom of Great Britain took control of Florida, the community of Spaniards and Native Americans were moved to Havana. Florida returned to Spanish control 20 years later, but there was no official resettlement of the island. Informally the island was used by fishermen from Cuba and from the British Bahamas, who were later joined by others from the United States after the latter nation's independence. While claimed by Spain, no nation exercised *de facto* control over the community there for some time.

Kharg Island, Iran is a continental island in the Persian Gulf belonging to Iran. The island is located 25 km (16 mi) off the coast of Iran and 483 km (300 mi) northwest of the Strait of Hormuz. Administered by the adjacent coastal Bushehr Province, Kharg Island provides a sea port for the export of oil and extends Iranian territorial sea claims into the Persian Gulf oil fields. Located on Kharg Island is Kharg, the only city in the Kharg District.

Mentioned in the Hudud al-'alam as a good source for pearls around 982 CE, Kharg was visited by Jean de Thévenot in 1665, who recorded trade at the time with Isfahan and Basra. In 1753 the Dutch Empire established both a trading post and a fort on the island. In 1766 the Dutch fort was captured by Mir Mahanna, the governor of Bandar Riq.

The island was briefly occupied in 1838 by the British to block the Siege of Herat (1838) but was soon returned.

Once the world's largest offshore crude oil terminal and the principal sea terminal for Iranian oil, the Kharg Island facilities were put out of commission in the fall of 1986. Heavy bombing of the Kharg Island facilities from 1982 through 1986 by the air forces of the government of Iraq during the Iran-Iraq War all but destroyed most of the terminal facilities. Kharg Island was situated in the middle of the Darius Oilfield, also destroyed by the intensive bombing. Repair to all facilities has been very slow, even after the war ended in 1988.

In 2009, Iran exported and swapped 950 million barrels of crude oil via southern Kharg oil terminal.

Kingston, Jamaica is the capital and largest city of Jamaica, located on the southeastern coast of the island. It faces a natural harbor protected by the Palisadoes, a long sand spit which connects the town of Port Royal and the Norman Manley International Airport to the rest of the island. In the Americas, Kingston is the largest predominantly English-speaking city south of the United States.

The local government bodies of the parishes of Kingston and St. Andrew were amalgamated by the Kingston and St. Andrew Corporation Act of 1923, to form the Kingston and St. Andrew Corporation (KSAC). Greater Kingston or the "Corporate Area" refers to those areas under the KSAC; however, it does not solely refer to Kingston Parish, which only consists of the old downtown and Port Royal. Kingston Parish had a population of 96,052, and St. Andrew parish had a population of 555,828 in 2001. Kingston is only bordered by Saint Andrew to the east, west and north. The geographical border for the parish of Kingston encompasses the following communities, Tivoli Gardens, Denham Town, downtown Kingston, National Heroes Park, Kingston Gardens, Rae Town, Bournemouth Gardens, Norman Gardens, Springfield, Rennock Lodge, and Port Royal along with portions of Allman Town, Franklyn Town and Rollington Town.

The city proper is bounded by Six Miles to the west, Stony Hill to the north, Papine to the northeast and Harbor View to the east, communities in urban and suburban Saint Andrew. Communities in rural St. Andrew such as Gordon Town, Mavis Bank, Lawrence Tavern, Mt. Airy and Bull Bay would not be described as being in Kingston city.

Two parts make up the central area of Kingston: the historic Downtown, and New Kingston. Both are served by Norman Manley International Airport and also by the smaller and primarily domestic Tinson Pen Aerodrome.

Leros, Greece is a Greek island and municipality in the Dodecanese in the southern Aegean Sea. It lies 317 km (171 nautical miles) from Athens's port of Piraeus, from which it can be reached by an 11-hour ferry ride (or by a 45-minute flight from Athens). Leros is part of the Kalymnos regional unit. The island has been also called in Italian: *Lèro* and in Turkish: *İleriye*.

The island is 74 square kilometres (29 sq mi) and has a coastline of 71 km (44 mi). The municipality includes the populated offshore island of Farmakonisi (pop. 10), as well as several uninhabited islets, including Levitha and Kinaros, and had a 2011 census population of 7,917, although this figure swells to over 15,000 during the summer peak. It is known for its imposing medieval castle of the Knights of Saint John possibly built on a Byzantine fortress. Nearby islands are Patmos, Lipsi, Kalymnos, and the small islands of Agia Kyriaki and Farmakos. In ancient times it was considered the island of Parthenos Iokallis and linked to the Hellenistic and Roman literature on Meleager and the Meleagrides. The administrative center and largest town is Agia Marina, with a population of 2,672 inhabitants. Other sizable towns are Lakkíon (pop. 1,990), Xirókampos (908), Kamára (573), and Álinda (542).

Thucydides stressed the special importance of the bays and the harbours of Leros during the Peloponnesian War (431 BC - 404 BC), where Leros supported the democratic Athenians. After the end of the war Leros came under the sovereignty of the Spartans. The island had a famous sanctuary of the goddess Artemis.

It then followed the fate of the rest of the Dodecanese Islands during the years of Alexander the Great and his successors, the Roman years and the Byzantine period. After the division of the Roman Empire, Leros was part of the Byzantine Empire. On the island of Farmaco east from Leros, a few miles from Didyma on the Turkish coast, Julius Caesar was held as a hostage by local pirates for forty days.

Lisbon, Portugal is the capital city and largest city of Portugal with a population of 547,631 within its administrative limits on a land area of 84.8 km^2 (33 sq mi). The urban area of Lisbon extends beyond the administrative city limits with a population of over 3 million[3] on an area of 958 km^2 (370 sq mi), making it the 11th most populous urban area in the European Union. About 3,035,000 people live in the Lisbon Metropolitan

Area (which represents approximately 27% of the population of the country). Lisbon is the westernmost large city located in Europe, as well as its westernmost capital city and the only one along the Atlantic coast. It lies in the western Iberian Peninsula on the Atlantic Ocean and the Tagus River.

Lisbon is recognized as a global city because of its importance in finance, commerce, media, entertainment, arts, international trade, education, and tourism. It is one of the major economic centers on the continent, with a growing financial sector and the largest/second largest container port on Europe's Atlantic coast. Lisbon Portela Airport serves over 15.3 million passengers annually (2012); the motorway network and the high-speed rail system of (Alfa Pendular) link the main cities of Portugal. The city is the seventh-most-visited city in Southern Europe, after Istanbul, Rome, Barcelona, Madrid, Athens, and Milan, with 1,740,000 tourists in 2009. The Lisbon region is the wealthiest region in Portugal, GDP PPP per capita is 26,100 euros (4.7% higher than the average European Union's GDP PPP per capita). It is the tenth richest metropolitan area by GDP on the continent amounting to 110 billion euros and thus €39,375 per capita, 40% higher than the average European Union's GDP per capita. The city occupies 32nd place of highest gross earnings in the world. Most of the headquarters of multinationals in the country are located in the Lisbon area and it is the ninth city in the world in terms of quantity of international conferences. It is also the political centre of the country, as seat of Government and residence of the Head of State. It is the seat of the district of Lisbon and the centre of the Lisbon region.

Lisbon is one of the oldest cities in the world, and the oldest city in Western Europe, predating other modern European capitals such as London, Paris and Rome by hundreds of years. Julius Caesar made it a municipium called *Felicitas Julia*, adding to the name *Olissipo*. Ruled by a series of Germanic tribes from the fifth century, it was captured by the Moors in the eighth century. In 1147, the Crusaders under Afonso Henriques reconquered the city and since then it has been a major political, economic, and cultural centre of Portugal. Unlike most capital cities, Lisbon's status as the capital of Portugal has never been granted or confirmed officially – by statute or in written form. Its position as the capital has formed through constitutional convention, making its position as *de facto* capital a part of the Constitution of Portugal.

Lisbon hosts two agencies of the European Union: the European Monitoring Centre for Drugs and Drug Addiction (EMCDDA) and the European Maritime Safety Agency (EMSA). Called the "Capital of the Lusophone world", the Community of Portuguese Language Countries has its headquarters in the city, in the Palace of the Counts of Penafiel.

Lisbon has two sites listed by UNESCO as a World Heritage Site: Belém Tower and Jerónimos Monastery. Furthermore, in 1994, Lisbon was the European Capital of Culture and in 1998 organized an Expo '98 (*1998 Lisbon World Exposition*).

Lisbon enjoys a Mediterranean climate. Among all the metropolises in Europe, it has the warmest winters, with average temperatures 15 °C (59 °F) during the day and 8 °C (46 °F) at night from December to February. The typical summer season lasts about six months, from May to October, although also in November, March and April temperatures sometimes reach around 20 °C (68.0 °F).

Londonderry. While the city is more usually known as Derry, Londonderry is also used and remains the legal name.

The old walled city lies on the west bank of the River Foyle, which is spanned by two road bridges and one footbridge. The city now covers both banks (*Cityside* on the west and *Waterside* on the east). The city district also extends to rural areas to the southeast. The population of the city proper (the area defined by its 17th-century charter) was 83,652 in the 2012 Census, while the Derry Urban Area had a population of 105,066. The district is administered by Derry City Council and contains both Londonderry Port and City of Derry Airport.

The Greater Derry area, that area within about 20 miles (32 km) of the city, has a population of 237,000.

This comprises the districts of Derry City and parts of Limavady district, Strabane district, and East Donegal (including Raphoe and St Johnston), along with Inishowen.

Derry is close to the border with County Donegal, with which it has had a close link for many centuries. The person traditionally seen as the 'founder' of the original Derry is Saint Colmcille, a holy man from Tír Chonaill, the old name for almost all of modern County Donegal (of which the west bank of the Foyle was a part before c. 1600). Derry and the nearby town of Letterkenny form the major economic core of northwest Ireland.

In 2013, Derry will become the inaugural city to be designated UK City of Cu**Londonderry, Ireland** is the second-largest city in Northern Ireland and the fourth-largest city on the island of Ireland. The name Derry is an anglicization of the Irish name *Daire* or *Doire* meaning "oak grove". In 1613, the city was granted a Royal Charter by King James I and the "London" prefix was added, changing the name of the city to Londondelture, having been awarded the title in July 2010.

Lorient, France is a commune and a seaport in the Morbihan department in Brittany in north-western France.

Beginning around 3000 BC, settlements in area of Lorient are attested by the presence of megalithic architecture. Ruins of Roman roads (linking Vannes to Quimper and Port-Louis to Carhaix) confirm Gallo-Roman presence.

In 1664, Colbert founded the French East Indies Company.[1] In June 1666, an ordinance of Louis XIV granted lands of Port-Louis to the company, along with Faouédic on the other side of the roadstead. One of its directors, Denis Langlois, bought lands at the confluence of the Scorff and the Blavet rivers, and built slipways. At first, it only served as a subsidiary of Port-Louis, where offices and warehouses were located. The following years, the operation was threatened of being abandoned several times, but in 1675, during the Franco-Dutch War, the French East Indies Company decided to scrap its base in Le Havre, too exposed during wartime, and transferred its infrastructures to l'Enclot, out of which Lorient will grow. The company then erected a chapel, workshops, forges, and offices, leaving Port-Louis permanently.[3]

The French Royal Navy opened up a base there in 1690, under the impulse of Colbert de Seignelay, who inherited his father's position as Secretary of State of the Navy. At the same time, privateers from Saint-Malo took shelter there. In 1700, the town grew out of l'Enclot following a law forcing people to leave the domain to move to the Faouédic heath. In 1702, there were about 6,000 inhabitants in Lorient, though activities slowed, and the town began to decline.

Mahon, Menorca conventionally known as **Port Mahon** in English, is a municipality and the capital of Minorca, located in the eastern part of the autonomous community of the Balearic Islands, Spain. Mahon has the second deepest natural harbor in the world: 5 km long and up to 900 meters wide. The water is deep but it remains mostly clear due to it being slightly enclosed.

Its population in 2009 was estimated to be 29,495 inhabitants.

The name's origin is attributed to the Carthaginian general Mago Barca, brother to Hannibal, who is thought to have taken refuge there in 205 BC. After the fall of the Western Roman Empire, it was part of the Byzantine Empire; it suffered raids from Viking and Arabs, until the Islamic Caliphate of Córdoba conquered it in 903.

Mahon was captured in 1287 from the Moors by Alfonso III of Aragon and incorporated into the Kingdom of Majorca, a vassal kingdom of the Kingdom of Aragon. Its harbor, one of the most strategically important in the western Mediterranean, was re-fortified.

In 1535, the Ottomans under Hayreddin Barbarossa attacked Mahon and took 6,000 captives as slaves back to Algiers, in the Sack of Mahon.

Minorca was captured by the British during the War of the Spanish Succession in 1708, and its status as a British possession was confirmed by the Treaty of Utrecht in 1713. During the island's years as a British dependency in the 18th century, Mahon served as its capital and residence for the governor, the most famous being General Richard Kane.

The island changed hands several times during the eighteenth century, with France and Spain both capturing it. In 1783 the Peace of Paris returned the town to control of the Spanish but it was occupied for a final time by the British during the Capture of Minorca in 1798 before being returned to Spain for good in 1802.

Marseilles, France is the second largest city in France after Paris and the centre of the second largest metropolitan area in France after Paris. To the east, starting in the small fishing village of Callelongue on the outskirts of Marseille and stretching as far as Cassis, are the Calanques, a rugged coastal area interspersed with small fjords. Further east still are the Sainte-Baume, a 1,147 m (3,763 ft) mountain ridge rising from a forest of deciduous trees, the town of Toulon and the French Riviera. To the north of Marseille, beyond the low Garlaban and Etoile mountain ranges, is the 1,011 m (3,317 ft) Mont Sainte Victoire. To the west of Marseille is the former artists' colony of l'Estaque; further west are the Côte Bleue, the Gulf of Lion and the Camargue region in the Rhône delta. The airport lies to the north west of the city at Marignane on the Étang de Berre.

The city's main thoroughfare, the wide boulevard called the Canebière, stretches eastward from the Old Port (Vieux Port) to the *Réformés* quarter. Two large forts flank the entrance to the Old Port—Fort Saint-Nicolas on the south side and Fort Saint-Jean on the north. Further out in the Bay of Marseille is the Frioul archipelago which comprises four islands, one

of which, If, is the location of Château d'If, made famous by the Dumas novel *The Count of Monte Cristo*. The main commercial centre of the city intersects with the Canebière at rue St Ferréol and the Centre Bourse (the main shopping mall). The centre of Marseille has several pedestrianised zones, most notably rue St Ferréol, Cours Julien near the Music Conservatory, the Cours Honoré-d'Estienne-d'Orves off the Old Port and the area around the Hôtel de Ville. To the south east of central Marseille in the 6th arrondissement are the Prefecture and the monumental fountain of Place Castellane, an important bus and metro interchange. To the south west are the hills of the 7th arrondissement, dominated by the basilica of Notre-Dame-de-la-Garde. The railway station—Gare de Marseille Saint-Charles—is north of the Centre Bourse in the 1st arrondissement; it is linked by the Boulevard d'Athènes to the Canebière.

Mayport, FL is a major United States Navy base in Jacksonville, Florida. It contains a protected harbor that can accommodate aircraft carrier-size vessels, ship's intermediate maintenance activity (SIMA) and a military airfield (Admiral David L. McDonald Field) with one asphalt paved runway (5/23) measuring 8,001 x 200 ft. (2,439 x 61 m).[1]

Since its commissioning in December 1942, NS Mayport has grown to become the third largest naval surface fleet concentration area in the United States. Mayport's operational composition is unique, with a busy harbor capable of accommodating 34 ships and an 8,001-foot (2,439 m) runway capable of handling most any aircraft in the Department of Defense inventory.

Naval Station Mayport is also home to the Navy's United States Fourth Fleet, reactivated in 2008 after being deactivated in 1950.

The base has historically served as the homeport to various conventionally powered aircraft carriers of the Atlantic Fleet, including the *Shangri-La*, *Franklin D. Roosevelt*, *Forrestal*, *Saratoga* and, most recently, the *John F. Kennedy*. With the decommissioning of all conventionally powered aircraft carriers by the Navy, no carriers are presently assigned to Mayport. However, both houses of Congress have passed legislation authorizing about US $75 million for dredging and upgrades at Mayport to accommodate a nuclear-powered aircraft carrier.

On January 29, 2010, the *Quadrennial Defense Review Report* stated that a nuclear aircraft carrier would be homeported at NAS Mayport. The action will help protect the fleet against a potential terror attack, accident or natural disaster, because all east coast aircraft carriers are currently based at Naval Station Norfolk, according to the report. West coast aircraft carriers are split between Naval Station San Diego and Naval Base Kitsap in Washington State. Robert Gates, Secretary of Defense, stated, "Having a single (nuclear carrier) homeport has not been considered acceptable on the west coast and should not be considered acceptable on the east coast." The decision was opposed by elected officials in Virginia, who would lose 3,500 sailors and their dependents, $425 million in revenue each year, and most importantly, 6,000 support jobs. The Hampton Roads Chamber of Commerce estimated the loss at 11,000 jobs and $650 million per year. Infrastructure changes and facility construction at Mayport are estimated to take five years and cost over half a billion dollars. The 2011 budget commits $590 million during the fiscal years from 2011 to 2019, so a carrier may not move to Mayport until 2019.[7] However, an amphibious group is coming sooner, between 2013 and 2016.

The Virginia congressional delegation has fought the loss of even one carrier's boost to their economy by citing other areas such as shipbuilding to spend the navy's tight budget.

Mersin, Turkey is a large city and a port on the Mediterranean coast of southern Turkey. It is part of an interurban agglomeration – the Adana-Mersin Metropolitan Area – and lies on the western part of Çukurova, a geographical, economical and cultural region. According to Evliya Çelebi, the city is named after the Mersinoğullari clan; another theory is that it is made from the myrtle which grows abundantly in the region.

Mersin is important for Turkey's economy, and Turkey's largest seaport is located there. Mersin's nickname within Turkey is "Pearl of the Mediterranean" and the city will host the 2013 Mediterranean Games.

According to the Turkish Statistical Institute, as of 2011 the Mersin Metropolitan Municipality had a population of 913,958. Mersin's population is 1.674.568 with all provinces.

This coast has been inhabited since the 9th millennium BC. Excavations by John Garstang of the hill of Yumuktepe have revealed 23 levels of occupation, the earliest dating from ca. 6300 BC. Fortifications were put up around 4500 BC, but the site appears to have been abandoned between 350 BC and 300 BC.

In subsequent centuries, the city became a part of many states and civilizations including the Hittites, Assyrians, Persians, Greeks, Seleucids and Lagids. During the Ancient Greek period, the city bore the name **Zephyrion** and was mentioned by numerous ancient authors. Apart from its natural harbor and strategic position along the trade routes of southern Anatolia, the city profited from trade in molybdenum (white lead) from the neighboring mines of Coreyra. Ancient sources attributed the best molybdenum to the city, which also minted its own coins.

Miami, Florida is a city located on the Atlantic coast in southeastern Florida and the county seat of Miami-Dade County. The 42nd largest city proper in the United States, with a population of 413,892, it is the principal, central, and most populous city of the Miami metropolitan area, and the most populous metropolis in the Southeastern United States. According to the U.S. Census Bureau, Miami's metro area is the eighth most populous and fourth-largest urban area in the United States, with a population of around 5.5 million.

Miami is a major center and a leader in finance, commerce, culture, media, entertainment, the arts, and international trade. In 2010, Miami was classified as an Alpha- World City in the World Cities Study Group's inventory. In 2010, Miami ranked seventh in the United States in terms of finance, commerce, culture, entertainment, fashion, education, and other sectors. It ranked thirty-third among global cities. In 2008, *Forbes* magazine ranked Miami "America's Cleanest City", for its year-round good air quality, vast green spaces, clean drinking water, clean streets and city-wide recycling programs. According to a 2009 UBS study of 73 world cities, Miami was ranked as the richest city in the United States, and the world's fifth-richest city in terms of purchasing power. Miami is nicknamed the "Capital of Latin America", is the second-largest U.S. city (after El Paso, Texas) with a Spanish-speaking majority, and the largest city with a Cuban-American plurality.

Downtown Miami and South Florida are home to the largest concentration of international banks in the United States, and many large national and international companies. The Civic Center is a major center for hospitals, research institutes, medical centers, and biotechnology industries. For more than two decades, the Port of Miami, known as the "Cruise Capital of the

World," has been the number one cruise passenger port in the world. It accommodates some of the world's largest cruise ships and operations, and is the busiest port in both passenger traffic and cruise lines.

Midway Island is a 2.4-square-mile (6.2 km^2) atoll in the North Pacific Ocean. As its name suggests, Midway is roughly equidistant between North America and Asia, and lies almost halfway around the world from Greenwich, England. It is near the northwestern end of the Hawaiian archipelago, about one-third of the way from Honolulu, Hawaii to Tokyo, Japan. Midway Atoll is an unorganized, unincorporated territory of the United States, and the former home of the Midway Naval Air Station (former ICAO PMDY). For statistical purposes, Midway is grouped as one of the United States Minor Outlying Islands. It is less than 140 nautical miles (259 km; 161 mi) east of the International Date Line, about 2,800 nautical miles (5,200 km; 3,200 mi) west of San Francisco, and 2,200 nautical miles (4,100 km; 2,500 mi) east of Tokyo. The Midway Atoll National Wildlife Refuge, encompassing 590,991.50 acres (239,165.77 ha) of land and water (mostly water) in the surrounding area, is administered by the United States Fish and Wildlife Service (FWS).

Midway was the focal point of the Battle of Midway, one of the most important naval battles of the Pacific Campaign in World War II. The battle, fought between June 4 and June 6, 1942 near the islands, saw the United

States Navy defeat a Japanese attack against the Midway Islands, marking a turning point in the war in the Pacific Theater.

Travel to the atoll in 2013 will not be possible through either organized tour companies or as a Fish and Wildlife Service volunteer, due to budget cuts in the US government's 2013 fiscal budget, suspending visitor and volunteer programs. The visitor program (which reopened the atoll to visitors in January 2008) hosted 332 visitors in 2012. The tours have focused on the ecology of Midway and its military history. The economy is derived solely from governmental sources and tourist fees. All food and manufactured goods are imported. The refuge and most of its surrounding area are part of the larger Papahānaumokuākea Marine National Monument.

The location of Midway in the Pacific became important to the military. Midway was a convenient refueling stop on transpacific flights, and was also an important stop for Navy ships. Beginning in 1940, as tensions with the Japanese were rising, Midway was deemed second only to Pearl Harbor in importance to protecting the U.S. west coast. Airstrips, gun emplacements and a seaplane base quickly materialized on the tiny atoll. The channel was widened, and Naval Air Station Midway was completed. Architect Albert Kahn designed the Officer's quarters, the mall and several other hangars and buildings. Midway was also an important submarine base. Midway's importance to the U.S. was brought into focus on

December 7, 1941 with the Japanese attack on Pearl Harbor. Midway was attacked for the first time on December 7, 1941, and the Japanese force was successfully repulsed in the first American victory of the war. A Japanese submarine bombarded Midway on February 10, 1942. Four months later, on June 4, 1942, a naval battle near Midway resulted in the U.S. Navy exacting a devastating defeat of the Japanese Navy. Four Japanese fleet aircraft carriers, the *Akagi*, *Kaga*, *Hiryu* and *Soryu*, were sunk, along with the loss of hundreds of Japanese aircraft, losses that the Japanese would never be able to replace. The U.S. lost the aircraft carrier USS *Yorktown* (CV-5), along with a number of its carrier- and land-based aircraft that were either shot down by Japanese forces or bombed on the ground at the airfields. The Battle of Midway was, by most accounts, the beginning of the end of the Japanese Navy's control of the Pacific Ocean.

From August 1, 1941 to 1945, it was occupied by U.S. military forces. In 1950, the Navy decommissioned Naval Air Station Midway, only to re-commission it again to support the Korean War. Thousands of troops on ships and aircraft stopped at Midway for refueling and emergency repairs. From 1968 to September 10, 1993, Midway Island was a Navy Air Facility. During the Cold War, the U.S. established an underwater listening post at Midway to track Soviet submarines. The facility remained secret until its demolition at the end of the Cold War. U.S. Navy WV-2 (EC-121K) "Willy Victor" radar aircraft flew night and day as an extension of the Distant Early Warning Line, and antenna fields covered the islands.

With about 3,500 people living on Sand Island, Midway also supported the U.S. troops during the Vietnam War. In June 1969, President Richard Nixon held a secret meeting with South Vietnamese President Nguyen Van Thieu at the Officer-in-Charge house or "Midway House".

Navarin Bay, Greece also known as Pylos under its Italian name **Navarino**, which in turn originates from the Turkic Avars, is a town and a former municipality in Messenia, Peloponnese, Greece. Since the 2011 local government reform it is part of the municipality Pylos-Nestoras, of which it is the seat and a municipal unit. It was the capital of the former Pylia Province. It is the main harbour on the Bay of Navarino. Nearby villages include Gialova, Pyla, Elaiofyto, Schinolakka, and Palaionero. The town of Pylos has 2,767 inhabitants, the municipal unit of Pylos 5,287 (2011).

Mycenean Pylos is an important archaeological site located on the western coast of the Peloponnese in Greece. The Bronze Age site, located at modern *Epano Englianos* some 9 km north-east of the bay, was first excavated by Carl Blegen in 1952. Blegen dubbed the remains of a large Mycenean palace excavated there the Palace of Nestor, after the Homeric ruler Nestor, who ruled over "Sandy Pylos" in the *Iliad*. Linear B tablets recovered from the site by Blegen clearly demonstrate that the site was called Pylos (Mycenaean Greek: *Pulos*, Linear B: *Pu-ro*) by its Mycenean inhabitants. The site of Mycenean Pylos was abandoned sometime after the 8th century BCE, and was apparently unknown in the Classical Period.

Old Pylos, the location of the town in Classical times, is to the north of the bay, see also Old Navarino castle.

The bay of Pylos was the site of two important naval battles:

- the Battle of Pylos, in 425 BC during the Peloponnesian War
- The Battle of Navarino, in 1827 during the Greek War of Independence.
- In the Middle Ages, Pylos was named Avarino (Αβαρίνος), probably after a body of Avars who settled there. "Of the Avars" (Greek: των Αβαρίνων) could later have become the place-name Navarino (Greek: Το Ναυαρίνον) by epenthesis. Hopf's theory that the name came from the Navarrese Company is chronologically unsustainable.[5] Another theory suggests it is a Slavic name meaning "place of maples".
- The Venetian name was "Zonklon" (from Greek Ionchion), the Turkish name (1498-1821) "Anavarin" (with another round of epenthesis), and the local Greek name "Neokastron" 'new castle'.

- Other names recorded for the town and the castles are Avarmus, Abarinus, Albarinos, Albaxinus, Avarinos, Coryphasium, Iverin, Nelea, Port de Jonc, Porto Giunco, and Zunchio.

Naples, Italy is the capital of Campania and the third-largest municipality in Italy, after Rome and Milan. As of 2012, around 960,000 people live within the city's administrative limits. The Naples urban area, covering 1,023 km² (395 sq mi), has a population of between 3 million and 3.7 million, and is the 8th-most populous urban area in the European Union. Between 4.1 and 4.9 million people live in the Naples metropolitan area, one of the largest metropolises on the Mediterranean Sea.

Naples is one of the oldest continuously-inhabited cities in the world. Bronze Age Greek settlements were established on the site in the 2nd millennium BC, with a larger mainland colony – initially known as Parthenope – developing around the 9th–8th centuries BC, at the end of the Greek Dark Ages. The city was refounded as Neápolis in the 6th century BC and became a lynchpin of Magna Graecia, playing a key role in the merging of Greek culture into Roman society and eventually becoming a cultural centre of the Roman Republic. Naples remained influential after the fall of the Western Roman Empire, serving as the capital city of the Kingdom of Naples between 1282 and 1816. Thereafter, in union with Sicily, it became the capital of the Two Sicilies until the unification of Italy in 1861. During the Neapolitan War of 1815, Naples strongly promoted Italian unification.

Naples was the most-bombed Italian city during World War II. Much of the city's 20th-century periphery was constructed under Benito Mussolini's fascist government, and during reconstruction efforts after World War II. In recent decades, Naples has constructed a large business district, the Centro Direzionale, and has developed an advanced transport infrastructure, including an Alta Velocità high-speed rail link to Rome and Salerno, and an expanded subway network, which is planned to eventually cover half of the region. The city has experienced significant economic growth in recent decades, and unemployment levels in the city and surrounding Campania have decreased since 1999. However, Naples is still characterized by political and economic corruption and a thriving black market, and unemployment levels remain high.

Naples has the fourth-largest urban economy in Italy, after Milan, Rome and Turin. It is the world's 103rd-richest city by purchasing power, with an estimated 2011 GDP of US$83.6 billion. The port of Naples is one of the most important in Europe, and has the world's second-highest level of passenger flow, after the port of Hong Kong. Numerous major Italian companies, such as MSC Cruises Italy S.p.A, are headquartered in Naples. The city also hosts NATO's Allied Joint Force Command Naples, the SRM Institution for Economic Research and the OPE Company and Study Centre. Naples is a full member of the Eurocities network of European cities. The city was selected to become the headquarters of the European institution ACP/UE and as a City of Literature by UNESCO's Creative Cities Network. The Villa Rosebery, one of the three official residences of the President of Italy, is located in the city's Posillipo district.

Naples' historic city centre is the largest in Europe, covering 1,700 hectares (4,200 acres), and is listed by UNESCO as a World Heritage Site. Over the course of its long history, Naples has been the capital of duchies, kingdoms, and one Empire, and has consistently been a major cultural centre with a global sphere of influence, particularly during the Renaissance and Enlightenment eras. In the immediate vicinity of Naples are numerous sites of great cultural and historical significance, including the Palace of Caserta and the Roman ruins of Pompeii and Herculaneum. Culinarily, the city is synonymous with pizza, which originated in the city. Neapolitan music has furthermore been highly influential, credited with the invention of the romantic guitar and the mandolin, as well as notable contributions to opera and folk standards. Popular characters and historical figures who have come to symbolize the city include Januarius, the patron saint of Naples, the comic figure Pulcinella, and the Sirens from the Greek epic poem the *Odyssey*.

Newcastle, England is a city and metropolitan borough in Tyne and Wear, North East England. Historically the county town of Northumberland, of which it was part until 1974, it is situated on the north bank of the River Tyne centered 8.5 mi (13.7 km) from the North Sea. The city grew up in the area that was the location of the Roman settlement called Pons Aelius, though it owes its name to the castle built in 1080, by Robert (II), Duke of Normandy, "Curthose", William the Conqueror's eldest son. The city grew as an important centre for the wool trade and it later became a major coal mining area. The port developed in the 16th century and, along with the shipyards lower down the river, was amongst the world's largest shipbuilding and ship-repairing centers. These industries suffered decline and closure. Newcastle'e economy includes a place as a corporate headquarters, learning, digital technology, retail, tourism and cultural centre.

Among its main icons are Newcastle Brown Ale, a leading brand of beer, Newcastle United F.C., a Premier League team, and the Tyne Bridge. It has hosted the world's most popular half marathon, the Great North Run, since it began in 1981.

The city is at the urban core of the Tyneside conurbation, which is the sixth most populous conurbation in the United Kingdom. Newcastle is a member of the

English Core Cities Group and with Gateshead the Eurocities network of European cities.

The regional nickname for people from Newcastle and the surrounding area is Geordie.

Newport, Rhode Island is a city on Aquidneck Island in Newport County, Rhode Island, United States. It is located 23 miles (37 km) south of Providence, and 61 miles (98 km) south of Boston. Known as a New England summer resort and for the famous Newport Mansions, it is the home of Salve Regina University and Naval Station Newport which houses the United States Naval War College, the Naval Undersea Warfare Center, and a major United States Navy training center. A major 18th century port city, Newport now contains among the highest number of surviving colonial buildings of any city in the United States.[3] The city is the county seat of Newport County (a county that no longer has any governmental functions other than court administrative and sheriff corrections boundaries). Newport was known for being the city of some of the "Summer White Houses" during the administrations of Presidents Dwight D. Eisenhower and John F. Kennedy. The population was 24,672 at the 2010 census.

Since the colonial era, Rhode Island would rotate its legislative sessions between Providence, Newport, Bristol, East Greenwich and Kingston and did not have a fixed capital. In 1854 the sessions in the cities other than Providence and Newport were eliminated and finally in 1900, Newport was dropped. A constitutional amendment that year restricted the meetings of the legislature to Providence.[18] Connecticut was the only other state to have more than one capital at one time.

John Fitzgerald Kennedy and Jacqueline Bouvier were married in St. Mary's Church in Newport on September 12, 1953.

Presidents Kennedy and Eisenhower both made Newport the sites of their "Summer White Houses" during their years in office. Eisenhower stayed at Quarters A at the Naval War College and at what became known as the Eisenhower House, while Kennedy used Hammersmith Farm next door.

In the 20th century, immigrants from Portugal and the Caribbean began settling in Newport, adding to the rich diversity of the city.

Naval War College - The city has long been entwined with the United States Navy. From 1952 to 1973, it hosted the Cruiser-Destroyer Force of the U.S. Atlantic Fleet, and subsequently it has from time to time hosted smaller numbers of warships. It held the campus of the U.S. Naval Academy during the American Civil War (1861-65), when the undergraduate officer training school was temporarily moved north from Annapolis, Maryland. It remains home to the U.S. Naval War College and the Naval Education and Training Command (NETC), the center of Surface Warfare Officer training, and a large division of the Naval Undersea Warfare Center. The decommissioned aircraft carrier USS *Saratoga* (CV-60) is moored in an inactive status at the docks previously used by the Cruiser-Destroyer Force. The USS *Forrestal* (CV-59) shared the pier until June 2010.

The departure of the Cruiser-Destroyer fleet from Newport and the closure of nearby Naval Air Station Quonset Point in 1973 was devastating to the local economy. The population of Newport decreased, businesses closed, and property values plummeted. However, in the late 1960s, the city had begun revitalizing the downtown area with the construction of America's Cup Avenue, malls of stores and condominiums, and upscale hotels. Construction was completed on the Newport Bridge. The Preservation Society of Newport County began opening Newport's historic mansions to the public, and the tourist industry became Newport's primary commercial enterprise over the subsequent years.

New York City, New York is the most populous city in the United States and the center of the New York Metropolitan Area, one of the most populous urban agglomerations in the world. The city is referred to as **New York City** or the **City of New York** to distinguish it from the State of New York, of which it is a part. A global power city, New York exerts a significant impact upon commerce, finance, media, art, fashion, research, technology, education, and entertainment. The home of the

United Nations Headquarters, New York is an important center for international diplomacy and has been described as the cultural capital of the world.

Located on one of the world's largest natural harbors, New York City consists of five boroughs, each of which is a county of New York State. The five boroughs—The Bronx, Brooklyn, Manhattan, Queens, and Staten Island—were consolidated into a single city in 1898. With a Census-estimated 2012 population of 8,336,697 distributed over a land area of just 302.64 square miles (783.8 km^2), New York is the most densely populated major city in the United States. As many as 800 languages are spoken in New York, making it the most linguistically diverse city in the world. The New York City Metropolitan Area's population is the United States' largest, with 18.9 million people distributed over 6,720 square miles (17,400 km^2), and is also part of the most populous combined statistical area in the United States, containing 22.1 million people as of the 2010 Census.

New York traces its roots to its 1624 founding as a trading post by colonists of the Dutch Republic, and was named New Amsterdam in 1626. The city and its surroundings came under English control in 1664 and were renamed *New York* after King Charles II of England granted the lands to his brother, the Duke of York. New York served as the capital of the United States from 1785 until 1790. It has been the country's largest city since 1790. The Statue of Liberty greeted millions of immigrants as they came to America by ship in the late 19th and early 20th centuries and is a globally recognized symbol of the United States and its democracy.

Many districts and landmarks in New York City have become well known to its approximately 50 million annual visitors. Times Square, iconified as "The Crossroads of the World", is the brightly illuminated hub of the Broadway theatre district, one of the world's busiest pedestrian intersections, and a major center of the world's entertainment industry. The city hosts many world renowned bridges, skyscrapers, and parks. New York City's financial district, anchored by Wall Street in Lower Manhattan, has been called the world's leading financial center and is home to the New York Stock Exchange, the world's largest stock exchange by total market capitalization of its listed companies. Manhattan's real estate market is among the most expensive in the world. Manhattan's Chinatown incorporates the highest concentration of Chinese people in the Western Hemisphere. Providing continuous 24/7 service, the New York City Subway is one of the most extensive rapid transit systems worldwide. Numerous colleges and universities are located in New York, including Columbia University, New York University, and Rockefeller University, which have been ranked among the top 50 in the world.

Nice, France is the fifth most populous city in France, after Paris, Marseille, Lyon and Toulouse. The urban area of Nice extends beyond the administrative city limits with a population of about 1 million on an area of 721 km^2 (278 sq mi). Located on the south east coast of France on the Mediterranean Sea, Nice is the second-largest French city on the Mediterranean coast after Marseille.

The city is called *Nice la Belle* (*Nissa La Bella* in Niçard), which means *Nice the Beautiful*, which is also the title of the unofficial anthem of Nice, written by Menica Rondelly in 1912. Nice is the capital of the Alpes Maritimes department and the second biggest city of the Provence-Alpes-Côte d'Azur region after Marseille.

The area of today's Nice contains Terra Amata, an archaeological site which displays evidence of a very early use of fire. Around 350 BC, Greeks of Marseille founded a permanent settlement and called it Nikaia, after *Nike*, the goddess of victory. Through the ages, the town has changed hands many times. Its strategic location and port significantly contributed to its maritime strength. For years it was a dominion of Savoy, and then became part of France between 1792 and 1815, when it was returned to Piedmont-Sardinia until its final annexation by France in 1860.

The natural beauty of the Nice area and its mild Mediterranean climate came to the attention of the English upper classes in the second half of the 18th century, when an increasing number of aristocratic families took to spending their winter there. The city's main seaside promenade, the Promenade des Anglais ('the Walkway of the English') owes its name to the earliest visitors to the resort. For decades now, the picturesque Nicean surroundings have attracted not only those in search of relaxation, but also those seeking inspiration. The clear air and soft light has been of particular appeal to some of Western culture's most outstanding painters, such as Marc Chagall, Henri Matisse, Niki de Saint Phalle and Arman. Their work is commemorated in many of the city's museums, including *Musée Marc Chagall*, Musée Matisse and Musée des Beaux-Arts Jules Chéret. Nice has the second largest hotel capacity in the country and it is one of its most visited cities, receiving 4 million tourists every year. It also has the third busiest airport in France after the two main Parisian ones. It is the historical capital city of the County of Nice (*Comté de Nice*).

Norfolk, VA is an independent city in the Commonwealth of Virginia in the United States. With a population of 245,803 as of the 2012 Cooper Center population estimates, it is Virginia's second-largest city behind neighboring Virginia Beach.

Norfolk is located at the core of the Hampton Roads metropolitan area, named for the large natural harbor of the same name located at the mouth of Chesapeake Bay. It is one of nine cities and seven counties that constitute the Hampton Roads metro area, officially known as the Virginia Beach-Norfolk-Newport News, VA-NC MSA. The city is bordered to the west by the Elizabeth River and to the north by the Chesapeake Bay. It also shares land borders with the independent cities of Chesapeake to its south and Virginia Beach to its east. One of the oldest of the cities in Hampton Roads, Norfolk is considered to be the historic, urban, financial, and cultural center of the region.

The city has a long history as a strategic military and transportation point. Norfolk Naval Base is the world's largest such base, and the world's largest military alliance, the North Atlantic Treaty Organization has one of its two Strategic Command headquarters here. The city also has the corporate headquarters of Norfolk Southern Railway, one of North America's principal Class I railroads, and Maersk Line, Limited, who manages the world's largest fleet of US-flag vessels. As the city is bordered by multiple bodies of water, Norfolk has many miles of riverfront and bay front property. It is linked to its neighbors by an extensive network of Interstate highways, bridges, tunnels, and three bridge-tunnel complexes—the only bridge-tunnels in the United States.

The waterways which almost completely surround the Hampton Roads region play an important part in the local economy. As a strategic location at the mouth of the Chesapeake Bay, its protected deep-water channels serve as a major trade artery for the import and export of goods from across the Mid-Atlantic, Mid-West, and internationally.

In addition to commercial activities, Hampton Roads is a major military center, particularly for the United States Navy, and Norfolk serves as the home for the most important of these regional installations, Naval Station Norfolk, the world's largest naval station. Located on Sewell's Point Peninsula, in the northwest corner of the city, the installation is the current headquarters of the United States Fleet Forces Command (formerly known as the Atlantic Fleet), as well as being home port for the Second Fleet, which compromises approximately 62,000 active duty personnel, 75 ships, and 132 aircraft. The base also serves as the headquarters to the Allied Command Transformation (NATO) and the United States Joint Forces Command.

The region also plays an important role in defense contracting, with particular emphasis in the shipbuilding and ship repair businesses for the city of Norfolk. Major private shipyards located in Norfolk or the Hampton Roads area include: Huntington Ingalls Industries (formerly Northrop Grumman Newport News) in Newport News, BAE Systems Norfolk Ship Repair, General Dynamics NASSCO Norfolk, and Colonna's Shipyard Inc., while the US Navy's Norfolk Naval Shipyard is just across the Downtown Tunnel in Portsmouth. Most contracts fulfilled by these shipyards are issued by the Navy, though some private commercial repair also takes place. Over 35% of Gross Regional Product (which includes the entire Norfolk-Newport News-Virginia Beach MSA), is attributable to defense spending, and that 75% of all regional growth since 2001 is attributable to increases in defense spending.

Ochos Rios, Jamaica is a town in the parish of Saint Ann on the north coast of Jamaica. Although he landed in many spots along the Jamaican coast, many believe that Christopher Columbus first set foot on land in Ochos Rios. Just outside the city, travelers and residents can visit Columbus Park, where Columbus supposedly first came on land, and see maritime artifacts and Spanish colonial buildings.

It was once a fishing village but now caters to tourists. It is a port of call for cruise ships as well as for cargo ships loading sugar, limestone, and in the past, bauxite Scuba diving and other water sports are offered in the town's vicinity.

The name "Ochos Rios" is a misnomer because there are not eight rivers in the area. It is most likely a British corruption of the original Spanish name "Las Chorreras" ("the waterfalls"), a name given to the village because of the nearby Dunn's River Falls.

The north coast highway from the international airport at Montego Bay to Ochos Rios has been improved since 2000 and the journey is now an hour and forty five minutes' drive. On 26 August 2011, the Jamaican government announced a $21 million revitalization plan for the resort area.

The town has restaurants, night clubs in Margaritaville and Dolphin Cove, where tourists swim and interact with dolphins.

It is perhaps most notable for its use in *Dr. No*, the very first James Bond film, which was released in 1962. It was the home of Miss Taro, played by Zena Marshall, who was an adversary of Bond (Sean Connery) and in alliance with the main villain Dr Julius No (Joseph Wiseman). It also appears as the primary location for the horror sequel Piranha II: The Spawning, many of the scenes being photographed at the Mallards Beach-Hyatt, now the Sunset Jamaica Grande.

Ochos Rios is the name of the sixth track on the album *Sounding out the City* by El Michels Affair and was also featured in the 10cc song, *From Rochdale to Ochos Rios*.

Oran, Africa is a major city on the northwestern Mediterranean coast of Algeria, and the second largest city of the country. It is closely associated with its neighboring city, Aïn Témouchent. Located north-west of Algeria, 432 km from the capital Algiers.

It is the capital of the Oran Province (*wilaya*). The city has a population of 759,645 (2008), while the metropolitan area has a population of approximately

1,500,000, making it the second largest city in Algeria. Oran is a major port, and since the 1960s has been the commercial, industrial, and educational centre of western Algeria.

Oran was founded in 903 by Moorish Andalusi traders but was captured by the Spanish under Cardinal Cisneros in 1509. Spanish sovereignty lasted until 1708, when the city was conquered by the Ottomans. Spain recaptured the city in 1732. However, its value as a trading post had decreased greatly, so King Charles IV sold the city to the Turks in 1792. Ottoman rule lasted until 1831, when it fell to the French.

During French rule over Algeria, Oran was the capital of a *department* of the same name (number 92). In July 1940, the British navy shelled French warships in the port after they refused a British ultimatum to surrender which was designed to ensure the fleet would not fall into German hands. The action increased the hatred of the Vichy regime for Britain but convinced the world that the British would fight on alone against Nazi Germany and its allies. The Vichy government held Oran during World War II until its capture by the Allies in late 1942, during Operation Torch.

Before the Algerian War, 1954-1962, Oran had one of the highest proportions of Europeans of any city in North Africa. However, shortly after the end of the war, most of the Europeans and Sephardic Jews living in Oran fled to France. A massacre of Europeans, four days after the vote for Algerian independence, triggered the exodus to France. In less than three months Oran lost about half its population.

Palma de Mallorca is the major city and port on the island of Majorca (*Mallorca*) and capital city of the autonomous community of the Balearic Islands in Spain. The names *Ciutat de Mallorca* (City of Majorca) and *Ciutat* (City) were used before the War of the Spanish Succession and are still used by people in Majorca. However, the official name was *Mallorca*, the same as the island. It is situated on the south coast of the island on the Bay of Palma. As of the 2009 census, the population of the city of Palma proper was 401,270, and the population of the entire urban area was 517,285, ranking as the twelfth largest urban area of Spain. Almost half of the total population of Majorca lives in Palma. The Cabrera Archipelago, though widely separated from Palma proper, is administratively considered part of the municipality. Its airport, Son Sant Joan, serves over 22 million passengers each year. The Marivent Palace was offered by the city to the then Prince Juan Carlos I of Spain. The royals have since spent their summer holidays in Palma.

Palma was founded as a Roman camp upon the remains of a Talaiotic settlement. The turbulent history of the city saw it the subject of several Vandal sackings during the fall of the Roman Empire, then reconquered by the Byzantine, then colonized by the Moors (who called it

Medina Mayurqa), and finally established by James I of Aragon.

Shipmates – Palma 1957

After the conquest of Majorca, it was loosely incorporated into the province of Tarraconensis by 123 BC; the Romans founded two new cities: *Palma* on the south of the island, and *Pollentia* in the northeast - on the site of a Phoenician settlement. Whilst Pollentia acted as port to Roman cities on the northwestern Mediterranean Sea, Palma was the port used for destinations in Africa, such as Carthage, and Hispania, such as Saguntum, Gades, and Carthago Nova. Though no visible remains of this period are seen in present day Palma, archaeological discoveries still occur whenever excavating under the city centre.

Patras, Greece is Greece's third largest urban area and the regional capital of Western Greece, in northern Peloponnese, 215 km (134 mi) west of Athens. The city is built at the foothills of Mount Panachaikon, overlooking the Gulf of Patras.

The *Patras City Area* is a conurbation of 160.400 inhabitants, while its wider urban area, in the new Patras municipality, has a population of 213,984 (in 2011). Patras' core settlement has a history spanning four millennia, in the Roman period it had become a cosmopolitan center of the eastern Mediterranean whilst, according to Christian tradition, it was also the place of Saint Andrew's martyrdom.

Dubbed Greece's *Gate to the West*, Patras is a commercial hub, while its busy port is a nodal point for trade and communication with Italy and the rest of Western Europe. The city has two public universities and one Technological Institute, hosting a large student population and rendering Patras a major scientific centre with a field of excellence in technological education. The Rio-Antirio bridge connects Patras' easternmost suburb of Rio to the town of Antirrio, connecting the Peloponnese peninsula with mainland Greece.

Every year, in February, the city hosts one of Europe's largest and most colourful carnivals; notable features of the Patras Carnival include its mammoth-sized satirical floats and extravagant balls and parades, enjoyed by hundreds of thousands of visitors in a pleasant Mediterranean climate. Patras is also famous for supporting an indigenous cultural scene active mainly in the performing arts and modern urban literature. It was European Capital of Culture 2006.

Patras is 215 km (134 mi) west of Athens by road, 94 km (58 mi) northeast of Pyrgos, 7 km (4 mi) south of Rio, 134 km (83 mi) west of Corinth, 77 kilometers northwest of Kalavryta, and 144 km (89 mi) northwest of Tripoli. A central feature of the urban geography of Patras is its division into upper and lower sections. This is the result of aninterplay between natural geography and human settlement patterns; the lower section of the city (Kato Poli), which includes the 19th century urban core and the port, is adjacent to the sea and stretches between the estuaries of the rivers of Glafkos and Haradros. It is built on what was originally a bed of river soils and dried-up swamps. The older upper section (Ano Poli) covers the area of the pre-modern settlement, around the Fortress, on what is the last elevation of Mount Panachaikon (1,926 m (6,319 ft))

Patras is 215 km (134 mi) west of Athens by road, 94 km (58 mi) northeast of Pyrgos, 7 km (4 mi) south of Rio, 134 km (83 mi) west of Corinth, 77 kilometers northwest of Kalavryta, and 144 km (89 mi) northwest of Tripoli. A central feature of the urban geography of Patras is its division into upper and lower sections. This is the result of aninterplay between natural geography and human settlement patterns; the lower section of the city (Kato Poli), which includes the 19th century urban core and the port, is adjacent to the sea and stretches between the estuaries of the rivers of Glafkos and Haradros. It is built on what was originally a bed of river soils and dried-up swamps. The older upper section (Ano Poli) covers the area of the pre-modern settlement, around the Fortress, on what is the last elevation of Mount Panachaikon (1,926 m (6,319 ft)) before the Gulf of Patras.

USS Arizona Memorial in background

Pearl Harbor, HI is a lagoon harbor on the island of Oahu, Hawaii, west of Honolulu. Much of the harbor and surrounding lands is a United States Navy deep-water naval base. It is also the headquarters of the United

States Pacific Fleet. The attack on Pearl Harbor by the Empire of Japan on Sunday, December 7, 1941 brought the United States into World War II.

Following the overthrow of the Hawaiian Kingdom, the United States Navy established a base on the island in 1899. In 1941, the base was attacked by the Japanese military. Over the years, Pearl Harbor remained a main base for the US Pacific Fleet after World War II along with Naval Base San Diego. In 2010, the Navy and the Air Force merged their two nearby bases; Pearl Harbor joined with Hickham Air Force Base to create Joint Base Pearl Harbor-Hickham.

Pensacola, Florida is the westernmost city in the Florida Panhandle and the county seat of Escambia County, Florida, United States. As of the 2010 census, the city had a total population of 51,923. Pensacola is the principal city of the Pensacola metropolitan area, which had an estimated 455,102 residents in 2009.

Pensacola is a sea port on Pensacola Bay, which connects to the Gulf of Mexico. A large United States Naval Air Station, the first in the United States, is located southwest of Pensacola (near the community of Warrington) and is home to the Blue Angels flight demonstration team and the National Naval Aviation Museum. The main campus of the University of West Florida is situated north of the city center.

The area was originally inhabited by Muskogean peoples; the Pensacola people lived there at the time of European contact. Pensacola Bay was the site of Spanish explorer Tristán de Luna's short-lived settlement in 1559. In 1698 the Spanish established a presidio in the area, laying the foundation for the modern city. It changed hands several times over the next several years, and became the capital of West Florida during Florida's British (1763-1783) and second Spanish periods (1783-1821). Pensacola is nicknamed "The City of Five Flags" due to the five governments that have flown flags over it during its history: the flags of Spain (Castile), France, Great Britain, the Confederate States of America, and the United States. Other nicknames include "World's Whitest Beaches" (due to the white sand prevalent along beaches in the Florida panhandle), "Cradle of Naval Aviation" (Naval Air Station Pensacola is the home of both the legendary Blue Angels and the National Museum of Naval Aviation), "Western Gate to the Sunshine State", "America's First Settlement", "Emerald Coast", "Redneck Riviera", "Red Snapper Capital of the World", and "P-Cola".

The original inhabitants of the Pensacola Bay area were Native American peoples. At the time of European contact, a Muskogean-speaking tribe known to the Spanish as the Pensacola lived in the region. This name is not recorded until 1677, but the tribe appears to be the source of the name "Pensacola" for the bay and thence the city. The area's recorded history begins in the 16th century, when the first European explorers arrived. Pensacola Bay was visited by the expeditions of Pánfilo de Narváez in 1528 and Hernando de Soto in 1539, at which time it was known as the Bay of Ochuse.

The city has been referred to as "The Cradle of Naval Aviation". Naval Air Station Pensacola (NASP) was the first Naval Air Station commissioned by the U.S. Navy in 1914. Tens of thousands Naval Aviators have received their training there including John H. Glenn, USMC who became the first American to orbit the earth in 1962 and Neil Armstrong who became the first man to set foot on the moon in 1969. The Navy's Flight Demonstration Squadron, the Blue Angels, is stationed there.

The National Museum of Naval Aviation is located on the Naval Air Station and is free to the public. The museum cares for and exhibits hundreds of vintage Naval Aviation aircraft and preserves the history of Naval Aviation through displays, symposiums, IMAX movies and tours.

Corry Station Naval Technical Training Center serves as an annex for the main base and the Center for Information Dominance. CWO3 Gary R. Schuetz Memorial Health Clinic is at Corry Station, Naval Hospital Pensacola, as is the main Navy Exchange and Defense Commissary Agency commissary complex for both Corry Station and NAS Pensacola. The Army National Guard B Troop 1-153 Cavalry is stationed in Pensacola.

Philadelphia, PA is the largest city in the Commonwealth of Pennsylvania, the second largest city on the East Coast of the United States, and the fifth-most-populous city in the United States. It is located in the Northeastern United States along the Delaware and Schuylkill rivers, and it is the only consolidated city-county in Pennsylvania. As of the 2010 Census, the city had a population of 1,526,006, growing to 1,547,607 in 2012 by Census estimates. Philadelphia is the economic and cultural center of the Delaware Valley, home to over 6 million people and the country's sixth-largest metropolitan area. Within the Delaware Valley, the Philadelphia metropolitan division consists of five counties in Pennsylvania and has a population of 4,008,994. Popular nicknames for Philadelphia are *Philly* and *The City of Brotherly Love*, the latter of which comes from the literal meaning of the city's name in Greek.

In 1682, William Penn founded the city to serve as capital of Pennsylvania Colony. By the 1750s, Philadelphia had surpassed Boston to become the largest city and busiest port in British America, and second in the British Empire, behind London. During the American Revolution, Philadelphia played an instrumental role as a meeting place for the Founding Fathers of the United States, who signed the Declaration of Independence in 1776 and the Constitution in 1787. Philadelphia was one of the nation's capitals during the Revolutionary War, and the city served as the temporary U.S. capital while Washington, D.C., was under construction. During the 19th century, Philadelphia became a major industrial center and railroad hub that grew from an influx of European immigrants. It became a prime destination for African Americans during the Great Migration and surpassed two million occupants by 1950.

Philadelphia has shifted to an information technology and service-based economy. Financial activities account for the largest sector of the metro economy, and it is one of the largest health education and research centers in the United States. Philadelphia's history attracts many tourists, with the Liberty Bell receiving over 2 million visitors in 2010. The Delaware Valley contains the headquarters of twelve Fortune 500 corporations, four of which are in Philadelphia proper. With a gross domestic product of $388 billion, Philadelphia ranks ninth among world cities and fourth in the nation. The city is also the nation's fourth-largest consumer media market, as ranked by the Nielsen Media Research.

Philadelphia is known for its arts and culture. The cheesesteak and soft pretzel are emblematic of Philadelphia cuisine, which is shaped by the city's ethnic mix. The city has more outdoor sculptures and murals than any other American city, and Philadelphia's Fairmount Park is the largest landscaped urban park in the world. Gentrification of Philadelphia's neighborhoods continues into the 21st century and the city has reversed its decades-long trend of population loss.

Piraeus, Greece is a port city in the region of Attica, Greece. Piraeus is located within the Athens urban area, 12 km southwest from its city center (municipality of Athens), and lies along the east coast of the Saronic Gulf.

According to the 2011 census, Piraeus had a population of 163,688 people within its administrative limits, making it the fourth largest municipality in Greece and the second largest within the urban area of the Greek capital, following the municipality of Athens. The municipality of Piraeus and several other suburban municipalities within the regional unit of Piraeus form the greater Piraeus area, with a total population of 448,997.

Piraeus has a long recorded history, dating to ancient Greece. The city was largely developed in the early 5th century BC, when it was selected to serve as the port city of classical Athens and was transformed into a prototype harbour, concentrating all the import and transit trade of Athens. Consequently, it became the chief harbour of ancient Greece, but declined gradually after the 4th century AD, growing once more in the 19th century, especially after Athens' declaration as the capital of Greece. In the modern era, Piraeus is a large city, bustling with activity and an integral part of

Athens, acting as home to the country's biggest harbour and bearing all the characteristics of a huge marine and commercial-industrial centre.

The port of Piraeus is the chief port in Greece, the largest passenger port in Europe and the third largest in the world, servicing about 20 million passengers annually. With a throughput of 1.4 million TEUs, Piraeus is placed among the first ten ports in container traffic in Europe and the top container port in the Eastern Mediterranean. The city hosted events in both the 1896 and 2004 Summer Olympics held in Athens.

Piraeus, which roughly means 'the place over the passage', has been inhabited since the 26th century BC. In prehistoric times, Piraeus was a rocky island consisting of the steep hill of Munichia, modern-day Kastella, and was connected to the mainland by a low-lying stretch of land that was flooded with sea water most of the year, and used as a salt field whenever it dried up. Consequently, it was called the Halipedon, meaning the 'salt field', and its muddy soil made it a tricky passage. Through the centuries, the area was increasingly silted and flooding ceased, thus by early classical times the land passage was made safe. In ancient Greece, Piraeus assumed its importance with its three deep water harbors, the main port of Cantharus and the two smaller of Zea and Munichia, and gradually replaced the older and shallow Phaleron harbour, which fell into disuse.

Port of Spain, Trinidad also written as **Port-of-Spain**, is the capital of the Republic of Trinidad and Tobago and the country's third-largest municipality, after San Fernando and Chaguanas. The city has a municipal population of 49,031 (2000 census), a metropolitan population of 128,026 (1990 unofficial estimate) and a transient daily population of 250,000. It is located on the Gulf of Paria, on the northwest coast of the island of Trinidad and is part of a larger conurbation stretching from Chaguaramas in the west to Arima in the east with an estimated population of 600,000.

The city serves primarily as a retail and administrative centre and it has been the capital of the island since 1757. It is also an important financial services centre for the Caribbean and is home to two of the largest banks in the region.

The city is also home to the largest container port on the island and is one of several shipping hubs of the Caribbean, exporting both agricultural products and manufactured goods. Bauxite from the Guyanas and iron ore from Venezuela are trans-shipped via facilities at Chaguaramas, about five miles (8 km) west of the city. The pre-lenten Carnival is the city's main annual cultural festival and tourist attraction.

Today, Port of Spain is as a leading city in the Caribbean region. Trinidad hosted the Fifth Summit of the

Americas in 2009 whose guests included US President Barack Obama and US Secretary of State Hillary Clinton. Port of Spain also hosted the Commonwealth Heads of Government Meeting in 2009 and hosted a Commonwealth Business Forum in 2011.

Port Said, Egypt is a city that lies in north east Egypt extending about 30 kilometres (19 mi) along the coast of the Mediterranean Sea, north of the Suez Canal, with an approximate population of 603,787 (2010). The city was established in 1859 during the building of the Suez Canal.

Port Said has been ranked the second among the Egyptian cities according to the Human Development Index in 2009 and 2010, the economic base of the city is fishing and industries, like chemicals, processed food, and cigarettes. Port Said is also an important harbour for exports of Egyptian products like cotton and rice, but also a fueling station for ships that pass through the Suez Canal. It thrives on being a duty-free port, as well as a tourist resort especially during summer. It is home to the Lighthouse of Port Said (the first building in the world built from reinforced concrete).

There are numerous old houses with grand balconies on all floors, giving the city a distinctive look. Port Said's twin city is Port Fuad, which lies on the eastern bank of the canal. The two cities coexist, to the extent that there hardly is any town centre in Port Fuad. The cities are connected by free ferries running all through the day, and together they form a metropolitan area with over a million residents that extend both on the African and the Asian sides of the Suez Canal. The only other metropolitan area in the world that also spans two continents is Istanbul.

Port Said acted as a global city since its establishment and flourished particularly during the nineteenth and the first half of the twentieth century when it was inhabited by various nationalities and religions. Most of them were from Mediterranean countries, and they coexisted in tolerance, forming a cosmopolitan community. Referring to this fact Rudyard Kipling once said "If you truly wish to find someone you have known and who travels, there are two points on the globe you have but to sit and wait, sooner or later your man will come there: the docks of London and Port Said".

On January 27, 2013, Egypt's government was reported to have lost control of the city as a result of protests and attacks that were a part of the 2012-2013 Egyptian protests and a response to death sentences issued due to the Port Said Stadium disaster.

The name of Port Said first appeared in 1855, It was chosen by an International committee composed of Great Britain, France, the Russian Empire, Austria, Spain and Piedmont. It is a compound name which composed of two parts: Port (marine harbour) and Said (the name of the ruler of Egypt at that time), who granted Ferdinand de Lesseps the concession to dig the Suez Canal.

Port Au Prince, Haiti is the capital and largest city of the Caribbean country of Haiti. The city's population was 704,776 as of the 2003 census, and was officially estimated to have reached 897,859 in 2009.

The city of Port-au-Prince is on the Gulf of Gonâve: the bay on which the city lies, which acts as a natural harbor, has sustained economic activity since the civilizations of the Arawaks. It was first incorporated under the colonial rule of the French, in 1749, and has been Haiti's largest metropolis since then. The city's layout is similar to that of an amphitheatre; commercial districts are near the water, while residential neighborhoods are located on the hills above. Its population is difficult to ascertain due to the rapid growth of slums in the hillsides above the city; however, recent estimates place the metropolitan area's population at around 3.7 million, nearly half of the country's national population.

Port-au-Prince was catastrophically affected by an earthquake on January 12, 2010, with large numbers of structures damaged or destroyed. Haiti's government has estimated the death toll at 230,000 and says more bodies remain uncounted.

Prior to the arrival of Christopher Columbus, the island of Hispaniola was inhabited by people known as the

Taíno, who arrived in approximately 2600 BC in large dugout canoes. They are believed to come primarily from what is now eastern Venezuela. By the time Columbus arrived in 1492 AD, the region was under the control of Bohechio, Taíno cacique of Xaragua. He, like his predecessors, feared settling too close to the coast—such settlements would have proven to be tempting targets for the Caribes, who lived on neighboring islands. Instead, the region served as a hunting ground. The population of the region was approximately 400,000 at the time, but the Taínos were gone within 30 years of the arrival of the Spaniards.

Portsmouth, England is the second largest city in the ceremonial county of Hampshire on the south coast of England. Portsmouth is notable for being the United Kingdom's only island city; it is located mainly on Portsea Island. It is situated 64 miles (103 km) south west from London and 19 miles (31 km) south east of Southampton.

As a significant naval port for centuries, Portsmouth is home to the world's oldest dry dock still in use and also home to some famous ships, including HMS *Warrior*, the Tudor carrack *Mary Rose* and Lord Nelson's flagship, HMS *Victory*. Although smaller than in its heyday, the naval base remains a major dockyard and base for the Royal Navy and Royal Marine Commandos whose Headquarters resides there. There is also a thriving commercial ferryport serving destinations on the continent for freight and passenger traffic. The City of Portsmouth and Portsmouth Football Club are both nicknamed **Pompey**.

The Spinnaker Tower is a striking recent addition to the city's skyline. It can be found in the redeveloped former HMS *Vernon*, formerly a shore establishment or 'stone frigate' of the Royal Navy, now an area of retail outlets, restaurants, clubs and bars now known as Gunwharf Quays.

The City of Portsmouth has a population of 207,100 and is the only city in England with a greater population density (5,145 /km^2 (13,330 /sq mi)) than London (4,984 /km^2 (12,910 /sq mi)). The Portsmouth Urban Area, which includes Fareham, Portchester, Gosport and Havant, is the 13th largest urban area in the United Kingdom and the largest in Hampshire, with an estimated 520,000 residents Office of Population Censuses and Surveys Census 2011. Portsmouth combines with Southampton to form a single metropolitan area with a population over a million, one of the United Kingdom's most populous metropolitan areas.

Rhodes, Greece is an island in Greece, located in the eastern Aegean Sea. It is the largest of the Dodecanese islands in terms of both land area and population, with a population of 115,490 (2011 census), and also the island group's historical capital.

Administratively the island forms a separate municipality within the Rhodes regional unit, which is part of the South Aegean region. The principal town of the island and seat of the municipality is Rhodes. The city of Rhodes had 50,636 inhabitants in 2011. It is located northeast of Crete, southeast of Athens and southwest of the Anatolian coast in Turkey.

Historically, Rhodes was famous worldwide for the Colossus of Rhodes, one of the Seven Wonders of the Ancient World. The medieval Old Town of the City of Rhodes has been declared a World Heritage Site. Today, it is one of the most popular tourist destinations in Europe.

Rhodes is closer to Asia Minor than to the Greek mainland.

The island of Rhodes is shaped like a spearhead, 79.7 km (49.5 mi) long and 38 km (24 mi) wide, with a total area of approximately 1,400 square kilometres (541 sq mi) and a coastline of approximately 220 km (137 mi). The city of Rhodes is located at the northern tip of the island, as well as the site of the ancient and modern commercial harbors. The main air gateway (Diagoras International Airport, IATA code: RHO) is located 14 km (9 mi) to the southwest of the city in Paradisi. The road network radiates from the city along the east and west coasts.

Outside of the city of Rhodes, the island is dotted with small villages and beach resorts, among them

Faliraki, Lindos, Kremasti, Haraki, Pefkos, Archangelos, Afantou, Koskinou, Embona (Attavyros), Paradisi, and Trianta (Ialysos).

It is situated 363 km (226 mi) east-south-east from Greece mainland and only 18 km (11 mi) from the southern shore of Turkey.

Roosevelt Roads, Puerto Rico is a former United States Navy base in the town of Ceiba, Puerto Rico. The site is run today as José Aponte de la Torre Airport, a public use airport.

In 1919, the future U.S. President Franklin D. Roosevelt, then Assistant Secretary of the Navy, toured Puerto Rico, visiting Ceiba. When he returned to Washington, D.C., he expressed a liking for the terrain where the base now is. This was during the World War I era, and the United States could benefit from an air field in Ceiba. While Puerto Rico is a commonwealth, its territorial rights belong to the United States, which made it perfectly feasible, and ideal, for the American government to build an airplane base in Ceiba.

It took many years for the United States Government to become convinced of the need for an air base in Ceiba. When Adolf Hitler and Nazi-led Germany began to invade other European countries, the US, led by then President Roosevelt, entertained the idea of a Naval air station in Ceiba. With war in the European and Pacific theatres, they saw an airbase in the Caribbean as necessary. The base had been inaugurated, but scaled down to maintenance status with a public works office in 1944. From then until 1957, the base went through many shifts, being opened seven times and closed eight times. Meanwhile, it continued as a source of employment for the citizens of Ceiba.

In 1957, it was upgraded to Naval Station status. Fort Bundy was located there, but it crossed over to parts of Vieques, a fact which would become important in the future. An American military mission, the M3, was located there. It was part of the "Naval Computer and Telecommunications Station, Puerto Rico Base Communication Department". M3 had a fleet center, a technical control facility and a Tactical support communications department, among other things. The M3 was designated to help Puerto Rico, the United States and other Caribbean and Latin American countries to deal with drug trafficking, illegal immigration and other problems. The main purpose of the base was tactical support for land/sea/air maneuvers on Vieques Island.

For the next 47 years the base was utilized for flight practice, as well as other missions and control of the area's air space. In August 2002, a MC-130H airplane carrying seven airmen crashed in the town of Caguas, while en route from Roosevelt Roads to Rafael Hernández Airport in Aguadilla. All seven perished, in the largest air tragedy in Caguas history.

Rota, Spain Spanish name Base Naval de Rota, is a Spanish naval base commanded by a Spanish Rear Admiral and fully funded by the United States of America. Located in Rota, Spain, and near the Spanish town of El Puerto de Santa María, NavSta Rota is the largest American military community in Spain and houses US Navy and US Marine Corps personnel. There are also small US Army and US Air Force contingents on the base.

Described by the US Navy as the "Gateway to the Mediterranean", Naval Station Rota is home to an airfield and a seaport; the airfield has often caused the base to be misidentified as "Naval Air Station Rota." The base is the headquarters for Commander, U.S. Naval Activities Spain (COMNAVACTSPAIN), as well as a primary gateway for Air Mobility Command flights into Europe.

Naval Station Rota is strategically located near the Strait of Gibraltar and at the halfway point between the United States and Southwest Asia. Because of this ideal location, the base is able to provide invaluable support to both US Sixth Fleet units in the Mediterranean and to USAF Air Mobility Command units transiting to Germany and Southwest Asia. The Base and its tenant commands are located within the boundaries of the 6,100-acre (25 km^2) Spanish 'Base Naval de Rota.' Under the guidance of the Agreement for Defense Cooperation, the US and Spanish navies work together and share many facilities. The US Navy has the responsibility for maintaining the station's infrastructure, including a 670-acre (2.7 km^2)

airfield, three active piers, 426 facilities and 806 family housing units.

From Naval Station Rota Spain, the VLF-transmitter Guardamar, which uses Torreta de Guardamar, the tallest man-made structure in the European Union as antenna, is telecontroled.

Naval Station Rota provides support for US and NATO ships; supports the safe and efficient movement of US Navy and US Air Force flights and passengers; and provides cargo, fuel, and ammunition to units in the region. The Naval Station is the only base in the Mediterranean capable of supporting Amphibious Readiness Group post-deployment wash-downs. The base port also offers secure, pier side maintenance and backload facilities. Rota supports Amphibious Readiness Group turnovers and hosts Sailors and Marines from visiting afloat units. The base also provides Quality of Life support to Morón Air Base, ARG support sites at Palma de Majorca, NATO headquarters in Madrid and the Military Sealift Command's Maritime Prepositioning Squadron 1. Rota also supports NASA Space Shuttle missions, and ongoing operations in the European theater of operations. The piers in Rota are available for aircraft carriers of US and NATO, including *Príncipe de Asturias*, the only aircraft carrier owned by Spanish Navy.

The mission of US Forces at Rota, as well as other US Navy installations in the Mediterranean such as NAS Sigonella and Souda Air Base is to provide Command,

Control and Logistics Support to US and NATO Operating Forces. These three facilities are undergoing a transformation from Maritime Patrol Aircraft airfields to Multi-role "Hubs" providing crucial air-links for USAF strategic airlift and mobility in support of US European Command (EUCOM), Central Command (CENTCOM) and African Area contingency operations under CENTCOM, EUCOM and the evolving Africa Command (AFRICOM).

The base is used jointly by Spain and the United States. It remains under the Spanish flag and is commanded by a Spanish Vice Admiral. While the Spanish Navy is responsible for external security of the base, both Navies are charged with internal security. NAVSTA Rota is technically a tenant facility of the Rota Spanish Navy base, although as such the USA pays for all the expenses and capital improvements. As such, certain U.S. military customs are not observed, such as the display of a U.S. Flag, which is only allowed during the annual Fourth of July celebration.

Rotterdam, Netherlands is the second-largest city in the Netherlands and one of the largest ports in the world. Starting as a dam constructed in 1270 on the Rotte River, Rotterdam has grown into a major international commercial centre. Its strategic location at the Rhine-Meuse-Scheldt delta on the North Sea and at the heart of a massive rail, road, air and inland waterway distribution system extending throughout Europe is the reason that Rotterdam is often called the "Gateway to Europe".

In the province of South Holland, Rotterdam is in the west of Netherlands and the south of the Randstad. The population of the city was 616,250 on February 1, 2012. The population of the greater Rotterdam area, called "Rotterdam-Rijnmond" or just "Rijnmond", is approximately 1.3 million. The combined urban area of Rotterdam and The Hague is the 206th largest urban area in the world. One of Europe's most vibrant, multicultural cities, Rotterdam is known for its university (Erasmus), cutting-edge architecture, lively cultural life, striking riverside setting and maritime heritage. It is also known for the Rotterdam Blitz.

The largest port in Europe and one of the busiest ports in the world, the port of Rotterdam was the world's busiest port from 1962 to 2004, when it was surpassed by Shanghai. Rotterdam's commercial and strategic importance is based on its location near the mouth of the Nieuwe Maas (New Meuse), a channel in the delta formed by the Rhine and Meuse on the North Sea. These rivers lead directly into the centre of Europe, including the industrial Ruhr region.

During World War II, the German army invaded the Netherlands on May 10, 1940. Adolf Hitler had hoped to conquer the country in just one day, but his forces met unexpectedly fierce resistance. The Dutch army was finally forced to capitulate on May 15, 1940, following

Hitler's bombing Rotterdam on May 14 and threatening to bomb other Dutch cities. The heart of Rotterdam was almost completely destroyed by the Luftwaffe; 900 civilians were killed and 80,000 made homeless. The City Hall survived the bombing. Ossip Zadkine later strikingly captured the event with his statue *De Verwoeste Stad* ('The Destroyed City'). The statue stands near the *Leuvehaven*, not far from the Erasmusbrug in the centre of the city, on the north shore of the river *Nieuwe Maas*.

Santiago de Cuba is the second largest city of Cuba and capital city of Santiago de Cuba Province in the south-eastern area of the island, some 540 miles (870 km) south-east of the Cuban capital of Havana.

The municipality extends over 1,023.8 square kilometers (395.3 sq mi), and contains the communities of El Caney, Guilera, Antonio Maceo, Bravo, Castillo Duany, Leyte Vidal and Moncada.

Historically Santiago de Cuba has long been the second most important city on the island after Havana, and still remains the second largest. It is on a bay connected to the Caribbean Sea and is an important sea port. In 2004 the city of Santiago de Cuba had a population of about 494,337 people.

San Diego, CA is the eighth-largest city in the United States and second-largest city in California. The city is located on the coast of the Pacific Ocean in

Southern California, immediately adjacent to the Mexican border. The birthplace of California, San Diego is known for its mild year-round climate, natural deep-water harbor, extensive beaches, long association with the U.S. Navy, and recent emergence as a healthcare and biotechnology development center. The population was 1,322,553 based on latest population estimates for 2012.

Historically home to the Kumeyaay people, San Diego was the first site visited by Europeans on what is now the West Coast of the United States. Upon landing in San Diego Bay in 1542, Juan Cabrillo claimed the entire area for Spain, forming the basis for the settlement of Alta California 200 years later. The Presidio and Mission of San Diego, founded in 1769, were the first European settlement in what is now California. In 1821, San Diego became part of newly independent Mexico, and in 1850, became part of the United States following the Mexican-American War and the admission of California to the union.

The city is the county seat of San Diego County and is the economic center of the San Diego-Carlsbad-San Marcos metropolitan area as well as the San Diego-Tijuana metropolitan area. San Diego's main economic engines are military and defense-related activities, tourism, international trade, and manufacturing. The presence of the University of California, San Diego (UCSD), with the affiliated UCSD Medical Center, has helped make the area a center of research in biotechnology.

Original inhabitants of the region are now known as the San Dieguito and La Jolla people. The area of San Diego has been inhabited for more than 10,000 years by the Kumeyaay people. The first European to visit the region was Portuguese-born explorer Juan Rodríguez Cabrillo sailing under the flag of Castile. Sailing his flagship *San Salvador* from Navidad, New Spain, Cabrillo claimed the bay for the Spanish Empire in 1542 and named the site 'San Miguel'. In November 1602, Sebastián Vizcaíno was sent to map the California coast. Arriving on his flagship *San Diego*, Vizcaíno surveyed the harbor and what are now Mission Bay and Point Loma and named the area for the Catholic Saint Didacus, a Spaniard more commonly known as *San Diego de Alcalá*. On November 12, 1602, the first Christian religious service of record in Alta California was conducted by Friar Antonio de la Ascensión, a member of Vizcaíno's expedition, to celebrate the feast day of San Diego.

San Juan, Puerto Rico is the capital and most populous municipality in Puerto Rico, an unincorporated territory of the United States. As of the 2010 census, it had a population of 395,326 making it the 46th-largest city under the jurisdiction of the United States. San Juan was founded by Spanish colonists in 1521, who called it *Ciudad de Puerto Rico* ("Rich Port City"). Puerto Rico's capital is the second oldest European-established city in the Americas, after Santo Domingo, in the

Dominican Republic. Several historical buildings are located in San Juan; among the most notable are the city's former defensive forts, Fort San Felipe del Morro and Fort San Cristóbal, and La Fortaleza, the oldest executive mansion in continuous use in the Americas.

Today, San Juan is one of Puerto Rico's most important seaports, and is the island's manufacturing, financial, cultural, and tourism center. The population of the Metropolitan Statistical Area, including San Juan and the municipalities of Bayamón, Guaynabo, Cataño, Canóvanas, Caguas, Toa Alta, Toa Baja, Carolina and Trujillo Alto, is about 2 million inhabitants; thus, about half the population of Puerto Rico now lives and works in this area. San Juan is also a principal city of the San Juan-Caguas-Fajardo Combined Statistical Area. The city has been the host of numerous important events within the sports community, including the 1979 Pan American Games, 1966 Central American and Caribbean Games, 2006 and 2009 World Baseball Classics, the Caribbean Series and the Special Olympics and MLB San Juan Series in 2010.

In 1508, Juan Ponce de León founded the original settlement Caparra (named after the province Caceres, Spain, the birthplace of then-governor of Spain's Caribbean territories Nicolás de Ovando), which today is known as the Pueblo Viejo sector of Guaynabo, just to the west of the present San Juan metropolitan area. A year later, the settlement was moved to a site then called

Puerto Rico, Spanish for "rich port" or "good port", after its similar geographical features to the island of Gran Canaria in the Canary Islands. In 1521, the newer settlement was given its formal name, *San Juan Bautista de Puerto Rico*, in honor of John the Baptist, following the tradition of christening the town with both its formal name and the name which Christopher Columbus had originally given the island.

The ambiguous use of *San Juan Bautista* and *Puerto Rico* for both the city and the island led to a reversal in practical use by most inhabitants: by 1746, the name for the city (Puerto Rico) had become that of the entire island, while the name for the Island (*San Juan Bautista*) had become the name for the city.

Savannah, GA is the largest city and the county seat of Chatham County, in the U.S. state of Georgia. Established in 1733, the city of Savannah was the colonial capital of the Province of Georgia and later the first state capital of Georgia. A strategic port city in the American Revolution and during the American Civil War, Savannah is today an industrial center and an important Atlantic seaport. It is Georgia's fifth largest city and third largest metropolitan area.

Each year Savannah attracts millions of visitors, who enjoy the city's architecture and historic buildings: the birthplace of Juliette Gordon Low (founder of the Girl Scouts of the United States of America), the Georgia

Historical Society (the oldest continually operating historical society in the South), the Telfair Academy of Arts and Sciences (one of the South's first public museums), the First African Baptist Church (one of the oldest African-American Baptist congregations in the United States), Temple Mickve Israel (the third oldest synagogue in America), and the Central of Georgia Railway roundhouse complex (the oldest standing antebellum rail facility in America).

Savannah's downtown area, which includes the Savannah Historic District, the Savannah Victorian Historic District and 22 park-like squares, is one of the largest National Historic Landmark Districts in the United States (designated by the U.S. government in 1966). Downtown Savannah largely retains the original town plan prescribed by founder James Oglethorpe (a design now known as The Oglethorpe Plan). Savannah was the host city for the sailing competitions during the 1996 Summer Olympics held in Atlanta.

On February 12, 1733, General James Oglethorpe and his settlers landed at Yamacraw Bluff and were greeted by Tomochichi, the Yamacraws, and Indian traders John and Mary Musgrove. Mary Musgrove often served as a translator. The city of Savannah was founded on that date, along with the colony of Georgia. In 1751 Savannah and the rest of Georgia became a Royal Colony and Savannah was made the colonial capital of Georgia.

The city was named for the Savannah River, which probably derives from variant names for the Shawnee, a Native American people who migrated to the river in the 1680s. The Shawnee destroyed another Native people, the Westo, and occupied their lands at the head of the Savannah River's navigation on the fall line, near present-day Augusta. These Shawnee were known by several local variants, including Shawano, Savano, Savana and Savannah. Another theory is that the name Savannah refers to the extensive marshlands surrounding the river for miles inland, and is derived from the English term savanna, a kind of tropical grassland, which was borrowed by the English from Spanish *sabana* and used in the Southern Colonies. (The Spanish word comes from the Taino word *zabana*.) Still other theories suggest that the name Savannah originates from Algonquian terms meaning "southerner" or perhaps "salt".

Southport, NC is a city in Brunswick County, North Carolina, near the mouth of the Cape Fear River. It is part of the Wilmington Metropolitan Statistical Area. Its population was listed as 2,351 for the 2000 census.

Southport has been a popular filming location for television and movies, including film adaptations of the works of novelist Nicholas Sparks. The town can be seen in the television series *Dawson's Creek* and numerous movies, including: *I Know What You Did Last Summer*,

Summer Catch, *Domestic Disturbance*, *Crimes of the Heart*, *Nights in Rodanthe*, *A Walk to Remember* and *Safe Haven*.

Southport is the location of the North Carolina Fourth of July Festival, which attracts 40,000 to 50,000 visitors annually to enjoy its parade, fireworks, vendors from around the country, and other festivities.

The Southport area was explored as early as the 1500s by Spanish explorers. During the 18th century, British settlements along the Carolina coast lacked fortifications to protect against pirates and privateers, and numerous Spanish attackers exploited this weakness. In response to these attacks, Governor Gabriel Johnston in 1744 appointed a committee to select the best location to construct a fort for the defense of the Cape Fear River region. It was determined that the fort should be constructed at a site the mouth of the Cape Fear River. During the same year, France declared war against Britain, later known as King George's War, increasing the fort's need. Further, increasingly bold Spanish privateer raids led the North Carolina General Assembly to authorize the construction of "Johnston's Fort" in April 1745, which would come to be known as Fort Johnston. The Governor of South Carolina agreed to lend ten small cannons for the fort, and the legislature, in spring 1748, appropriated 2000 pounds for construction costs, and construction finally began. Southport developed around Fort Johnston.

Southport was founded as the town of Smithville in 1792. Joshua Potts had requested the formation of a town adjacent to Fort Johnston, and the North Carolina General Assembly formed a commission of five men to administer its founding. The town was named after Benjamin Smith, a Colonel in the Continental Army during the Revolutionary War and later governor of North Carolina. Smithville grew as a fishing village and through supporting military activity. Smithville was the county seat of Brunswick County from 1808 to 1887. In an effort to promote the town as a major shipping port, Smithville was renamed Southport in 1887. Smithville Township, in which Southport lies, and other local landmarks, such as the cemetery, retains the Smithville name.

St. George, Bermuda located on the island and within the parish of the same names, settled in 1612, was the first permanent English settlement on the islands of Bermuda. It is often described as the third successful English settlement in the Americas, after St. John's, Newfoundland, and Jamestown, Virginia. St. George's is claimed to be the oldest continuously inhabited English town in the New World.

Originally called *New London*, St. George's was first settled in 1612. This was three years after the first English settlers landed on St. George's Island on their way to Virginia. Led by Admiral Sir George Somers and Lieutenant-General Sir Thomas Gates, they had deliberately steered their ship, the *Sea Venture,* onto a reef. The survivors built two new ships, and most continued their voyage to Jamestown, but the Virginia Company laid claim to the island.

Two men remained behind to maintain the company's possession of the archipelago (a third stayed when the *Patience* returned later that year). By the Virginia Company's Third Charter in 1612, the boundaries of the new colony were extended out to sea to include Bermuda. The company sent a party of 60 new settlers to Bermuda to join the three men left behind by the *Sea Venture.* After a brief period on neighboring St. David's, the settlers started building structures at St. George's, located in a sheltered sound that kept ships protected from bad weather.

Suez Canal is an artificial sea-level waterway in Egypt, connecting the Mediterranean Sea and the Red Sea. Opened in November 1869 after 10 years of construction work, it allows transportation by water between Europe and Asia without navigation around Africa. The northern terminus is Port Said and the southern terminus is Port Tawfiq at the city of Suez. Ismailia lies on its west bank, 3 km (1.9 mi) from the half-way point.

When first built, the canal was 164 km (102 mi) long and 8 m (26 ft) deep. After multiple enlargements, the canal is 193.30 km (120.11 mi) long, 24 m (79 ft) deep and 205 meters (673 ft) wide as of 2010. It consists of the northern access channel of 22 km (14 mi), the canal itself of 162.25 km (100.82 mi) and the southern access channel of 9 km (5.6 mi).

The canal is single lane with passing places in the "Ballah By-Pass" and the Great Bitter Lake. It contains no locks; seawater flows freely through the canal. In general, the canal north of the Bitter Lakes flows north in winter and south in summer. The current south of the lakes changes with the tide at Suez.

The canal is owned and maintained by the Suez Canal Authority (SCA) of Egypt. Under international treaty, it may be used "in time of war as in time of peace, by every vessel of commerce or of war, without distinction of flag."

Ancient west-east canals have facilitated travel from the Nile to the Red Sea. One smaller canal is believed to have been constructed under the auspices of either Senusret II or Ramesses II. Another canal probably incorporating a portion of the first was constructed under the reign of Necho II and completed by Darius.

Thessaloniki, Greece is the second-largest city in Greece and the capital of the region of Central Macedonia as well as the capital of the Decentralized Administration of Macedonia and Thrace.[4] Its honorific title is Συμπρωτεύουσα (*Symprotévusa*), literally "co-capital", and stands as a reference to its historical status as the Συμβασιλεύουσα (*Symvasilévousa*), "coreigning" city of the Eastern Roman Empire, alongside Constantinople.

According to the preliminary results of the 2011 census, the municipality of Thessaloniki today has a population of 322,240, while the Thessaloniki Urban Area (the contiguous built up area forming the "City of Thessaloniki") has a population of 790,824; making it the fifth largest and most populated city in the Balkans and the second most populated city that is not a capital, after Istanbul. Furthermore, the Thessaloniki Metropolitan Area extends over an area of 1,455.62 km^2 (562.02 sq mi) and its population in 2011 reached a total of 1,006,730 inhabitants.

Thessaloniki is Greece's second major economic, industrial, commercial and political centre, and a major transportation hub for the rest of southeastern Europe; its commercial port is also of great importance for Greece and the southeastern European hinterland. The city is renowned for its festivals, events and vibrant cultural life in general, and is considered to be Greece's cultural capital. Events such as the Thessaloniki International Trade Fair and the Thessaloniki International Film Festival are held annually, while the city also hosts the largest bi-annual meeting of the Greek diaspora. In 2014 Thessaloniki will be the European Youth Capital.

Founded in 315 BC by Cassander of Macedon, Thessaloniki's history spans some 2,300 years. An important metropolis by the Roman period, Thessaloniki was the second largest and wealthiest city of the Byzantine Empire. Thessaloniki is home to numerous notable Byzantine monuments, including the Paleochristian and Byzantine monuments of Thessaloniki, a UNESCO World Heritage Site, as well as several Roman, Ottoman and Sephardic Jewish structures. The city's main university, Aristotle University, is the largest in Greece and the Balkans.

The earliest known letter by Paul the Apostle was written to the early Christian church in Thessaloniki and is identified as First Thessalonians; it is among the books in the New Testament whose authorship by Paul is generally regarded by scholars as being undisputed. A later letter to the same church follows in the Christian Bible as Second Thessalonians.

In addition to its historic roots, Thessaloniki is also a very popular tourist destination in Greece. In 2010, Lonely Planet ranked Thessaloniki as the world's fifth-best party city worldwide, comparable to other cities such as Dubai and Montreal. For 2013 National Geographic Magazine included Thessaloniki in its top tourist destinations worldwide.

Trieste, Italy is a city and seaport in northeastern Italy. It is situated towards the end of a narrow strip of Italian territory lying between the Adriatic Sea and Italy's border with Slovenia, which lies almost immediately south and east of the city. Trieste is located at the head of the Gulf of Trieste and throughout history it has been influenced by its location at the crossroads of Germanic, Latin and Slavic cultures. In 2009, it had a population of about 205,000 and it is the capital of the autonomous region Friuli Venezia Giulia and Trieste province.

Trieste was one of the oldest parts of the Habsburg Monarchy from 1382 until 1918. In the 19th century, it was the most important port of one of the Great Powers of Europe. As a prosperous seaport in the Mediterranean region, Trieste became the fourth largest city of the Austro-Hungarian Empire (after Vienna, Budapest, and Prague). In the fin-de-siecle period, it emerged as an important hub for literature and music. However, the collapse of the Austro-Hungarian Empire and Trieste's union to Italy after World War I led to some decline of its "Mittel-European" cultural and commercial importance. Enjoying an economic revival during the 1930s and throughout the Cold War, Trieste was an important spot in the struggle between the Eastern and Western blocs. Today, the city is in one of the richest regions of Italy, and has been a great centre for shipping, through its port (Port of Trieste), shipbuilding and financial services.

Tunis, Tunisia is the capital of both the Tunisian Republic and the Tunis Governorate. It is Tunisia's largest city, with a population of 2,256,320 as of 2011; the greater metropolitan area holds some 2,412,500 inhabitants.

Situated on a large Mediterranean Sea gulf (the Gulf of Tunis), behind the Lake of Tunis and the port of La Goulette (Halq al Wadi), the city extends along the coastal plain and the hills that surround it. At the centre of more modern development (from the colonial era and later) lies the old medina. Beyond this district lie the suburbs of Carthage, La Marsa, and Sidi Bou Said.

The medina is found at the centre of the city: a dense agglomeration of alleys and covered passages, full of intense scents and colors, boisterous and active trade, and a surfeit of goods on offer ranging from leather to plastic, tin to the finest filigree, tourist souvenirs to the works of tiny crafts shops.

Just through the Sea Gate (also known as the *Bab el Bahr* and the *Porte de France*) begins the modern city, or Ville Nouvelle, transversed by the grand Avenue Habib Bourguiba (often referred to by popular press and travel guides as "the Tunisian Champs-Élysées"), where the colonial-era buildings provide a clear contrast to smaller, older structures. As the capital city of the country, Tunis is the focus of Tunisian political and administrative life; it is also the centre of the country's commercial activity. The expansion of the Tunisian economy in recent decades is reflected in the booming development of the outer city where one can see clearly the social challenges brought about by rapid modernization in Tunisia.

U.S. Naval Base Subic Bay, Philippines was a major ship-repair, supply, and rest and recreation facility of the United States Navy located in Olongapo, Zambales, Philippines. The Navy Exchange had the largest volume of sales of any exchange in the world, and the Naval Supply Depot handled the largest volume of fuel oil of any navy facility in the world. The naval base was the largest overseas military installation of the United States Armed Forces after Clark Air Base in Angeles City was closed in 1991. Following its closure in 1992, it was transformed into the Subic Bay Freeport Zone by the Philippine government.

Subic Bay's famous strategic location, sheltered anchorages, and deep water was first made known when the Spanish explorer Juan de Salcedo reported its existence to the Spanish authorities upon his return to Manila after Salcedo arrived in Zambales to establish the Spanish crown but it would be a number of years before the Spanish would consider establishing a base there.

Cavite, which had been home to most of the Spanish fleet in the Philippines, suffered from unhealthy living conditions and was vulnerable in time of war and bad weather because of its shallow water and lack of shelter. Because of these, a military expedition was sent to Subic Bay in 1868 with orders to survey the bay to find out if it would be a suitable site for a naval yard. The Spanish explored the entire bay and concluded that it had much promise and thus reported their findings to Cavite. This report was not well-accepted in Manila as the Spanish command was reluctant to move to the provincial isolation of Subic. Finally, in 1884, a Royal Decree declared Subic Bay as a naval port.

On March 8, 1885, the Spanish Navy authorized construction of the *Arsenal en Olongapo* and by the following September, work started at Olongapo. Both the harbor and its inner basin were dredged and a drainage canal was built, as the Spanish military authorities were planning to make Olongapo and their Navy yard an "island." This canal also served as a line of defense and over which the bridge at the base's Main Gate passes. When the Arsenal was finished, the *Caviteño*, the *Santa Ana*, and the *San Quentin*, all of which were gunboats, were assigned for its defense. To complement these gunboats, coastal artilleries were planned for the east and west ends of the station, as well as on Grande Island.

Seawalls, causeways and a short railway were built across the swampy tidal flats. To finish these projects, thousands of tons of dirt and rock from Kalalake in Olongapo had to be brought in to be used as fill. The magnitude of this quarrying was so huge that a hill eventually disappeared and became a lagoon in the area now known as Bicentennial Park.

The main entrance to the Arsenal was the West Gate, which still stands at present. This gate was equipped with gun ports and also served as a jail. This gate was connected to the South Gate, which was near the water front, by a high wall of locally quarried stone.

Inside the Arsenal, the Spanish constructed a foundry, as well as other shops, which were necessary for the construction and repair of ships. The buildings were laid out in two rows on Rivera Point, a sandy patch of land jutting into the bay, and named after the incumbent Captain-General of the Philippines, Fernando Primo de Rivera. The Arsenal's showpiece was the station commandant's headquarters, which was a one-story building of molave and narra, and stood near today's Alava Pier and had colored glass windows.

The Spanish navy yard was constructed in the area that was last occupied by the U.S. Naval Ship Repair Facility.

Valencia, Spain is the capital of the autonomous community of Valencia and the third largest city in Spain after Madrid and Barcelona, with around 809,000 inhabitants in the administrative centre. Valencia is also Spain's third largest metropolitan area, with a population ranging from 1.7 to 2.3 million. The city has global city status. The Port of Valencia is the 5th busiest container port in Europe and the largest on the

Mediterranean Sea, with a trade volume of 4.21 million TEU's.

Shipmates – Valencia 1957

Valencia was founded as a Roman colony in 138 BC. The city is situated on the banks of the Turia, on the east coast of the Iberian Peninsula, fronting the Gulf of Valencia on the Mediterranean Sea. Its historic centre is one of the largest in Spain, with approximately 169 acres; this heritage of ancient monuments, views and cultural attractions makes Valencia one of the country's most popular tourist destinations. Major monuments include Valencia Cathedral, the *Torres de Serranos*, the *Torres de Quart*, the *Llotja de la Seda* (declared a World Heritage Site by UNESCO in 1996), and the *Ciutat de les Arts i les Ciències* (City of Arts and Sciences), an entertainment-based cultural and architectural complex designed by Santiago Calatrava and Félix Candela. The *Museu de Belles Arts de València* houses a large collection of paintings from the 14th to the 18th centuries, including works by Velázquez, El Greco, and Goya, as well as an important series of engravings by

Piranesi. The *Institut Valencià d'Art Modern* (Valencian Institute of Modern Art) houses both permanent collections and temporary exhibitions of contemporary art and photography.

Valencia is integrated into an industrial area on the *Costa del Azahar* (Orange Blossom Coast). Valencia's main festival is the *Falles*. The traditional Spanish dish, *paella*, originated in Valencia.

The city is situated on the banks of the Turia river, on the eastern coast of the Iberian peninsula and the western part of the Mediterranean Sea, fronting the Gulf of Valencia. At the time of its founding by the Romans it stood on a river island in the Turia, 6.4 km (4 mi) from the sea. The Albufera, a saltwater lagoon and estuary which lies about 11 km (7 mi) south of the city, is one of the largest lakes in Spain; it was bought by the City Council from the Crown of Spain for 1,072,980 pesetas in 1911, and today forms the main portion of the *Parc Natural de l'Albufera* (Albufera Nature Reserve), with a surface area of 21,120 hectares (52,200 acres). Because of its cultural, historical and ecological value, it was declared a natural park by the *Generalitat Valenciana* in 1986.

Venice, Italy is a city in northeastern Italy sited on a group of 118 small islands separated by canals and linked by bridges. It is located in the marshy Venetian Lagoon which stretches along the shoreline between the mouths of the Po and the Piave Rivers. Venice is renowned for the beauty of its setting, its architecture and its artworks. The city in its entirety is listed as a World Heritage Site, along with its lagoon.

Venice is the capital of the Veneto region. In 2009, there were 270,098 people residing in Venice's commune (the population estimate of 272,000 inhabitants includes the population of the whole Commune of Venezia; around 60,000 in the historic city of Venice (*Centro storico*); 176,000 in *Terraferma* (the *Mainland*), mostly in the large *frazioni* of Mestre and Marghera; 31,000 live on other islands in the lagoon). Together with Padua and Treviso, the city is included in the Padua-Treviso-Venice Metropolitan Area (PATREVE), with a total population of 1,600,000. PATREVE is only a statistical metropolitan area without degree of autonomy.

The name is derived from the ancient Veneti people who inhabited the region by the 10th century BC. The city historically was the capital of the Venetian Republic. Venice has been known as the "La Dominante", "Serenissima", "Queen of the Adriatic", "City of Water", "City of Masks", "City of Bridges", "The Floating City", and "City of Canals". Luigi Barzini described it in *The New York Times* as "undoubtedly the most beautiful city built by man". Venice has also been described by the *Times Online* as being one of Europe's most romantic cities.

The Republic of Venice was a major maritime power during the Middle Ages and Renaissance, and a staging area for the Crusades and the Battle of Lepanto, as well as a very important center of commerce (especially silk, grain, and spice) and art in the 13th century up to the end of the 17th century. This made Venice a wealthy city throughout most of its history. It is also known for its several important artistic movements, especially the Renaissance period. Venice has played an important role in the history of symphonic and operatic music, and it is the birthplace of Antonio Vivaldi.

While there are no historical records that deal directly with the founding of Venice, tradition and the available evidence have led several historians to agree that the original population of Venice consisted of refugees from Roman cities near Venice such as Padua, Aquileia, Treviso, Altino and Concordia (modern Portogruaro) and from the undefended countryside, who were fleeing successive waves of Germanic and Hun invasions. Some late Roman sources reveal the existence of fishermen on the islands in the original marshy lagoons. They were referred to as *incolae lacunae* ("lagoon dwellers"). The traditional founding is identified with the dedication of the first church, that of San Giacomo at the islet of Rialto (Rivoalto, "High Shore"), which is said to have been at the stroke of noon on 25 March 421.

Villefranche, France is a commune in the Alpes-Maritimes department in the Provence-Alpes-Côte d'Azur region on the French Riviera.

Villefranche-sur-Mer adjoins the city of Nice to the east along Mont Boron, Mont Alban and Mont Vinaigrier, and 10 km (6.2 mi) south west of Monaco. The bay (*rade*) of Villefranche is one of the deepest natural harbors of any port in the Mediterranean Sea and provides safe anchorage for large ships, reaching depths of 95 m (320 ft) between the Cape of Nice and Cap Ferrat; it extends to the south to form a 500 m (1700 ft) abyss known as the undersea Canyon of Villefranche at about one nautical mile off the coastline.

The town limits extend to the hills surrounding the bay climbing from sea level to an altitude of 520 m

(1750 ft) at Mont-Leuze, reflecting on land the features found offshore. The three "Corniches" or main roads linking Nice to Italy pass through Villefranche.

The site of what is now Villefranche and surrounding Beaulieu-sur-Mer and Saint-Jean-Cap-Ferrat has been settled since prehistoric times. Celto-ligurian tribes roamed the area and established farming communities on the surrounding hills. The Greeks and later the Romans used the natural harbour as a stop-over en route to the Greek settlements around the Western Mediterranean. After the conquest of Gaul by Julius Caesar, the Romans built an extension of the Via Aurelia (Aurelian Way), which passed through the settlement of Montolivo.

Wilhelmshaven, Germany is a coastal town in Lower Saxony, Germany. It is situated on the western side of the Jade Bight, a bay of the North Sea. Wilhelmshaven is the centre of the "Jade Bay" business region with around 330,000 inhabitants.

The adjacent Lower Saxony Wadden Sea National Park (part of the Wattenmeer UNESCO World Natural Heritage Site) provides the basis for the major tourism industry in the region.

The Siebethsburg castle, built before 1383, was occupied by pirates and destroyed in 1433 by the Hanseatic League. Four centuries later, the Kingdom of Prussia planned a fleet and a harbour on the North Sea. In 1853, Prince Adalbert of Prussia arranged the Jade

Treaty (*Jade-Vertrag*) with the Grand Duchy of Oldenburg, in which Prussia and the Grand Duchy entered into a contract: 3.13 km² of Oldenburgian territory at the Jade Bight should be ceded to Prussia. In 1869, King William I of Prussia (later also German Emperor) founded the town as an exclave of the Province of Hanover as a naval base for Prussia's developing fleet. All the hinterland of the city remained as part of the Duchy of Oldenburg.

A shipbuilder was established at Wilhelmshaven, the *Kaiserliche Werft Wilhelmshaven* (Imperial Shipyard Wilhelmshaven). On 30 June 1934, the "pocket battleship" *Admiral Graf Spee* was launched at Wilhelmshaven.

In 1937, Wilhelmshaven and Rüstringen merged and the united city, named Wilhelmshaven, became a part of the Free State of Oldenburg.

Two thirds of the town's buildings were destroyed during bombing by the Allies of World War II. On 5 May 1945, Polish forces under General Stanisław Maczek captured Wilhelmshaven and took the surrender of the entire garrison, including some 200 ships of the Kriegsmarine. They remained as part of the allied occupation forces. During World War II *Alter Banter Weg* (No. 1582 Wilhelmshaven) was a subcamp of the Neuengamme concentration camp. In 1947 the city council decided to seek a new emblem for the city. After several designs were rejected by the Control Commission for Germany - British Element (CCG/BE) an emblem of a Frisian warrior (*Rüstringer Friese*) was chosen, designed after a nail man erected in the city during the first world war to collect war donations.

Yokosuka, Japan is a city in Kanagawa Prefecture, Japan. As of June 2012, the city has an estimated population of 414,960 and a population density of 4,120 people per km². It covered an area of 100.7 km². Yokosuka is the 11th most populous city in Greater Tokyo, 12th in the Kantō region.

Yokosuka occupies most of Miura Peninsula, and is bordered by the mouth of Tokyo Bay to the east and Sagami Bay on the Pacific Ocean on the west.

The adventurer William Adams (inspiration for a character in the novel *Shōgun*), the first Briton to set foot in Japan, arrived at Uraga aboard the Dutch trading vessel *Liefde* in 1600. In 1612, he was granted the title of samurai and a fief in Hemi within the boundaries of present-day Yokosuka, due to his services to the Tokugawa shogunate. A monument to William Adams (called *Miura Anjin* in Japanese) is a local landmark in Yokosuka.

Chapter 8

A SAILOR'S LIFE

A Sailor's Life

I'm sitting here and thinking

Of days I've left behind

And I think I'll put on paper

What's running through my mind?

The people on the outside

Think a sailor's life is swell

But I'll let you in on something mate,

A sailor's life is Hell.

A sailor has one consoling thought

So gather close and I will tell,

When I die I will go to Heaven

Cause I've served my life in Hell.

I've scrubbed a million bulkheads,

I've chipped ten miles of paint,

For meaner places this side of Hell,

I swear to you there ain't.

I've stood a million hours

Just waiting for my mail,

And I've stood a million watches

On every special detail.

I've shined a million miles of brass

And I've scrubbed my dirty duds,

I slung a million hammocks

And I've peeled a million spuds.

I've cruised a million miles
And I've made a million ports,
I've spent the night in dirty jails
For trying to be a sport.

But when those final taps are sounded
And I lay aside life's cares,
I'll take my final shore leave
Right up those Golden Stairs.

'Tis then Saint Peter will greet me
And loudly he will yell….
Take your front seat in heaven, Sailor
Cause you've served your hitch in hell.

(More truth than poetry)

Sailor's Creed

"I am a United States Sailor.

I will support and defend the Constitution of the United States of America and I will obey the orders of those appointed over me.

I represent the fighting spirit of the Navy and those who have gone Before me to defend freedom and democracy around the world.

I proudly serve my country's Navy Combat team with honor, courage and Commitment.

I am committed to excellence and the fair treatment of all."

Military Life
By: Colonel Stu McIntosh, USAF Retired

Editor's Note: Although Colonel Stu McIntosh never served in our Navy, he is a veteran and his take on life in the military seems right on!

Occasionally, I venture back to one or another military post, where I'm greeted by an imposing security guard who looks carefully at my identification card, hands it back and says, "Have a good day, Sir!"

Every time I go back to any Military Base it feels good to be called by my previous rank, but odd to be in civilian clothes, walking among the servicemen and servicewomen going about their duties as I once did, many years ago.

The military is a comfort zone for anyone who has ever worn the uniform. It's a place where you know the rules and know they are enforced -- a place where everybody is busy, but not too busy to take care of business.

Because there exists behind the gates of every military facility an institutional understanding of respect, order, uniformity, accountability and dedication that becomes part of your marrow and never, ever leaves you.

Personally, I miss the fact that you always knew where you stood in the military, and who you were dealing with. That's because you could read somebody's uniform from 20 feet away and know the score.

Service personnel wear their careers on their uniforms, so to speak. When you approach each other, you can read their name tag, examine their rank and, if they are in dress uniform, read their ribbons and know where they've served.

I miss all those little things you take for granted when you're in the ranks, like breaking starch on a set of fatigues fresh from the laundry and standing in a perfectly straight line military formation that looks like a mirror as it stretches to the endless horizon.

I miss the sight of troops marching in the early morning mist, the sound of boot heels thumping in unison on the tarmac, the bark of drill instructors and the sing-song answers from the squads as they pass by in review.

To romanticize military service is to be far removed from its reality, because it's very serious business -- especially in times of war. But, I miss the salutes I'd throw at senior officers and the crisp returns as we crisscrossed with a "by-your-leave" sir.

I miss the smell of jet fuel hanging heavily on the night air and the sound of engines roaring down runways and disappearing into the clouds.

I even miss the hurry-up-and-wait mentality that enlisted men gripe about constantly, a masterful invention that bonded people more than they'll ever know or admit.

I miss people taking off their hats when they enter a building, speaking directly and clearly to others and never showing disrespect for rank, race, religion or gender.

I miss being a small cog in a machine so complex it constantly circumnavigates the Earth and so simple it feeds everyone on time, three times a day, on the ground, in the air or at sea.

Mostly, I don't know anyone who has served who regrets it, and doesn't feel a sense of pride when they pass through those gates and re-enter the world they left behind with their youth.

Face it guys - we all miss it............Whether you had one tour or a career, it shaped your life.

Little Known Tidbit of Naval History
By: Unknown

The U.S.S. Constitution (Old Ironsides), as a combat vessel, carried 48,600 gallons of fresh water for her crew of 475 officers and men. This was sufficient to last six months of sustained operations at sea. She carried no evaporators (i.e. fresh water distillers).

However, let it be noted that according to her ship's log, "On July 27, 1798, the U.S.S. Constitution sailed from Boston with a full complement of 475 officers and men, 48,600 gallons of fresh water, 7,400 cannon shot, 11,600 pounds of black powder and 79,400 gallons of rum."

Her mission: "To destroy and harass English shipping." Making Jamaica on 6 October, she took on 826 pounds of flour and 68,300 gallons of rum.

Then she headed for the Azores, arriving there 12 November. She provisioned with 550 pounds of beef and 64,300 gallons of Portuguese wine.

On 18 November, she set sail for England. In the ensuing days she defeated five British men-of-war and captured and scuttled 12 English merchant ships, salvaging only the rum aboard each.

By 26 January, her powder and shot were exhausted. Nevertheless, although unarmed she made a night raid up the Firth of Clyde in Scotland. Her landing party captured a whiskey distillery and transferred 40,000 gallons of single malt Scotch aboard by dawn. Then she headed home.

The U. S. S. Constitution arrived in Boston on 20 February 1799, with <u>no cannon shot, no food, no powder, no rum, no wine, no whiskey,</u> and 38,600 gallons of water.

<u>GO NAVY!</u>

Why We Call A Ship A She

By: Rear Admiral Francis D. Foley, US Navy (Retired)
Originally published in the Naval History magazine,
November/December 1998

A Salty retired U.S. Navy flag officer shuns the current trend toward political correctness.

Ships are referred to as "she" because men love them, but this encompasses far more than just that. Man-o'-war or merchantman, there can be a great deal of bustle about her as well as a gang of men on deck, particularly if she is slim-waisted, well-stacked, and has an inviting super-structure. It is not so much her initial cost as it is her upkeep that makes you wonder where you founder. She is greatly admired when freshly painted and all decked out to emphasize her cardinal points. If an aircraft carrier, she will look in a mirror when about to be arrested, and will wave you off if she feels you are sinking too low or a little too high, day or night. She will not hangar around with duds, but will light you off and launch you into the wild blue yonder when you muster a full head of steam.

Even a submarine reveals her topsides returning to port, heads straight for the buoys, knows her pier, and gets her breast-lines out promptly if she is single-screwed. On departure, no ship leaves port asleep, she always leaves awake. She may not mind her helm or answer to the old man when the going gets rough, and can be expected to kick up her heels on a family squall.

A ship costs a lot to dress, sometimes blows a bit of smoke, and requires periodic overhauls to extend her useful life. Some have a cute fantail, others are heavy in the stern, but all have double bottoms which demand attention. When meeting head-on, sound a recognition signal; whistle! If she does not answer up, come about and start laying alongside, but watch to see if her ship is slowing… perhaps her slip is showing? Then proceed with caution until danger of collision is over and you can fathom how much latitude she will allow.

If she does not remain on an even keel, let things ride, feel your way, and do not cross the line until you determine weather the "do" point is right for a prolonged blast. Get the feel of the helm, stay on the right tact, keep her so, and she will pay off handsomely. If she is in the roaring forties, however, you may be in the dangerous semi-circle, so do not expect much "luff<' especially under bare poles. She may think you are not under command or control and shove off. If she edges aweigh, keep her steady as she goes, but do not sink into the doldrums. Just remember that "to furnish a ship requireth much trouble, but to furnish a woman the cost is double!"

To the women who now help us "man" our ships, my apologies for the foregoing. Only the opening phrase presents my true feelings. After all, a ship's bell€ will always remain her most prized possession, and every good ship has a heart, just like yours. A trick at the wheel, like you, would have been welcome aboard when I was on "she" duty for 40 years. May God bless you all, sweetheart!

Admiral Foley was a long-time contributor to Naval History and the U.S. Naval Institute Proceedings. He lived in Annapolis, Maryland.

Good Point!

At Naval History's editorial offices, in the presence of the author, the editor reacted to the above with a resounding: "most of our readers will love it; the women will hate it!" Coincidentally, the U.S. Naval Institute's chief financial officer, obviously sensitive to such statements, overheard and inquired: "The women will hate what?" She then heard of plans to publish "Why We Call A Ship A She." Unaware of the author's presence, she asked: "If they call ships she, then why do they name them Arleigh Burke?" To that, Admiral Foley responded, "Good Point!"

A Sailor Once

*** I liked standing on the bridge wing at sunrise with salt spray in my face and clean ocean winds whipping in from the four quarters of the globe. The ship beneath me feeling like a living thing as her engines drove her swiftly through the sea.

*** I liked the sounds of the Navy - the piercing thrill of the boatswains pipe, the syncopated clangor of the ship's bell on the quarterdeck, the harsh squawk of the 1MC, and the strong language and laughter of sailors at work.

*** I liked Navy vessels -- nervous darting destroyers, plodding fleet auxiliaries and amphibs, sleek submarines and steady solid aircraft carriers.

*** I liked the proud names of Navy ships: Midway, Lexington, Saratoga, Coral Sea, Antietam, Valley Forge - memorials of great battles won and tribulations overcome.

*** I liked the lean angular names of Navy "tin-cans" and escorts - Barney, Dahlgren, Mullinix, McCloy, Damato,

Leftwich, Mills - mementos of heroes who went before us and the others - San Jose, San Diego, Los Angeles, St. Paul, Chicago - named for our cities.

*** My ships Washoe County, Windham County, Terrell County, Saratoga, Dale, and Richmond K Turner. Also don't forget Porter and William D Porter.

*** I liked the tempo of a Navy band blaring through the topside speakers as we pulled away from the oiler after refueling at sea.

*** I liked Liberty Call and the spicy scent of a foreign port.

*** I even liked the never-ending paperwork and all-hands working parties as my ship filled herself with the multitude of supplies, both critical and mundane in order to cut ties to the land and carry out her mission anywhere on the globe where there was water to float her.

*** I liked sailors, officers and enlisted men from all parts of the land, farms of the Midwest, small towns of New England, from the cities, the mountains and the prairies, from all walks of life. I trusted and depended on them as they trusted and depended on me - for professional competence, for comradeship, for strength and courage. In a word, they were "shipmates"; then and forever.

*** I liked the surge of adventure in my heart, when the word was passed: "Now set the special sea and anchor detail - all hands to quarters for leaving port," and I liked the infectious thrill of sighting home again, with the waving hands of welcome from family and friends waiting pier side.

*** The work was hard and dangerous; the going rough at times; the parting from loved ones painful, but the companionship of robust Navy laughter, the "all for one and one for all" philosophy of the sea was ever present.

*** I liked the serenity of the sea after a day of hard ship's work, as flying fish flitted across the wave tops and sunset gave way to night.

*** I liked the feel of the Navy in darkness - the masthead and range lights, the red and green navigation lights and stern light, the pulsating phosphorescence of radar repeaters - they cut through the dusk and joined with the mirror of stars overhead. And I liked drifting off to sleep lulled by the myriad noises large and small that told me that my ship was alive and well, and that my shipmates on watch would keep me safe.

*** I liked quiet mid watches with the aroma of strong coffee - the lifeblood of the Navy permeating everywhere. *** And I liked hectic watches when the exacting minuet of haze-gray shapes racing at flank speed kept all hands on a razor edge of alertness.

*** I liked the sudden electricity of "General quarters, general quarters, all hands man your battle stations," followed by the hurried clamor of running feet on ladders and the resounding thump of watertight doors as the ship transformed herself in a few brief seconds from a peaceful workplace to a weapon of war - ready for anything.

*** And I liked the sight of space-age equipment manned by youngsters clad in dungarees and sound-powered phones that their grandfathers would still recognize.

*** I liked the traditions of the Navy and the men and women who made them. I liked the proud names of Navy heroes: Halsey, Nimitz, Perry, Farragut, John Paul Jones and Burke. A sailor could find much in the Navy: Comrades-in-arms, pride in self and country, mastery of the seaman's trade. An adolescent could find adulthood.

*** In years to come, when sailors are home from the sea, they will still remember with fondness and respect the ocean in all its moods - the impossible shimmering mirror calm and the storm-tossed green water surging over the bow. And then there will come again a faint whiff of stack gas, a faint echo of engine and rudder orders, a vision of the bright bunting of signal flags snapping at the yardarm, a refrain of hearty laughter in the wardroom and Chief's quarters and mess decks.

*** Gone ashore for good they will grow wistful about their Navy days, when the seas belonged to them and a new port of call was ever over the horizon.

*** Remembering this, they will stand taller and say, "I WAS A SAILOR ONCE. I WAS A PART OF THE NAVY, AND THE NAVY WILL ALWAYS BE A PART OF ME."

Ways to Simulate Your Days in the Navy

Have your wife wake you up every 2 hours by shaking you & shinning a flashlight in your eyes then say: "Sorry, wrong rack."

Make sure you wet your toilet paper rolls before using them.

Have your family & friends vote on a movie they want to see, and then take them to a different movie.

Stand in a closet for 8 hours; call your wife every hour while in there and say: "All is secure."

Save up your dirty underwear, sweaty tees and socks. Put them in a laundry bag hang it over your bed. Make sure it hangs about 10" from your nose.

Invite a group of friends over. Stand on the front porch; make them show their I.D. before they come inside.

Install your shower head at chest level then use cold water to shower.

Replace the water in your humidifier with machine oil. Then turn on high.

Dress in your best suit, stand in the driveway at attention for an hour in a cold drizzle. Have your mother-in-law come out and criticize you.

Use 18 scoops of coffee in a 12 cup coffee pot. Let in sit 5-6 hours before drinking.

When you get the midnight munchies; fix yourself a peanut butter and jelly sandwich on cold white stale bread. Eat it with a bowl of cold soup.

Good Sailor Bars

GOOD SAILOR BARS...A MUST READ FOR ALL FORMER SAILORS

This is no doubt one of the best descriptions of a good sailor bar that I have ever read. Whoever wrote this certainly knew what he was talking about. Talk about walking (or crawling) down memory lane?

Our favorite liberty bars were unlike no other watering holes or dens of iniquity inhabited by seagoing men. They had to meet strict standards to be in compliance with the acceptable requirement for a sailor beer-swilling dump.

The first and foremost requirement was a crusty old gal serving suds. She had to be able to wrestle King Kong to parade rest. Be able to balance a tray with one hand, knock sailors out of the way with the other hand and skillfully navigate through a roomful of milling around drunks. On slow nights, she had to be the kind of gal who would give you a back scratch or put her foot on the table so you could admire her new ankle bracelet some "mook" brought her back from a Hong Kong liberty.

A good barmaid had to be able to whisper sweet nothings in your young sailor ear like, "I love you no shit, you buy me Honda??" "Buy a pack of Clorets and chew up the whole thing before you get within heaving range of any gal you ever want to see again."

And, from the crusty old gal behind the bar, "Hey animals, I know we have a crowd tonight, but if any of you guys find the head facilities fully occupied and start pissing down the floor drain, you're gonna find yourself scrubbing the deck with your white hats!"

The barmaids had to be able to admire great tattoos, look at pictures of ugly bucktooth kids and smile. Be able to help haul drunks to cabs and comfort 19 year-olds who had lost someone he thought loved him in a dark corner booth.

They could look at your ship's identification shoulder tab and tell you the names of the Skippers back to the time you were a Cub Scout.

If you came in after a late night maintenance problem and fell asleep with a half eaten Slim-Jim in your hand, they tucked your pea coat around you, put out the cigarette you left burning in the ashtray and replaced the warm draft you left sitting on the table with a cold one when you woke up. Why? Simply because they were one of the few people on the face of the earth that knew what you did, and appreciated what you were doing.

And if you treated them like a decent human being and didn't drive 'em nuts by playing songs they hated on the juke box, they would lean over the back of the booth and park their soft, warm tits on your neck when they sat two San Miguel beers in front of you.

And the Imported table wipe down guy and glass washer, trash dumper, deck swabber and paper towel replacer. The guy had to have baggy tweed pants and a gold tooth and a grin like a 1950 Buick. And a name like "Ramon", "Juan", "Pedro" or "Tico". He had to smoke unfiltered Luckies, Camels or Raleighs. He wiped the tables down with a sour wash rag that smelled like a billy goat's crotch and always said, "How are choo navee mans tonight? He was the indispensable man. The guy with credentials that allowed him to borrow Slim-Jims, Beer Nuts and pickled hard boiled eggs from other beer joints when they ran out where he worked.

The establishment itself. The place had to have walls covered with ship and squadron plaques. The walls were adorned with enlarged unit patches and the dates of previous deployments. A dozen or more old yellowed photographs of fellows named "Buster", "Chicago", "P-Boat Barney", "Flaming Hooker Harry", "Malone", "Honshu Harry", "Jackson", "Douche Bag Doug", and "Capt Slade Cutter" decorated any unused space. It had to have the obligatory Michelob, Pabst Blue Ribbon and "Beer Nuts sold here" neon signs. An eight-ball mystery beer tap handle and signs reading; "Your mother does not work here, so clean away your frickin' trash." "Keep your hands off the barmaid." "Don't throw butts in urinal." "Barmaid's word is final in settling bets." "Take your fights out in the alley behind the bar!" "Owner reserves the right to waltz your worthless sorry ass outside." "Shipmates are responsible for riding herd on their ship/squadron drunks." This was typical signage found in any good liberty bar.

You had to have a juke box built along the lines of a Sherman tank loaded with Hank Williams, Mother Maybelle Carter, Johnny Horton, Johnny Cash and twenty other crooning goobers nobody ever heard of. The damn thing had to have "La Bamba", Herb Alpert's "Lonely Bull" and Johnny Cash's "Don't take your guns to town".

The furniture in a real good liberty bar had to be made from coal mine shoring lumber and was not fully acceptable until it had 600 cigarette burns and your ship's numbers or "F**k the Navy" carved into it. The bar had to have a brass foot rail and at least six Slim-Jim containers, an oversized glass cookie jar full of Beer-Nuts, a jar of pickled hard boiled eggs that could produce rectal gas emissions that could shut down a sorority party, and big glass containers full of something called Pickled Pigs Feet and Polish Sausage.

Only drunk Chiefs and starving Ethiopians ate pickled pig's feet and unless the last three feet of your colon had been manufactured by Midas, you didn't want to get anywhere near the Polish Napalm Dogs.

No liberty bar was complete without a couple of hundred faded ship or airplane pictures and a "Shut the hell up!" sign taped on the mirror behind the bar along with several rather tasteless naked lady pictures.

The pool table felt had to have at least three strategic rips as a result of drunken competitors and balls that looked as if a gorilla baby had teethed on the sonuvabitches.

Liberty bars were home and it didn't matter what country, state, or city you were in. When you walked into a good liberty bar, you felt at home. These were also establishments where 19 year-old kids received an education available nowhere else on earth. You learned how to "tell" and "listen" to sea stories. You learned about sex at $10.00 a pop -- from professional ladies who taught you things your high school biology teacher didn't know were anatomically possible. You learned how to make a two cushion bank shot and how to toss down a beer and shot of Sun Torry known as a "depth charge."

We were young and a helluva long way from home. We were pulling down crappy wages for twenty-four hours a day, seven days a-week availability and loving the life we lived. We didn't know it at the time, but our association with the men we served with forged us into the men we became. And a lot of that association took place in bars where we shared the stories accumulated in our, up to then, short lives. We learned about women and that life could be tough on a gal.

While many of our classmates were attending college, we were getting an education slicing through the green rolling seas in WestPac, experiencing the orgasmic rush of a night cat shot, the heart pounding drama of the return to the ship with the gut wrenching arrestment to a pitching deck. The hours of tedium, boring holes in the sky late at night, experiencing the periodic discomfort of turbulence, marveling at the creation of St. Elmo's Fire, and sometimes having our reverie interrupted with stark terror.

But when we came ashore on liberty, we could rub shoulders with some of the finest men we would ever know, in bars our mothers would never have approved of, in saloons and cabarets that would live in our memories forever.

Long live those liberties in WestPac and in the Med - They were the greatest! "Any man who may be asked in this century what he did to make his life worthwhile I think can respond with a good deal of pride and satisfaction, I SERVED IN THE UNITED STATES NAVY."

Then and Now
Author Unknown
Provided by: Michael Besse, Radioman (RM-2)

Years on board the Johnston: 1967 to 1968

Then	Now
If you smoked, you had an ashtray on your desk.	If you smoke, you get sent outside and treated like a leper, if you're lucky.
Mail took weeks to come to the ship.	If the ship is near land, there's a mob topside to see if their cell phones work.
If you left the ship it was in Blues or Whites, even in home port.	The only time you wear Blues or Whites is for ceremonies.
You wore bell bottoms	Bell Bottoms are gone and

everywhere on the ship.	14 year-old girls wear them everywhere.
You wore a Dixie cup all day, with every uniform.	It's not required and you have a choice of different hats.
Say "DAMN", people knew you were annoyed and avoided you.	Say "DAMN", you'd better be talking about a hydroelectric plant.
The Ships Office yeoman had a typewriter on his desk for doing daily reports.	Everyone has a computer with Internet access and they wonder why no work is getting done.
We painted pictures of pretty girls on airplanes to remind us of home.	We put the real thing in the cockpit.
Your girlfriend was at home, praying you would return alive.	She is on the same ship, praying your condom worked.
If you got drunk off duty, your buddies would take you back to the ship so you could sleep it off.	If you get drunk off duty, they slap you in rehab and ruin your career.
Canteens were made out of steel and you could heat coffee or hot Chocolate in them.	Canteens are made of plastic, you can't heat them because they'll melt and anything inside always tastes like plastic.

Our top officers were professional sailors first. They commanded respect.	Our top officers are politicians first. They beg not to be given a wedgie.
They collected enemy intelligence and analyzed it.	They collect our pee and analyze it.
If you didn't act right, they'd put you on extra duty until you straightened up.	If you don't act right, they start a paper trail that follows you forever.
Medals were awarded to heroes who saved lives at the risk of their own.	Medals are awarded to people who show up for work most of the time.
You slept in a barracks, like a soldier.	You sleep in a dormitory, like a college kid.
You ate in a Mess Hall or Galley. It was free and you could have all the food you wanted.	You eat in a Dining Facility. Every slice of bread or pat of butter costs, and you can only have one.
If you wanted to relax, you went to the Rec Center, played pool, smoked and drank beer.	You go to the Community Center and can still play pool, maybe.
If you wanted a quarter beer and conversation, you could go to the Chief's or	The beer will cost you three dollars and someone is watching to see how

Officers' Club.	much you drink.
The Exchange had bargains for sailors who didn't make much money.	You can get better merchandise and cheaper at Walmart.
If an Admiral wanted to make a presentation, he scribbled down some notes and an YN spent an hour preparing a bunch of charts.	The Admiral has his entire staff spending days preparing a Power Point Presentation.
We called the enemy things like "Commie Bastards" and "Reds" because we didn't like them.	We call the enemy things like "Opposing Forces" and "Aggressors or Insurgents" so we won't offend them…Allah Akabar ya'll.
We declared victory when the enemy was dead and all his things were broken.	We declare victory when the enemy says he is sorry and won't do it again.
A commander would put his butt on the line to protect his people.	A commander will put his people on the line to protect his butt.

Thank God I was in the "OLD NAVY". And proud of it.

The Five Most Dangerous Things in the U.S. Navy

A Seaman saying, "I learned this in Boot Camp..."

A Petty Officer saying, "Trust me, sir..."

A Lieutenant JG saying "Based on my experience..."

A Lieutenant saying, "I was just thinking..."

A Chief chuckling, "Watch this shit..."

"MAKE SMOKE!"

With the whistle and clang of GQ
That shivers the nerves of each bloke,
Comes the order to task force and beaches,
Short, sharp and simple, "MAKE SMOKE!"

There are orders that nettle and irk you
And pin you right down to the yoke,
But the one with the bell, that cuts loose all hell,
Is that nine-letter order – "MAKE SMOKE!"

Now the Admiral is usually quiet
Even sips on a punch or a coke,
But he churns himself into a warlord,
When he issues that order – "MAKE SMOKE!"

If flag plot the officers bull fest
Of women and wind it's a joke,
Till the Admiral yells, with the clanging of bells,
That soul searing order – "MAKE SMOKE!"

If you've got a pat hand in a card game
Set to clean out the boys in a stroke,
Better keep what you've got, because like as not,
The order will come to – "MAKE SMOKE!"

So when this war is all over
And your friends ask you why you're a soak,
Just tell them of old Okinawa,
And TURNER and HALL and SMOKE!

Chapter 9

ON THE LIGHTER SIDE

I hope we can all laugh as we look back over the years and think about all the issues each of us had as individuals in the Navy - the good, the bad and the funny. Please take no offense to the following jokes - they are only intended to remind us of our time in the U.S. Navy.

A Retired Navy Chief

It seems that a retired Navy Chief walked into a drug store and asked to talk to a male pharmacist. The elderly woman he was talking to said that she was the pharmacist and as she and her also widowed elderly sister owned the store, there were no males employed there. She then asked if she could help the gentleman. The chief said that it was something that he would be much more comfortable discussing with a male pharmacist. The female pharmacist assured him that she was completely professional and whatever it was that he needed to discuss, he could be confident that she would treat him with the highest level of professionalism. The old chief agreed and began by saying, "'This is tough for me to discuss, but I have a permanent erection. It causes me a lot of problems and severe embarrassment, and I was wondering what you could give me for it."The pharmacist said, "Just a minute, I'll go talk to my sister."When she returned, she said, "We discussed it at length and the absolute best we can do is, 1/3 ownership in the store, a company car, and $3,000 a month plus living expenses."

Four Old Men

Four old retired guys are walking down a street in Yuma, Arizona. They turn a corner and see a sign that says, 'Old Timers Bar - ALL drinks 10 cents'. They look at each other, and then go in, thinking this is too good to be true. The old bartender says in a voice that carries across the room, "Come on in and let me pour one for you! What'll it be, Gentlemen?"

There seemed to be a fully-stocked bar, so each of the men ordered a martini. In short order, the bartender serves up four iced martinis, shaken, not stirred, and says, "That'll be 10 cents each, please."

The four men stare at the bartender for a moment. Then look at each other. They can't believe their good luck. They pay the 40 cents, finish their martinis, and order another round. Again, four excellent martinis are produced with the bartender again saying, "That's 40 cents, please."

They pay the 40 cents, but their curiosity is more than they can stand. They have each had two martinis and so far they have spent less than a dollar.

Finally one of the men says, "How can you afford to serve martinis as good as these for a dime a piece?"

"I'm a retired tailor from Phoenix," the bartender said, "and I always wanted to own a bar. Last year I hit the Lottery jackpot for $125 million and decided to open this place. Every drink costs a dime! Wine, liquor, beer, it's all the same."

"Wow!!!! That's quite a story," says one of the men.

The four of them sipped at their martinis and couldn't help but notice seven other people at the end of the bar who didn't have drinks in front of them, and hadn't ordered anything the whole time they were there.

One man gestures at the seven at the end of the bar

without drinks and asks the bartender, "What's with them?"

The bartender says, "Oh, they're all old retired Navy guys. They're waiting for Happy Hour when drinks are half price."

Old Radioman Salt

A crusty old battleship admiral died and found himself standing before Saint Peter at the pearly gates. Peter welcomed him warmly, "Come right in, Admiral! You've served your country well and you may enter Heaven!"

The admiral looked through the gates and stepped up to Saint Peter, "Just one thing, sonny. I hope there are no Chiefs here. They are the rudest, most obnoxious variety of human ever, and if there are any of them here, I'm not going in; I'd rather go to the other place."

"Don't worry, admiral," said Saint Peter. "No Chief has ever made it into Heaven. You'll find none of 'em here."

So, the admiral goes on into Heaven. Moments later, he comes upon an amazing sight. It is a swaggering figure in khakis, garrison cap cocked slightly on his head, a mostly empty bottle of Jack Daniel's in one hand, and a beautiful woman on either arm. Incensed, the admiral rushes back to Saint Peter and gets in his face. "Hey!

You said there were no Chiefs here! So what the hell is THAT??"

"Don't worry, admiral," says Saint Peter gently. "That's God. He just THINKS he's a Radioman Chief."

Old Sailor and an Old Marine

An old Sailor and an old Marine were sitting at the VFW arguing about who'd had the tougher career.

"I did 30 years in the Corps," the Marine declared proudly, "and fought in three of my country's wars. Fresh out of boot camp, I hit the beach at Okinawa, clawed my way up the blood-soaked sand, and eventually took out an entire enemy machine gun nest with a single grenade. As a sergeant, I fought in Korea alongside General MacArthur. We pushed back the enemy inch by bloody inch, all the way up to the Chinese border, always under a barrage of artillery and small arms fire. Finally, as a Gunny Sergeant, I did three consecutive combat tours in Vietnam. We humped through the mud and razor grass for 14 hours a day, plagued by rain and mosquitoes, ducking under sniper fire all day, and mortar fire all night. In a firefight, we'd fire until our arms ached and our guns were empty, then we'd charge the enemy with bayonets!"

"Ah," said the Sailor with a dismissive wave of his hand, "Lucky bastard! All shore duty, huh?"

The Old Sailor and the Working Girl

An old retired sailor puts on his old uniform and heads for the docks once more, for old time's sake. He engages a prostitute and takes her up to a room. He's soon going at it as well as he can for a guy his age, but needing some reassurance, he asks, "How am I doing?"

The prostitute replies, "Well, old sailor, you're doing about three knots."

"Three knots?" he asks. "What's that supposed to mean?" She says, "You're knot hard, you're knot in, and your knot getting your money back."

The Pope and a Navy Chief

The Pope dies of old age and finds himself at the gates of Heaven. At 0300 he knocks on the gate and a very sleepy-eyed watchman opens the gate and asks, "Waddyah want?"

"I'm the recently deceased Pope and have done 68 years of godly works and thought I should check in here."

The watchman checks his clipboard and says, "I ain't got no orders for you here. Just bring your stuff in and we'll sort this out in the morning."

They go to an old WWII barracks, 3rd floor, open bay. All the bottom racks are taken and all empty lockers have no doors. The Pope stows his gear under a rack and climbs into an upper bunk.

The next morning he awakens to sounds of cheering and clapping. He goes to the window and sees a flashy Jaguar convertible parading down the clouds from the golden headquarters building. The cloud walks are lined with saints and angels cheering and tossing confetti. In the back seat sits a Navy Chief; his Aircrew Wings glistening on his chest, a cigar in his mouth, a can of San Miguel beer in one hand, and his other arm around a voluptuous blonde Angel with magnificent halos.

This sight disturbs the Pope and he runs downstairs to the Master-at-Arms shack and says, "Hey, what gives? You put me, the Pope with 68 years of godly deeds, in an open bay barracks, while this Navy Chief, who must've committed every sin known and unknown to man is staying in a mansion on the hill and getting a hero's welcome. How can this be?"

The Master at Arms calmly looks up and says, "Hey, we get a Pope up here every 20 or 30 years, but we've never had a Navy Chief before.

NOW THEY TELL ME

During a commercial airline flight a Navy Chief was seated next to a young mother with a baby in arms. When her baby began crying during the descent for landing, the mother began nursing her infant as discretely as possible.

The Chief pretended not to notice and upon debarking, he gallantly offered his assistance to help with the various baby-related articles. When the young mother expressed her gratitude, he responded, "Gosh, that's a good looking baby...and he sure was hungry!" Somewhat embarrassed, the mother explained that her pediatrician said breast feeding would help alleviate the pressure in the baby's ears. The Chief sadly shook his head, and in true US Navy fashion exclaimed........ And all these years I've been chewing gum.

NAVAL OFFICERS and NAVY CHIEFS

A group of Chiefs and a group of Naval Officers take a train to a conference. Each Naval Officer holds a ticket. But the entire group of Chiefs has bought only one ticket for a single passenger. The Naval Officers are just shaking their heads and are secretly pleased that the arrogant Chiefs will finally get what they deserve. Suddenly one of the Chiefs calls out: "The conductor is coming!" At once, all of the Chiefs jump up and squeeze into one of the toilets. The conductor checks the tickets of the Naval Officers. When he notices that the toilet is occupied he knocks on the door and says: "Ticket, please!" One of the Chiefs slides the single ticket under the doors and the conductor continues merrily on his round. For the return trip the Naval Officers decide to use the same trick. They buy only one ticket for the entire group but they are baffled as they realize that the Chiefs didn't buy any tickets at all. After a while one of the Chiefs announces again: "The conductor is coming!" Immediately all the Naval Officers race to a toilet and lock themselves in. All the Chiefs leisurely walk to the other toilet. Before the last Chief enters the toilet, he knocks on the toilet occupied by the Naval Officers and says: "Ticket, please!"

Moral of the story? -- Officers like to use the methods of the Chiefs, but they don't really understand them.

SEAMANSHIP TEST

One time during the underway watch the OOD decided to test a Chief Petty Officer's seamanship.

"Chief, what would you do if the forward watch fell off the side of the ship?" "Easy, sir, I'd call 'Man Overboard' and follow the Man Overboard procedures."

"What would you do if an officer fell overboard?" "Hmmm," The Chief said, "Which one, sir?"

"DOES THAT ANSWER YOUR QUESTION?"

"Yes Master Chief" replied the young Ensign. "But what about Lieutenant Commander and Commander?"

"That, sir, goes waaaay back in history - back to the Garden of Eden. You see we've always covered our pricks with leaves."

The Chief and the Parrot

The old Chief finally retired from the Navy and got that chicken ranch he always wanted. He took with him his lifelong pet parrot. First morning at 0430, the parrot squawked and said, "Off yer hocks and don yer socks. Reveille!"

The old chief told the parrot, "We are no longer in the Navy. Go back to sleep." The next morning, the parrot did the same thing. The old Chief told the parrot, "Look, if you keep this up, I will put you out in the chicken pen."

Again the parrot did it, and true to his word, the Chief put the parrot in the chicken pen. About 0630, the Chief was awakened by one heck of a ruckus in the chicken pen. He went out to see what the matter was.

The parrot had about 40 white chickens in formation and on the ground laid 3 bruised and beaten brown ones. The parrot was saying, "By God, when I say fall out in dress whites, I don't mean !&@$*%# khakis!"

A MASTER CHIEF AND THREE LIEUTENANTS

One day, a Master Chief went to the Officer's Club with his Captain to eat lunch. When they entered the main dining room, they found the place was crowded. They did notice three Lieutenants sitting at a table with two empty chairs, so the Captain asked them if they could join them. They promptly invited them to join them. They ordered lunch and joined them in conversation as they ate. At one point, the Master Chief mentioned he had observed characteristics about many officers from which he could determine the sources of their commissioning. The Lieutenants were eager to hear about this and asked if he could tell how each of them had been commissioned.

The Master Chief turned to the Lieutenant on his left and said he went through ROTC. The Lieutenant confirmed that was correct and asked how he had noted this. The Master Chief replied that the Lieutenant, through his conversation, seemed to have a strong academic background but limited military experience.

The Master Chief then told the Lt on his right that he had gone through OCS with previous enlisted service. The Lieutenant confirmed this was correct and also asked how he had determined this. The Master Chief said, again through his conversation, that the Lieutenant seemed to have a firm military background and a lot of common sense.

The Lieutenant across the table from the Master Chief asked if he had determined his source of commission. The Master Chief replied that the Lieutenant had graduated from the United States Naval Academy. The Lieutenant stated that was correct and asked if he had noticed his high level of intelligence, precise military bearing, or other superior qualities acquired at the United States Naval Academy. The Master Chief replied that it was none of these that led to his determination. He had simply observed the Lieutenant's class ring while he was picking his nose.

ROUTE TO BECOMING AN ADMIRAL

Three men are sitting stiffly side by side on a long commercial flight. After they're airborne and the plane has leveled off, the man in the window seat abruptly says, distinctly and confidently, in a low voice, "Admiral , United States Navy, retired. married, two sons, both surgeons."

After a few minutes the man in the aisle seat states through a tightlipped smile, "Admiral, United States Navy, retired, married, two sons, both judges."

After some thought, the fellow in the center seat decides to introduce himself. With a twinkle in his eye he proclaims: "Master Chief Petty Officer, United States Navy, retired. never married, two sons, both Admirals."

A WISE OLD MASTER CHIEF ONCE SAID

A young Ensign approaches the crusty old Master Chief and asked about the origin of the commissioned officer insignias.

"Well," replied the Master Chief," the insignias for the Navy are steeped in history and tradition.

First, we give you a gold bar representing that you are very valuable but also malleable.

The silver bar also represents significant value, but is less malleable.

Now, when you make Lieutenant, your value doubles, hence the two silver bars.

As a Captain, you soar over the military masses, hence the eagle.

As an Admiral, you are, obviously, a star.

THE CHIEF AND THE GUNNY

An old Chief and an old Gunny were sitting at the VFW arguing about who'd had the tougher career. "I did 30 years in the Corps," the Gunny declared proudly, "and fought in three of my country's wars. Fresh out of boot camp I hit the beach at Okinawa, clawed my way up the blood soaked sand, and eventually took out an entire enemy machine gun nest with a single grenade.

"As a sergeant, I fought in Korea alongside General Mac Arthur. We pushed back the enemy inch by bloody inch all the way up to the Chinese border, always under a barrage of artillery and small arms fire. "Finally, as a gunny sergeant, I did three consecutive combat tours in Vietnam . We humped through the mud and razor grass for 14 hours a day, plagued by rain and mosquitoes, ducking under sniper fire all day and mortar fire all night. In a fire fight, we'd fire until our arms ached and our guns were empty, then we'd charge the enemy with bayonets!"

"Ah," said the Chief with a dismissive wave of his hand, "all shore duty, huh?"

RUM & COKE

A minister was seated on a plane bound from Hong Kong to the US with a stopover in Honolulu.

After the stopover a crusty old Chief Petty Officer boarded and as fate would have it he was seated next to the minister.

After the plane was airborne, to continue on its journey, drink orders were taken.

The Flight Attendant asked the CPO if he wanted a drink? The CPO asked for Rum & Coke, which was prepared and placed before him.

The flight attendant then asked the minister if he would like a drink.

He replied in disgust.....

"I'd rather be savagely raped by a dozen whores than let liquor touch my lips."

The ole Chief then handed his drink back to the attendant and said,

"Me too, I didn't know we had a choice."

Old Sailors Sit and Chew the Fat
Author - Larry Dunn, RMCM(SS)(NAC), USN (Ret)

OLD SAILORS SIT AND CHEW THE FAT ABOUT THINGS THAT USED TO BE,
OF THE THINGS THEY'VE SEEN, THE PLACES THEY'VE BEEN,
WHEN THEY VENTURED OUT TO SEA.

THEY REMEMBERED FRIENDS FROM LONG AGO,
THE TIMES THEY HAD BACK THEN.
THE MONEY THEY SPENT, THE BEER THEY DRANK,
IN THEIR DAYS AS SAILING MEN.

THEIR LIVES ARE LIVED IN DAYS GONE BY,
WITH THOUGHTS THAT FOREVER LAST.
OF BELL BOTTOM BLUES, WINGED WHITE HATS,
AND GOOD TIMES IN THEIR PAST.

THEY RECALL LONG NIGHTS WITH A MOON SO BRIGHT
FAR OUT ON A LONELY SEA.
THE THOUGHTS THEY HAD AS YOUTHFUL LADS,

WHEN THEIR LIVES WERE WILD AND FREE.

THEY KNEW SO WELL HOW THEIR HEARTS WOULD SWELL
WHEN OLD GLORY FLUTTERED PROUD AND FREE.
THE UNDERWAY PENNANT SUCH A BEAUTIFUL SIGHT
AS THEY PLOWED THROUGH AN ANGRY SEA.

THEY TALKED OF THE CHOW OL' COOKIE WOULD MAKE
AND THE SHRILL OF THE BOS UN'S PIPE.
HOW SALT SPRAY WOULD FALL LIKE SPARKS FROM HELL
WHEN A STORM STRUCK IN THE NIGHT.

THEY REMEMBER OLD SHIPMATES ALREADY GONE
WHO FOREVER HOLD A SPOT IN THEIR HEART,
WHEN SAILORS WERE BOLD, AND FRIENDSHIPS WOULD HOLD,
UNTIL DEATH RIPPED THEM APART.

THEY SPEAK OF NIGHTS IN PIG ALLEY AND GUT
ON MANY A FOREIGN SHORE,
OF THE BEER THEY'D DOWN AS GATHERING AROUND,
TELLING JOKES AND SEA STORIES GALORE.

THEIR SAILING DAYS ARE GONE AWAY,
NEVER AGAIN WILL THEY CROSS THE BROW.
THEY HAVE NO REGRETS, THEY KNOW THEY ARE BLESSED,
FOR HONORING A SACRED VOW.

THEIR NUMBERS GROW LESS WITH EACH PASSING DAY

```
AS THE FINAL MUSTER BEGINS,
THERE'S NOTHING TO LOSE, ALL HAVE PAID DUES,
AND THEY'LL SAIL WITH SHIPMATES AGAIN.

I'VE HEARD THEM SAY BEFORE GETTING UNDERWAY
THAT THERE'S STILL SOME SAILING TO DO,
THEY'LL SAY WITH A GRIN THAT THEIR SHIP HAS COME IN
AND THE GOOD LORD NEEDS A GOOD CREW.
```

Navy Chiefs are Honorable

One day, while a Navy Chief was cutting a branch of a tree above a river, his axe fell into the river. When he cried out, the Lord appeared and asked, "Why are you crying?" The Chief replied that his axe had fallen into the water, and he needed the axe to make his living. The Lord went down into the water and reappeared with a golden axe. "Is this your axe?" the Lord asked. The Chief replied, "No."

The Lord again went down and came up with a silver axe. "Is this your axe?" the lord asked. Again the Chief replied, "No." The Lord went down again and came up with an iron axe. "Is this your axe?" the Lord asked. The Chief replied, "Yes."

The Lord was pleased with the Chief's honesty and gave him all three axes to keep, and the Chief went back to the ship happy.

Sometime later the Chief was walking with his wife along the riverbank, and his wife fell into the river. When he cried out, the Lord again appeared and asked him, "Why are you crying?" "Oh Lord, my wife has fallen into the water!" The Lord went down into the water and came up with Angelina Jolie. "Is this your wife?" the Lord asked. "Yes," cried the Chief.

The Lord was furious. "You lied! That is an untruth!" The Chief replied, "Oh, forgive me, my Lord. It is a misunderstanding. You see, if I had said 'no' to Angelina Jolie, you would have come up with Cameron Diaz. Then if I said 'no' to her, you would have come up with my wife. Had I then said 'yes' you would have given me all three. Lord, I am poor old seagoing Chief, and am not able to take care of all three wives in a way that they should be, so that's why I said yes to Angelina Jolie."

The moral of this story is: Whenever a Navy Chief lies, it is for a good and honorable reason, and for the benefit of others. That's my story, and I'm sticking to it.

MARINE CORPS, ARMY & NAVY RULES
(author unknown)

MARINE CORPS RULE:

1. Be courteous to everyone, friendly to no one.

2. Decide to be aggressive enough, quickly enough.
3. Have a plan.
4. Have a back-up plan, because the first one probably won't work.
5. Be polite. Be professional. But, have a plan to kill everyone you meet.
6. Do not attend a gunfight with a handgun whose caliber does not start with a 4.
7. Anything worth shooting is worth shooting twice. Ammo is cheap. Life is expensive.
8. Move away from your attacker. Distance is your friend. (Lateral & diagonal preferred.)
9. Use cover or concealment as much as possible.
10. Flank your adversary when possible. Protect yours.
11. Always cheat; always win. The only unfair fight is the one you lose.
12. In ten years nobody will remember the details of caliber, stance, or tactics. They will only remember who live.
13. If you are not shooting, you should be communicating your intention to shoot.

US Army Rules

1. Curse bitterly when receiving operational order.
2. Make sure there is extra ammo and extra coffee.
3. Curse Bitterly.
4. Curse Bitterly.
5. Do not listen to 2nd LTs; it can get you killed.

6. Curse Bitterly.

US Navy Rules

1. Go to Sea.
2. Drink Coffee.
3. Deploy the Marines.

Job Description

Years ago on a U.S. Navy ship's open house visit day, an elderly lady asked if she could talk with some ship's officers. She was escorted to the wardroom where she found four officers.

She asked the first what he did and he explained that he was the Navigator and his job was to keep the ship headed in the right direction.

She turned to the next one and asked what he did. He explained that he was the Engineer and his job was to provide propulsion and power to the ship at all times.

She turned to the next one and asked what he did. He explained that as the Captain he was responsible for everything on the ship.

She then turned to the fourth officer who explained he was the Executive Officer. She then asked, "Well young man, what is your job?"

He replied "Ma'am, I am the Captain's Sexual Advisor."

Somewhat shocked, she said, "I beg your pardon, but what do you mean by that?"

"Very simple Ma'am. The Captain has told me on several occasions that when he wants my f***ing advice, he'll ask me!"

www.ingramcontent.com/pod-product-compliance
Lightning Source LLC
Chambersburg PA
CBHW080527170426
43195CB00016B/2487